Places visited by Ivor Herbert and included in the book

Herbert's Travels

— ALSO BY IVOR HERBERT —

BOOKS
The Filly, Red Rum, Arkle, Six At The Top, Spot The Winner, Longacre,
Come Riding, Over Our Dead Bodies!, Scarlet Fever, Winter's Tale, The
Winter Kings, The Queen Mother's Horses, The Diamond Diggers, The
Way To The Top, Point-to-Point, Eastern Windows, Vincent O'Brien's
Great Horses (with Jacqueline O'Brien), Revolting Behaviour.

TELEVISION
Odds Against?
The Queen's Horses
Derby 200
Classic Touch
Stewards' Enquiry

VIDEO
Tattersalls
Keeneland's Golden Year
Grand National Campaign
To Ride Like a Champion
The Slip Anchor Story
Newmarket – Centre of the Racing World

CINEMA
The Great St Trinian's Train Robbery

THEATRE
Night of the Blue Demands (with Frank Launder)

Herbert's Travels

—IVOR HERBERT—

Ivor Herbert

Best wishes

PELHAM BOOKS

For all my travelling companions –
particularly the family.

First published in Great Britain by
Pelham Books Ltd
27 Wrights Lane
London W8 5TZ
1987

British Library Cataloguing in Publication Data

Herbert, Ivor
Herbert's travels.
1. Travel — Handbooks, manuals, etc.
I. Title
910'.2'02   G151

ISBN 0-7207-1742-6

Typeset by Wilmaset, Birkenhead
Printed in Great Britain by
Billings & Son Ltd, Worcester

— CONTENTS —

Introduction   page   ix

PART 1 – **Weekend Breaks**   1
Florence   3
Vienna   7
Amsterdam   10
The Loire   14
Rome   18
Paris   22
Brussels   27
Champagne   31
Marbella   35
Barbizon   39
Bruges   42

PART 2 – **European Holidays**   47
Provence   49
Switzerland (summer)   53
Greece – The Peloponnese   57
Package to Club Tropicana, Majorca   61
Majorca – Cala Ratjada   65
Paxos   70
Menorca   74
Portugal – The Coast of Estoril   78
Hungary   82
The Camargue   86
Madeira   90
Rhine Cruise   94
Cyprus   99
Portugal – Algarve   103
Biarritz and the Basque Country   107

Spain – Andalucia's White Villages   111
Corfu   115
Morocco   119
Gozo   124
Camping in Brittany   128
Turkey   132

PART 3 – **Long Haul**   137
New Orleans and the Mississippi Cruise   139
Egypt and the Nile   144
Jamaica   148
Miami and the Bahamas Cruise   152
Mauritius   157
Kenya Safari   161
Canyonlands, U.S.A.   165
Lanzarote   168
EPCOT, Disneyworld   172
Thailand   175
New York   180
Hong Kong   186

Index   191

— INTRODUCTION —

The conception of 'Herbert's Travels' as a succession of series in *The Mail on Sunday* sprang from its editor Stewart Steven. Seizing on an idiosyncratic piece I had written about a weekend with a stranger in New York city, he cried, 'This tells me more about the place than years of the usual travel rubbish. Write more.'

He provided what every writer needs from an editor: initial and continuing enthusiasm, coupled with fair criticism. This new type of personal, often highly critical travel writing could well have been censored by an editor keener on oiling to advertisers than entertaining his readers.

My experiences round the world usually run to enough notes to produce five thousand words a place. In *The Mail on Sunday* there is room for about one thousand words. This book includes some paragraphs and phrases which appeared in my series and I am grateful to Stewart for permitting – indeed encouraging – their reappearance in book form together with the new material.

Contact numbers and travel data have been contributed by the stalwart Sarah Whitfield-King who expertly ran the Travel Desk and made all my arrangements for the first three years of 'Herbert's Travels'. Her successor Wendy Driver carries on the good work.

I must also record my gratitude to 'La belle Veronique' otherwise Veronica Wadley, Deputy Features Editor who handled my copy with zeal and sympathy until selfishly deserting us first, for marriage, and worse for promotion (but on the wrong side of Fleet Street).

Thanks are due again to Andrea Hessay for translating my writing into type and to Candida Chilton for checking the proofs. The detailed cross-reference index has been compiled by Jenni Leslie in the belief that this book, in addition to amusing, may be of practical help in discovering the sort of holidays readers want but may not know where to find.

Ivor Herbert,
Bradenham, Bucks.

Spring 1987

— ILLUSTRATIONS —

1 & 2   Menorca (the author)

3   Gozo (the author)

4, 5, 6 & 7   Kenya (the author)

8 & 9   Provence (the author)

10   Bruges (the author)

11   Lanzarote (the author)

12, 13, 14 & 15   Egypt (the author)

16 & 17   Turkey (the author)

18   Vienna (the author)

19   Paxos (the author)

20   Anti-Paxos (the author)

21   Jamaica (the author)

22   Sintra, Portugal (the author)

23   Portugal, Algarve (Portuguese National Tourist Office)

24, 25 & 26   Bangkok (the author)

2 , 28, 29 & 30   Greece (the author)

31 & 32   Hungary (Danube Travel)

33   Rome (Italian State Tourist Office)

34   Florence (Italian State Tourist Office)

35   Madeira (Portuguese National Tourist Office)

36, 37   Switzerland (the author)

The individual photographs used on the jacket are also the copyright of the author.

— Part 1 —
Weekend Breaks

— FLORENCE —

Our Florence apartment's newness and neatness were surprising, for it has been constructed in the Palazzo Ricasoli. It perched above an old courtyard with falcon views across red Renaissance roof-tops. As we walked to breakfast in our closest corner café – cappuccinos, hot omelettes folded into paper napkins by boldly smiling Florentine ladies – they were wrestling with cars in the sepia back streets.

Jammed into one another, sometimes double-parked, the cars were rocked and shoved and semi-hoisted, by frantic Florentines seeking to go about their morning's business.

Thank God we hadn't hired Mr Hertz or Mr Avis as I'd planned. One of this sweet city's joys is that feet can get you everywhere and cars almost nowhere. Even wide streets are banned to them and Florence's beauties are clustered round corners visible only on foot, by the slow approach and upward gaze.

Inured to loveliness and majesty, the Florentines ignore it, like foolish old men too accustomed to their beautiful wives. They read racing form and cackle politics with their backs to the Duomo's sea-green flanks and the Baptistry's legendary bronze doors – attitudes which seem extraordinary to the eager visitor. But then I don't recall going on and on about the loveliness of Henry VI's College Chapel and School Yard at Eton. American tourists used to stop and stare to hear us prattling about games and girlfriends.

The Magic of Italy girl, Irish-Italian with an English lover and tangled hair, met us at Pisa Airport in the flamingo glow of a November dusk. It was an astonishing 72°F. She drove us to Florence and handed us safely over to the mouse-like concierge of the Residence Palazzo Ricasoli.

Foreign flats, unlike hotel rooms, make you wonder about living there. From our terrrace I sniffed urban smells of coffee grinding, bread baking and leather. The travelling companion would be hunting handbags and shoes. But the terrace, I thought, would make a fair place for writing. Some authors need to face a blank wall to avoid views. I need height and the stimulation of watching something when the wrist and fingers ache. All of us can be sparked by the special feel of a place, natural or man-made. Florence has all that abundantly.

Our un-chic area had a whiff of Bloomsbury's muddle about it. Out of ancient doorways looking as if they led into Oxford colleges, students hurried or stood before the oddest shops – antiques mixed with electricians and motor spares – heads bobbing together like busy cockerels while righting the world or dreaming that another Dante might appear.

The travelling companion fingered impossible antiques like gigantic stoves. 'Amazingly cheap,' she declared. 'Would go very well in the corner of the dining room.'

The Via San Gallo became the Via De'Ginori and there stands my favourite place in Florence: the church and cloisters of San Lorenzo. Round here small artisan shops jostle together and there's a busy market where bright expensive clothes – looking as if they had fallen out of the back of smart Alfa-Romeos – can be bought for almost nothing.

The grand shops, smelling deliciously expensive, are in the Via Strozzi and in the Via de'Calzaioli. 'Go to just three and spend a long time in each,' I said, 'so that I can sit and read the guide book, while pretty girls come up and ask if they can help me.'

Just before San Lorenzo, I spotted iron gates ajar on to a courtyard. Out of it emerged an interested American hum. A guide was lecturing classy New Englanders – always distinguished by the men's floppy khaki hats with Brigade of Guards blue-red-blue ribbons and similar belts. Their womenfolk are slim. The vast bulk of America's working classes, most of whom earn as much as British managers are – perhaps consequently – wobblingly fat.

Illicitly we slipped in through the wrought-iron rusty gates past the muttering gardener, for this was the Medici-Riccardi Palace, begun 550 years ago for Cosimo Medici. As a town resident it ranks halfway in stature between London's Apsley House and Buckingham Palace, but it has a strong country feel. What is more, though civil servants now toil there, it still feels surprisingly lived in.

We scurried through the courtyards where they used to stage plays and squeezed into Michelozzo's gloriously tiny chapel. There we goggled at the Fresco of the Three Magi – marvellous stuff, for all the nobs in it are Medici portraits dressed in the highest fashion of 1450. Today, in the streets outside, Florentine youths dress like Teddy Boys.

One of friendship's true tests is liking at first sniff the same restaurants abroad. We passed several restaurants we immediately didn't take to, and grew hungry as we walked. We came to the Piazza della Repubblica, which is the city centre with pretty but costly cafés like the Bar Gilli and the Paszkowski, good for grappa. The bank cashier had warned us 'Ten thousand lira just to sit down!' He burst into 'God Save the Queen'. I responded politely with our regimental slow march which comes from an Italian opera. I thought it unlikely we would be doing this in our local Barclays.

South of the Piazza we came to the restaurant La Posta. A great table of sea food in the entrance instantly enticed. The red-haired proprietress waved us in to a vast fishy hors-d'oeuvre.

'I must have vino pronto', declared the travelling companion in Italian to the waiter, 'for I'm exhausted from walking the streets.'

Guffaws of laughter arose from the next door Italian and French tables. Two American pooftas eyeing each other opposite, looked up and smirked nervously. The bill for an excellent meal with masses of vino was £30.

Sightseeing stretches legs and minds. Past the Palazzo Vecchio and up into and around the Uffizi. No crowds in November. The rooms are vast and the guides are proudly kind. Ours, small with a twisted foot, let us in free up steep stairs into the secret Chamber of the Four Elements.

Walls built at odd angles to fill the available space make the palace homely. It displays glorious pictures pinched by and recovered from people like Goering ('Leda and the Swan' suitably enough), another illegally exported to Boston and rescued, and several Tintoretto's once nicked by hellish Hitler.

A bevy of American girl students gaze at their darkly slim Italian guide. 'Okay, so Florence gets to be capital of all Italy,' he declaims, 'so big spring cleaning job here at Uffizi Palace, okay?' I suppose that his cocky form of tuition continues all through the night.

Over the Ponte Vecchio, of course, where once in those dire post-war Labour days with no foreign money I had to sell my father's gold cigarette case to pay for the hotel room.

We got a lovely long view upstream of the Ponte Vecchio from the Ponte alla Carraia – two scullers were dipping the stippled evening Arno – on our way from the Hotel Lugarno to Harry's Bar. The Lurgarno has such a splendid riverside setting that the travelling companion began asking for prices for a spring weekend. It would not be cheap: two vodkatinis cost £8.

I had feared the Bar might be honking with American tourists. But there were only two Americans and both were old Florence residents: a rich old biddy in a plastic hat with her cringeing female companion. Next to us, an Italian publisher made play over photographs with a local beauty and her lusty hound. The girl was cool with the man but fed her dog with the excellent stream of hot what-nots they bring with the drinks.

We searched up a shadowy stairwell in a mediaeval building for a friend's daughter studying in Florence. I'd love mine, too, to go there if I could afford it after school. Smaller, less dangerous by far than Rome, and feelings of Europe's astonishing artistic rebirth tickling your lungs all day.

Best meal: at the Paoli in the Via dei Tavolini. Faded frescos, one by Annigoni when still a poor student in Florence before he found fame and his glamorous mistress, Juanita, and became society's darling of portrait painters.

Trattoria Cammillo in the Borgo San Jacopo buzzed with Italian zest but the food was average Italian stodge at £41 for two. We found dull food, too, except for the starter – buffalo cheese toasted with tomatoes – but tremendous soaring views from the little-known roof-top restaurant of the Hotel Baglioni, opposite the station.

Best lasting things: the church of San Lorenzo, its quiet sludge-yellow walled cloisters round a green glow of a courtyard like a magic carpet back into the century when Florence ruled all. 'The Quietness of the Cloisters must not be Troubled' declaims a sensible notice.

In the light and happy church there's the Chapel of the Espousal of Our Lady, where Florentines take their engagement rings to be blessed. On its altar rails are the words 'O Lord, who has united our hearts and You, give us the joy always to love each other ... Grant the grace to bind ourselves to You.'

TRAVEL FACTS

Alitalia, 27–28 Piccadilly, London W1 (01–602 7111)
Magic of Italy, 47 Shepherd's Bush Green, London W12 (01–743 9555)
Pegasus, 24a Earls Court Gardens, London SW5 (01–370 6851)
Sovereign, 17–27 High Street, Hounslow, Middx (01–897 4545)
Italian State Tourist Office, 1 Princes St., London W1 (01–408 1254)

— VIENNA —

Sitting on a bench at a wooden table in a wine pub in Grinzing village, on the hill above Vienna, I thought suddenly how much I enjoy Europe. Africa, the Orient, the States, the Caribbean all have their potent lures but ...

I swig another *viertel* and *spritzer* to quench the blazing, fresh-grated horseradish with our smoked ham. But there is this bond between Europeans of shared history and the same, and therefore often disputed, interests. And Austria's always been at the crossroads of Europe, particularly now as neutrals on point-duty. I felt, despite the villains they've thrown up, warm towards the Austrians and ordered another *viertel*.

These wine pubs (known as *heurigers*) in Grinzing front their own vineyards which tip into the tumbled, beamy, egg yolk-coloured courtyards. It's as if fields of vines and Cotswold hamlets nuzzled into Islington and Wandsworth. *Viertels* are one-quarter bottles produced from their own new wine.

Two Austrians in braces, like characters from the other side's *Dad's Army*, play accordion and violin. Huddled round their table behind the pot-bellied stove, locals of salad days and wrinkled evenings chant old songs. They try me with *Waltzing Matilda* – there is a young Australian couple in the inn – before settling for *Daisy, Daisy*, the latest British song they remember.

The Aussies drink with a Colorado couple they had met the previous night at one of Vienna's two dozen concerts or operas. They are joined by an old Swiss with a girl far too young and too fair for him, who looked and looked across the crowded room, and so we joined them, too. Vienna is a coupling place.

It's also markedly un-Kraut like. They hate Prussians, dislike the Czechs, love the Hungarians (with whom they made a vast empire) and admire the Poles. They find us funny. They're funny themselves. Chambermaids, taxi-drivers, waitresses and even people in the streetcars openly joke, frankly enjoy themselves. How often are fellow travellers on a London 'bus belles of the ball and stars at a party? But the Viennese have this theatrical inclination.

There's a dashing new exhibition, *Dream and Truth*, in the Künstlerhaus on the Karlsplatz. This square gives you a good flavour of the city. Here is its batty old Heath Robinson metro-station, preserved like a joke. Opposite is that very grand, ice-creamily baroque church. Between them: public gardens. And inside the museum this lively reminder that Vienna, at the century's start, was the leaping heart of music, architecture, art nouveau and Dr Freud, Gustav Klimt, and Mahler.

Friederike is to meet me at the Opera House on the Ring. But I nip off first to a pavement café near the famous Sachers and Kärntnerstrasse, their Bond Street, mercifully without cars. Above is a plaque: 'W. H. Auden lived here', the poet who'd weaned me off Rupert Brooke and Housman when I was at Cambridge.

These pavement cafés – there's a good one opposite the National Theatre in the Rathausplatz – are fine sport and I never had those revoltingly-rich, sticky cakes. Friederike and I travel by Metro – it's spotless and swift – and lunch at Smutny's in Elizabethstrasse. It's a typical, family-run, stout Viennese eating place, and I foolishly order a typical dish – enough beef, ham and potatoes to feed five burgomeisters. But Friederike's dish of wild mushrooms is delicious. You need to be picky. If Brussels is in Division One eating-wise and Cairo at the bum end of Division Four, Vienna is about halfway up Division Two.

Lots of Vienna is named after last century's stunningly sexy and restless Empress Elisabeth, 'Sissy', who rode like smoke across the hunting fields of England pursuing our foxes, and pursued by our lusty squires. She ended violently, too; this woman who must have been marvellous to know. She was assassinated in unlikely Switzerland.

The tiny hotel Amadeus, though new, is cosy and squeezed into an old street behind the city's centre, the soaring spire of St Stephan's Cathedral. That is Vienna's old heart, then come the grand boulevards round the Ring, and the boring suburbs until – swoosh – you're into the curling hills and vineyards. Main walkways radiate from St Stephan. The Graben are a fine mix of mediaeval, baroque and art nouveau. We have coffee in Lehman's, full of fortyish Viennese ladies with bobbing hats and young lovers necking.

Just off is the students' café, Hawelka, decor and waiters unchanged for decades. Opposite the Amadeus is a good restaurant, the Grünewald, with a handsome patronne, whose hand her regular clients hungrily kiss. 'It'll be expensive,' warned Friederike, who never takes a taxi when a tram will do. But £15 a head is really peanuts for a luxurious restaurant in a Western capital.

While I'm ogling at the marvellous carvings round St Stephan's pulpit, there's a burst of cherubic singing: schoolchildren practising anthems beneath the pumping elbows of their choirmaster.

Then it's the Spanish Riding School horses practising in their huge tiered ballroom in the Hofburg, the Imperial Palace. Evening performances are sold out and even at 10 am there's a queue for rehearsals. Better to walk in with the experts at about 11.

I fill in time in the tremendous National Library and down tiny alleys off Kohlmarkt and the Michaelerplatz. In the afternoon, a street car to Schönbrunn Palace which I'd supposed was. in the country. 'No,' said Friederike, 'that's Mayerling, the hunting lodge, and not much to see there.'

If you accept the maddening top storey on the Schönbrunn to accommodate the Emperor's Chancellor (spiral staircase; secret consultations). It's a superb palace with some of the best furniture I've ever seen. And its grounds are almost as fine as Versailles.

We lunch in Beim Novak, in the Richtergasse, famous with Viennese gourmets. Out to the Prater, an adequate amusement park with that overrated 'Great Wheel' from *The Third Man*. You get a better view from the hilltop restaurant at Kählenberg.

And so to the Belvedere Palace (great pictures, good site) built for that brave homosexual general, Prince Eugen, who conquered the Turks. Officers of his persuasion are often wildly courageous in front of their troops on the battlefield.

Then to the opera, the Italian *Barber of Seville*, sung in German, with Figaro cheekily played by a tiny Oriental called Kwang Dong Kim. Typical of Vienna's cosmopolitan verve, I thought, slipping out to a Greek restaurant, the Olivenhain, just behind the Volksoper.

TRAVEL FACTS

Austrian Airlines, 50–51 Conduit St., London W1 (01–439 0741)
Sovereign, Hodford House, 17–27 High St., Hounslow, Middx
(01–897 4545)
Pegasus, 24a Earls Court Gardens, London SW5 (01–370 6851)
American Express, Portland House, Stag Place, Victoria St.,
London SW1 (linkline 0345 010333)
Austrian Tourist Office, 30 St George's St., London W1 (01-629
0461)

— AMSTERDAM —

I went to Amsterdam for a weekend because it's only a short hop from Britain and, by Europe's artificially kept up prices, a cheap ticket. (American air fares are one quarter of ours.) I also wanted to explore two aspects which, although outwardly poles apart, provide sensory satisfactions: the picture museums and the window tarts.

'Bruges for churches, Amsterdam for museums,' pronounced my expert friend from Agnews of Bond Street, giving the sort of brief guide-line travellers need. Bruges, so different, is a singular joy in Belgium. Across the border we found in the often dreary, grubby Dutch city pleasures and disappointments equally arrayed.

The big plus was the Pulitzer on the Princess Canal, one of the best hotels I have stayed in – and I perch in about one hundred and fifty a year round the world.

The Pulitzer is both artistic and efficient, a rare two to tango. A cunning modernisation of nineteen old houses, it reflects the happy swing away from the soul-depressing Identikit cubes of the mass-produced, mass-satisfying, hotel chains.

Our bedroom with its early eighteenth century brick walls and beams, overlooked a silent garden full of trees and statues. The concentric pattern of old Amsterdam is easy to grasp, though some of the radial canals look at first glance muddlingly the same. The pattern runs: canal, narrow road (hard to find car parking space), tall narrow houses (because of the old tax on width, like our old window tax), back gardens, then the next row's back gardens, houses again, street, and the next canal. High up, looking back over the garden was peaceful. And yet our bathroom was super modern de luxe and, conversely our beds were old-fashionedly turned down by cheerful maids. Who said all Dutch were dull?

The hotel was trebly welcome. The approach to the city is first boring, then ugly. Outside the old semi-circle Amsterdam is St Pancras all over and often grimier. The Royal Palace looks like an empty prison needing a wash and the Dam, its square, could be Wolverhampton or Wupperthal.

But beyond that dreariness and the odd sad junky group, lie the jesting ladies, displaying breasts and whatnots in their windows on both sides of pretty canals. All, except some less-frequented Eurasians who looked sulky, giggled like girls enjoying a successful social dance which, in a way, they are.

The twenty-year old blonde star, who had the best pink-lit corner berth, played with her poodle and rocked seductively on her oscillating stool, during the brief spells she wasn't working behind her curtains. A Scandinavian, she was young, shapely and beautiful enough to model anywhere and was openly enjoying the oldest and – by others' accounts – disagreeable and boring profession. She leaned in her black leotard over her half-stable door between bouts, smoking a quick cigarette and joking with a group of men playing, suitably, a Dutch version of Find the Lady on the narrow humped-back bridge over the canal from the Damstraat.

Amazingly, these girls don't mind being stared at by outside ladies who earn their livings wearing more clothes in less horizontal positions. The streets froth with strolling, staring couples. The women, some young with youthful pimply boyfriends, some into corpulent middle-age with their pot-bellied, peeping old hubbies, often showed not disapproval but envy of the girls displayed in the windows.

The Rijksmuseum is a titanic St Pancras. But what joys it holds from the comic supporting characters of 450 years ago in serious scenes like the Resurrection, through the glorious Rembrandts with his supernatural lighting, and the Vermeers (some little houses he painted still remain, unscathed by tasteless modernisation or the last war's bombs), right up to the dashing nineteenth century landscapes.

We foolishly tried to see all round in two half-days. You need four, with breaks across the canal, the Singel, around the Leidesplan, a large and busy square abutted by cafés and restaurants like the Oyster Bar. There are also 'brown bars' (pubs, really, where you can eat soundly and cheaply). On the canal side of the Leidesplan Square is the bizarre art deco of the Hotel American, where I downed four drams of fiery spicy Genever, a good sort of gin, provided by vouchers from Time Off – a sound idea from a travel operator.

Then on springier steps, we headed off past the better canal boat station to lap up the dazzle and feel the stress of the Van Goghs in his light, bright museum. Quite different viewers here. In the Rijks, too many foreigners dragged on guided tours, slumped on brown benches, resembling suddenly, as real life does after the theatre, living parodies of art. In the Van Gogh, dirty haired youths and neat old ladies briskly shared awe and joy. A happy place, to which I long to return.

We had been warned (by the Belgians) that we would most certainly be mugged in Amsterdam but we saw no violence, though one white-faced female junky came wailing after us, swerving past the clanking trams across the Leidesplan.

We found a very up market 'brown bar', the Gijsbrecht van Amstel, on the Heren Canal, where people drift in after midnight to drink and gossip. Great value for good French cuisine at £32 for two with lots to drink. The clientèle (no Americans for once) were locals and neither fat nor dull, but lean, distinguished and in sparkling form. Having at last, through North Sea oil, a booming economy, the Dutch national spirit has been transformed. Brits would laugh more if we got out of the mire. If the Dutch can, why can't we? The Dutch don't pretend to be a super power and try to live like one on a poor nation's income. They, too, had their empire and shrugged it off with no lasting regrets. One of its legacies is good Indonesian cooking.

There's a surprising Indonesian restaurant called the Speciall in a dingy Fulham-like street opposite the Westerkirk and the house in which the brave and tragic girl, Anne Frank, hid for so long from the atrocious occupying Nazis. The Speciall looks nothing from the outside and to my alarm takes no credit cards. So, plonking my petrol and tip money on the table, I asked the patron to feed us as much as he could for the £16 lying there. This amused him greatly and we had a huge and delicious meal of Rijsstafel: 18 different dishes.

Above our heads I noticed, as we left this excellent, humbly decorated place full of cheerful and underdressed people, a photograph of a familiar figure hanging on the bamboo walls. It was of Prince Philip in the restaurant in one of his ultra smart double-breasted suits. Catching my smile of surprised recognition, the patron murmured discreetly, 'Brought last summer by one of our old clients.'

TRAVEL FACTS

KLM, Time & Life Building, New Bond St., London W1
(01–568–9144)
British Airways, PO Box 10, Heathrow Airport, Hounslow, Middx
(01–759 2525)
British Midland, Donington Hall, Castle Donington, Derby (0332
810552)
Time Off, 2a Chester Close, Chester St., London SW1 (01–235
8070)
American Express, Portland House, Stag Place, Victoria St.,
London SW1 (linkline 0345 010333)
Travelscene, 94 Baker St., London W1 (01–935 1025)
22a Cheapside, Bradford, W. Yorks (0274 392911)
Netherlands National Tourist Office, 25–28 Buckingham Gate,
London SW1 (01–630 0451)

— THE LOIRE —

A decent holiday needs two complementary activities. Going round some of the one thousand châteaux which stud the wide green valleys of the Loire and Cher nicely balances eating at the score of Michelin-rosetted restaurants from Orleans to Angers.

The *Red Guide* is still dependable for food; less so for hotels. I used to like the Château de Pray, near Amboise. Then shabby and tapestried, it's now been tarted up with a flashing sign which should have warned us off. Food moderate – our only bad meal in three days – in a dining room full of Americans. It's probably now on some US stop-over list and thus incurs an influx of tourists chewing gum over cocktails, then smoking between, even during courses. No cook however humble stands for such ignorant offensiveness. Thus are good chefs driven away to points less obviously on the circuit.

It's a pity about de Pray. The situation is super on the Loire's south bank with woods all around. And I've had some happy times there. Maybe new management will restore the good old feel.

You need two châteaux a morning, nicely spaced, to work up appetites for lunch, then two more to do the same for dinner. A short siesta after lunch is always to be recommended and this, for comfort's sake, means booking into your chosen hotel the night before.

We reach Orleans in under two hours from Charles de Gaulle, one of the world's few attractive airports. (Luton, Athens and Agadir are the pits and Heathrow's Terminal 3 in summer is dreadful.)

Governments should, like the French, value tourists' first impressions. Though it's misty, we zap southwards on Autoroute 10 in high good humour. My companion, as good a looker as she is a cook, runs a delectable restaurant in her Hampshire millhouse. Judging the Loire cuisine among the world's best, she's out to pinch its secrets.

The châteaux prove as diverse as the menus. French, a prettier sounding language than ours, is infinitely poorer, having only Latin and no Anglo-Saxon roots, the blend which makes ours such a rich mixture full of nuances. French must use one word to lump together places as different as the grim castles of Loches and Chinon, colossal palaces like Chambord (suddenly leaping up like a mad St Pancras in the midst of a silent forest), or regal Blois above its town, a thousand elegant manors like Beauregard (some of these could be in the

Cotswolds), and fairy tale places like the river-bridging Chenonceaux across the Cher. Actually, nowhere is like Chenonceaux ...

Orleans possesses the restaurant, La Cremaillière, in which we will eat our last magnificent lunch on the way home. Michelin finds us this but misleads us over the sort of comfortable, charming country hotel one wants for a weekend châteaux-visiting. Places in Olivet along the river *read* all right but they turn out sadly suburban like thirties things along the Thames near Staines.

So, as dusk washes rose-pink over the Loire's sandbanks, we hurry on south-westwards. The southern road along the valley is far prettier than the north and, nearing Blois, runs along a floodbank giving great views of châteaux, willows, islands and grey-stone villages across the mirror-water.

Labourers on bikes wobble down poplar avenues. Harvested maize towers in stacks. Tiny vineyards drowse. Shooters with whimpering dogs crunch across stubble. In forests of oak, beech and chestnut, the deer and wild boar rustle.

In undistinguished little Cléry, there's suddenly a huge basilica. We stop to snoop. It's lemon pale and chilly but a board proclaims that Louis XI is buried here, as surprisingly as if a great English king lay in Chipping Sodbury.

Another inscribed notice lists all the kings, French and foreign, who've made pilgrimages here. At the bottom leaps out the name Mountbatten. What on earth was our Royal Family's beloved Uncle Dickie doing in this village twenty years earlier? I search for someone to explain this mystery. Two portly village women waddle out of a side chapel where they've lit up the gloom with their candles.

'Mountbatten anglais,' they explain approvingly, 'Allemand, non.' They cross themselves. Heads are shaken then put together as they kneel as if to pray but, in fact, to complain as the French do, because they love it, about the rising cost of food. I refrain, for reasons of loyalty and decorum, from explaining the Mountbatten Battenberg German ancestry.

Six hundred years ago a ploughman here turned up a mysterious statue of the Virgin. The chapel built to house it was burnt down by English troops in 1428. The Loire Valley was for centuries full of battles, murders, mistresses, plots, poisons and saints like Joan, so you get a good dose of melodramatic history and not just pretty pictures when you tour it.

Louis XI promised his weight in silver (a reverse of the Aga Khan gold swop) to build this basilica at Cléry for the Virgin. Here stands his sarcophagus. The two Frenchwomen, moaning about Mitterand, drift out into the dusk.

We find our hotel. On the outskirts of little St Dye-sur-Loire and with its feet in the water stands the Manoir Bel Air. Three generations of its owners sit round the kitchen drinking wine and watching telly. A curving staircase, a room overlooking the river, and when we say we're dining out no-one's affronted. Just a note with our key, 'Please lock front door and turn out hall light.' It's like being at home.

To Blois first to stretch legs down streets of timbered mediaeval houses closed to cars. The palace broods above, empty windows gazing across the town, with that wonderfully grand exterior staircase built for Francois I and the creepy room where Henri III had the Duc de Guise murdered.

So through the forest past Chambord to Bracieux to dine at Le Relais (two Michelin rosettes) among other reverential gastronomes. M. Robin's menu proclaims 'Cooking is a voyage in a secret country. Let us guide you to it ...'

He proposes, with menus from 158 francs up to 240 francs, 'the colours, scents and tastes of the season.' The essence of the nouvelle cuisine spreads over six delicate courses. Even at £30 a head, it's fabulous value to include two bottles of wine (one a rare red Sancerre) and a Marc to finish. Compare this with the pre-cooked muck they chuck at you in Chelsea.

Next morning we go round Chambord and Beauregard picking country tracks through silent forests. The companion is a dab hand with maps too. The large-scale Michelin (no. 64 for the Loire) lets travellers into the real France.

Chambord has been partly furnished since my last visit when I sat with a wife on our hotel bedroom windowsill in the park getting a free look at the *son et lumière*. Nice simple little hotel, too, the St. Michel.

But the château is still a great gloomy hulk. Could courts and kings ever have liked living here? Outside, horses whinny from the old stables and I hail mistakenly a boyish girl as 'M'sieu'. Evidently they still breed Joan of Arc types here. 'Do you want a ride in the forests?' she asks. Then, laughing: 'Or hire a carriage for your wedding?' I shake my head and don't translate. Here were the stables of that violent, dashing seducer, the Marechal de Saxe, bastard of a Polish king, who filled this park with savage Ukranian horses. They were the mounts of his Tartar and negro cavalry troops whom he would hang from a tree for the slightest slip.

Plus ça change ... I was once filming on the Loire for Ranks with a

Menorca Most of Menorca is quite unspoilt. Up on the north coast at Reclau we could be on a Scottish loch, but we're finishing a good lunch at 3.30 pm. in October

Menorca "Villa Seekers" had indeed sought well in the "urbanisation" of San Jaime

Gozo A splendid mix of Italian culture suddenly squashed on primitive Middle East

Kenya
Going home to
Kikorok Lodge in the
Masai Mara, we stop
for a stately, home-bound
giraffe, neck decorated with
hitch-hiking birds

Kenya
It's easy to
believe that
lionesses are cuddly
as labradors. Within
15 minutes these had
stalked and killed
a deer

Kenya The locals
literally at the bottom
of our garden at
Kikorok. We had just
finished tea and sandwiches,
black buttered to our
bungalow 50 yards away.

<u>Provence</u> In the hills west of Grasse lie many quiet, old villages, tourist-free, yet only 40 minutes from the squashed sardine and concrete coastline.

<u>Provence</u> A real pleasure of France is a long summer lunch with family and friends. This is "La Joliette" et La Garoupe, less spoilt than most of the coast between Nice and Cannes.

<u>Bruges</u> One of my favourite small cities. Easily walkable, it's also wonderful to see by boat. Its silence, broken only by bells, is exceptional in Europe, and it makes a beautiful weekend break.

<u>Lanzarote</u> This looks tough and barren but it's on the road from a really pretty village, Femes, high up on the hills, down to Playa Blanca. Delicious fish in the restaurant of the same name and good bathing round the corner at Papagayo.

Egypt. If you like Greek architecture,
Egyptian is heavy. Greece lets light in
on minds, too, while Egypt feels
constrictive, often menacing, making
mankind feel like scarabs.

Egypt. Our floating and comfortable
home, "Nile Beauty" on the left, and
one of the feluccas which we hired
for a day's sail down the Nile.

Egypt. I had to cuff our
coachman for whipping
his horse —after two
warnings.

Egypt. Camels are surly, but quite
fun to ride. You can feel from their
rock and roll another reason why
they are called 'ships of the desert'.
Shortly after this, fisticuffs and oaths
flew among the camelkeepers at the
foot of the pyramid of Cheops.

former German bomber pilot as my cameraman. He'd been stationed at Tours during the war. 'We used to dine really well in a good hotel near Saumur,' he told me. 'Friendly landlord, too. Probably locked up now for collaborating with us. Let's see.' Indeed, the patron had just returned from his long prison sentence. When the former Luftwaffe officer strode in to greet him, the wretch shook like a white blancmange, thinking the past was back to haunt him.

France's enemies are now within, thinks the aristocratic owner of pretty park-surrounded Beauregard, a château no-one seems to know. We summon a girl to guide us by clanking a rusty bell high up on the wall. While waiting, I read the owner's manifesto to his visitors. 'France, country of culture and tourism, will soon be denuded of all its historic houses and its treasures by these unjust new taxes ...' *Plus ça change* again to that worldwide cry.

The upstairs saloon is floored with Delft tiles and walled solidly with seventeenth century portraits. 'I'd love to spend a weekend here with the owners,' muses the companion. They, French-style, live mainly in Paris.

To lunch at Montrichard in an amazing one-room tollhouse, half-filled with an immense glowing grill, and perched up on the river bridge. Then on to Chenonceaux, as lovable as the famous two women who lived there, Diane de Poitiers and Catherine de Medici. Each gave it one of the two grand gardens which still embrace it along its river banks.

'A weekend on the Loire like this,' said the companion when we parted, 'is more of a holiday than a month on any boring yacht in the Mediterranean.'

TRAVEL FACTS

Air France, 69 Boston Manor Rd., Brentford, Middx (01–499 7511)
Townsend Thoresen, Enterprise House, Channel View Rd., Dover, Kent (0304 203388)
French Leave, 21 Fleet St., London EC4 (01–583 8383)
VFB, 1 St Margaret's Terrace, Cheltenham, Glos (0242 35515)
Winter Inn, Park Street, Hovingham, York (065382 425)
French Government Tourist Office, 178 Piccadilly, London W1 (01–499 6911)

— ROME —

'Better punctual trains than freedom.' Mussolini's dictum had been the subject of my first grown-up essay as a ten-year old – 'Right or wrong? Give your reasons' – by an enlightened prep. school 'beak'.

Decades later, and certainly free, I was delighted when the Trans-Europe Express from Florence slid into Rome on the dot. Among the babbling foreigners, taxi grabbers and beggars for tips, who constitute the capital's main railway station, I hoped that I, too, had been able to enlighten the odd ten-year old in my time.

The taxi darkly whizzed up and down most of the seven hills which make the place such an agreeable tangle. Is any other capital so hilly? Rain splashed on rush-hour jams across the Tiber. The Castel Sant' Angelo (mausoleum, grim prison and fortress) gleamed in spotlights. Suddenly, there was St Peter's. On its broad, triumphal approach, lined by the former palaces of nobles oiling their way into the bribable, often disgusting old Popes' favours, we find our Hotel Columbus.

Very old porters in livery, a back courtyard bereft of cars – but who was that black-hatted Mafia type sneaking in? – and hardly another guest. Yet our room was high up under the roof where servants in the old days must have slept. It had an excellent view of St Peter's dome and the pines on the rural hillside – provided you bent right down and cricked your neck.

On our last day, a team in dazzling tracksuits from behind the Iron Curtain pranced along the faded corridors. The hotel, they said, belonged to the Vatican and was only let to tenants for management.

'You'd think,' said my travelling companion, 'that the Pope would let us have a bathroom of our own. We'll complain at Wednesday's audience.'

There's no difficulty about getting a public audience with the Pope. All you do is write ahead to the Governor of Vatican City and collect your tickets on the Monday.

Once, stopping in Rome with a former wife, and gawping up at the Basilica, we'd been swept like twigs by a flood of pilgrims into St Peter's. We'd seen at only arms length the tiny, ivory-pallored Pope, borne along in a chair aloft. He continuously passed down on either side of the aisle one or other of his two little white skull caps. These the devout clutched, kissed and handed back agog. We Prots felt imposters at a private feast.

This time we walked in marbled moonlight round the great empty square (a circle in fact) lined by Bernini's cohort of a colonnade below the steps. The hot dog stands and the souvenir junk stalls were blessedly closed. The obelisk which took nine hundred men to raise one April day four centuries ago shafted up at the moon. Only one other couple, hand in hand, looked up at Michelangelo's immense pale-blue dome. Under the archways into the square, two tramps huddled under vile blankets: one black man and one bearded ancient with his head in a cardboard box.

Round the roof of St Peter's we capered next day, taking the lift on the left of the Basilica. Staying out by the Vatican means you're a long way from Rome's bustling hub and voluptuous shops. But from the roof of St Peter's what a view ... !

Down the lift again (you pay for everything in the Church of Rome, it seems) and then into and round the claustrophobic Treasury. With the world's millions starving to death outside, we found too much richness, too many nauseating casefuls of gold and precious stones for Papal finery.

We fled to the High Altar over St Peter's Tomb. Rich, too. But here a humble American priest is showing a small group round. 'Do join us,' he quietly invites. We are enthralled by his simplicity. He points out a wooden crucifix. Something to do with an American saint, he murmurs, patting an Italian child's head. And I never knew that the United States had produced a saint.

Next day, not far across the river from our hotel, we dined at the Passetto, recommended by our helpful rep from Magic of Italy. It proved the best meal so far of our Italian trip. A neat and serious restaurant, with a very friendly staff recommending as an hors-d'oeuvre 'Roman vegetables' – artichokes, stuffed tomatoes, zucchini, peppers and so on. Then pasta with special truffles, then osso buco for me and opposite suckling pig – 'of such delicacy, it's unbearable! Wonderful!' cried the lady. But the bill was £56.

After dinner, we strolled in that marvellous square, the Navona, with the Bernini Fountain of the Rivers. Below our feet an ancient stadium had once roared. Now irregular baroque buildings in strawberry red, orange, mulberry and lemon, and two churches frame the three fountains.

In the light beaming from the café, students disgorge licking ice creams, swinging arms and singing. A bearded artist paints a pale, nervous girl under the lamplight by the fountain. A young, savage gipsy girl curses us for not buying a bunch of roses from her. It is November and children play with leaping dogs in and out of the shadows.

Such etched scenes, being both beautiful and busy with locals, are the essence of travel. So, too, is shopping, I suppose. But my tolerance threshold here is five minutes to buy a necessary shirt or shoes.

My companion, however, like a blonde borzoi, hunts through all the shops both sides of the Via Condotti, and indeed all the other rich streets which lure ladies outwards from the Spanish Steps: Bulgari, Gucci, Ferragamo, Valentino, Armani all lead us in.

We took the underground there from the Vatican to save a pound. The lady suddenly spends what sounded awfully like a couple of million lire on a very dashing coat. But she calculates this thereafter on a special female shopper's rate of exchange which makes it seem to her the give-away bargain of the year.

Thus triumphant, we walked down the Corso (once a city racetrack) to the Piazza del Popolo and an excellent lunch at the *dal Bolognese* on the corner. Outside: rather full of American tourists but excellent for people-watching across the square. Inside: serious Roman businessmen in the comfortable ambience of a London club.

On to the Santa Maria to see the Caravaggios (but the church is locked) and so, puffing up the cliff edge into the Borghese Gardens. These, by their very hilliness, are made far more rural than Hyde Park.

Past the Hippodromo, redolent of dung and competing children squeaking, and out of the gardens again at the top of the Via Veneto. Even in November, we can sit, slightly sheltered by glass screens against the paparazzi, gunmen and bomb throwers, outside the long, mirrored Café de Paris.

That evening to the Pantheon, built twenty-seven years before Christ's birth and thus a century before the Romans started to civilise us ancient Brits. This healthily makes us feel like central Africans should feel in Paris or mid-Westerners anywhere in Europe. It's bracing for the traveller to be made to feel a barbarian once in a while.

Close to the Pantheon is a tremendous fish restaurant, Rosetta. Hectic atmosphere, delicious, delicate food, horrific bill, and worth every mouthful. Home naturally via the Fontana de Trevi – coins fly in and earnest wishes fly up for our respective children.

This might have brought our final bonus. For security diverts us from the mundane route to Rome's little charter airport. From the Baths of Caracalla (what a name to conjure with) instead we amble and jolt all down the tomb-lined, green and charming Appian Way, as if an overgrown bridle path could suddenly be found in Knightsbridge.

TRAVEL FACTS

Alitalia, 27–28 Piccadilly, London W1 (01–602 7111)
British Airways, PO Box 10, Heathrow Airport, Hounslow, Middx (01–759 2525)
Magic of Italy, 47 Shepherd's Bush Green, London W12 (01–743 9555)
Pegasus, 24a Earl's Court Gardens, London SW5 (01–370 6851)
American Express, Portland House, Stag Place, Victoria St., London SW1 (linkline 0345 010333)

— PARIS —

'But you must be completely mad!' expostulated the attractive French girl on Biarritz station. 'Even to think to drive your daughters with your car through central Paris. Ze traffic. Ze crowds. Ze little bandits!'

Claire was seeing us off on the night express Mototrain from Spain – an excellent way to traverse one of France's longest, least pretty sections. She is a Bordelaise not a Parisienne and so did not know that August is Paris's emptiest month. Just as British upper classes explain: 'But no-one, darling, actually lives in Slough', so their Parisian counterparts maintain: 'In August, the city is completely empty'.

Claire persisted: 'Go instead to Versailles'. Versailles, much further from Paris than one ever allows for, is essential viewing even though I have always preferred the far less ostentatious Fontainebleau set in particularly attractive countryside. But Versailles has a number of diversions for younger tourists. You must not just pad round all those gigantic rooms, your fund of energetic interest drying out. I like boating on the lake, walking in the gardens, of course, and best of all Le Petit Trianon, pretty as ten pictures and reasonably sized enough for one to imagine living there.

But Versailles, where we had once lunched on tripper-grub (le sandwich like British Rail's horrors) in its fine but too trippery square, was closed. The heads of EEC governments were walled up inside, debating probably the latest nonsenses of wine lakes and butter mountains.

So it would be central Paris. I don't know whether it's possible really to *love* Paris, as Americans ingenuously sing. It's too big, too disdainful, too pock-marked in parts like an aging, arrogant duchess, to be loved. That doesn't stop its fascination.

What would give the girls a good, lively first impression? Not the Louvre, anyway. Old museums bore young minds. At any age, fine exhibits, like rich food, need to be taken in light snacks over several days. The Louvre takes eight hours to see properly. For this visit, its grand façade suffices since it forms the other end of that glorious shaft down from the Arc de Triomphe, which makes the backbone of Paris. This would be our target.

The Gare d'Austerlitz celebrates yet another Napoleonic victory over our allies. Do French visitors to London, I wonder, mind being constantly reminded of their defeat at Waterloo? Compared with dour King's Cross, Austerlitz is clean, sprightly and free – at least at breakfast-time – of hookers, pimps, winos and bum boys.

The first impression was good. The station buffet (as on most French stations) is several cuts above its British counterpart. I recall one restaurant listed by Michelin on the centre platform of a small station somewhere in the Midi. And I call to mind several good meals in the stations at Toulouse and Toulon. But while drinking *chocolat* (compliments of French Railways) Kate, who usually forgets nothing, remembered that she had left her ear-rings in our *couchette*. The girls set forth boldly to find them. Fifty fretful minutes and five frantic platform searches later, the girls blithely turned up, not transported to Spain, but having made arrangements to contact our *conducteur* in the offices of the Wagons-Lit.

Angry with relief from anguish, I quarrelled with the poxy dwarf of a taxi driver – aren't we lucky with London's cabbies? – who was taking us with surly slowness to collect our car from the Motorail Terminus. At Boulogne and Biarritz, cars and passengers depart and arrive much more conveniently together.

Disgruntlement fled as we reached the Seine. For there were barges and *bâteaux mouches* busy in sunlight which blue-rinsed the river. The girls encouragingly oohed and aahed; and even more so over Nôtre Dame.

'This Ile de la Cité must be a very smart place to live!'

The Louvre loomed. But traffic was light. We had time for life's necessary thing: time to stand and stare. Only one driver shouted at us and that only because our door was ajar.

By fortune and the sense of direction I learned out fox hunting as a boy – 'Gives a lad a good eye across country!' a major had grunted when we started driving tanks – I found the Rue de Rivoli. Only a fool could not. It flanks the north side of the Louvre lying in the same north-westerly direction as the Champs Elysées. That, and the fact that the Seine flows first north-west, then due west opposite the Place de la Concorde, and then south-west, gives anyone a sound basis.

The Rue de Rivoli is a favourite street. Fine buildings on the right, then the Tuileries Gardens on our left. We swung into the Place de la Concorde, the sort of approach needed to enter this extraordinarily extravagant space in a city centre. We paused to look all round; back at the Tuileries, across towards the Seine. And then up that marvellous slope of the Champs Elysées.

The best view of all is from the terrace linking the Jeu de Paume (an exhibition was in progress) and the Orangerie, but the charm of a nearly empty Champs Elysées at 11 o'clock on an August morning was too good to miss. It's an excellent month to visit Paris. Some of the expensive restaurants and shops are shut, but few Brits can afford them. The remaining Parisians, short on custom and otherwise often on manners, too, try harder. Sales take place.

We dawdled up and down and I could blather: 'Down there's a restaurant where I used to dine with ...' and: 'There in the open I bought the horse-and-carriage prints in the hall at home for almost nothing ...' and: 'There's the nice hotel by the Etoile where the American cousins stayed ...'

The area south of the Arc de Triomphe is an excellent place for numerous hotels. Nor is it impossibly far for a pleasant stroll down the Champs Elysées for the shopping areas at the bottom and the smartest shops in the Faubourg St Honoré, Rue Royale, and Rue de la Paix, with big stores in the Rue de Rivoli, Rue de Sèvres and at the east end of the Boulevard Haussmann (which starts as the Avenue de Friedland where it joins the Champs Elysées at the Etoile).

Traffic round the Etoile which embraces the Arc is usually dodgem-crazy. Today, we could circle it thrice. 'There's the Bois de Boulogne. Wonderful restaurant, La Cascade, but hideously expensive. Out there is the racecourse, Longchamp.'

Up and down the Champs Elysées twice. 'But there are no smart shops here, Daddy. These only sell cars or airlines.'

When the scale is grand, how the French can build! And execute. 'Here,' I said, re-entering the Place de la Concorde, 'stood the guillotine. Louis XVI and Marie-Antoinette and about 1300 others, over there by the Tuileries railings, had their heads swished off into baskets.'

Agreeably yucking sounds. Then: 'What's that thing like Cleopatra's Needle in the middle?' pointing up at Rameses II's whopping obelisk from Luxor. Like ours on London's Embankment, it was presented last century by that obsequious Egyptian Viceroy called Mohamed Ali.

Then down the splendid Rue Royale and round the lovely Madeleine to the useful large 'Garage parking' in the square's north-west corner.

And then, of course, le window-shopping all down the Rue St Honoré as far as the Palais Royale and back up the other side, peering into a thousand windows. The daughters savagely criticised several styles, praised a few, and groaned at the prices. 'Those shoes can't be £200! Who could spend that?'

So, after coffee and Cokes on a corner of the Rivoli (grey-suited American businessmen earnestly dealing) into the sun-filled Tuileries. Under neat trees, poor men dozed on benches.

The gardens through which the King and his loathed Queen had been chased by the mob were devoid of locals and light on tourists. Tall, thin, very black men were peddling brass bangles and silly paper birds which flew into the trees.

'Pretty things, missy,' they pursued my daughters. I strode on while they tried different tongues on me. Once talk to pedlars and you're doomed. 'Only a pound, Daddy,' one daughter called out, betraying instantly not only our nationality but our interest.

Then, near the Louvre, came my first attack by Paris's notorious child bandits. 'Look! Look!' Two dark gipsy girls of twelve or so, about five feet high, jostled me holding out a tatty tear sheet for me to examine. As they did so, two swarthy bigger boys lunged at my hip pocket. I clipped one across his earhole. Grunting, he spun. Both fled.

The three of us kept close company walking to lunch near the car. We wanted neither a tourist trap nor anything grand but a bustling typical brasserie. There is just such a one on the corner of the Madeleine and the Rue Tronchet, called after the latter. It is elegant within and peopled by French businessmen. They, and French lorry drivers, are the best guides to good value food in France. Outside the restaurant, covered tables on the pavement were brisk with secretaries, office juniors, and trysting lovers snatching sandwiches between kisses.

Finally, due to Kate's skilled map-reading (always buy a large scale street map for big cities for everyone of whom you ask the way will either be too busy, or foreign) we contrived by devious back alleys to reach the autoroute without having to venture on Europe's most terrifying circuit, the Périphérique. Unless possessed of nerves of steel and driving a heavy lorry this inner circle road, which clutches the city in a roaring grip, must be avoided.

TRAVEL FACTS

Air France, 69 Boston Manor Rd., Brentford, Middx (01–499 6511)

British Airways, PO Box 10, Heathrow Airport, Hounslow, Middx (01–759 2525)

British Caledonian, Caledonian House, Crawley, W. Sussex (01–668 4222)

Paris Travel Service, Bridge House, Ware, Herts (0920 3922)

Thomson Holidays, Greater London House, Hampstead Rd., London NW1 (01–439 2211)

Time Off, 2a Chester Close, Chester St., London SW1 (01–235 8070)

French Government Tourist Office, 178 Piccadilly, London W1 (01–499 6911)

— BRUSSELS —

Loathing those battery blocks of heartless modern hotels, I asked Time Off to find for me in Brussels something old and characterful, like a decent burgundy.

They found the Astoria, built in 1909 and scarcely disturbed since. It's a pocket Ritz with gilt pillars, tall mirrors, a sweeping staircase and a uniformed porter who actually opens doors for you and humps your suitcase. Arriving in the ordinary, but expensive, 'businessman's hotel' is dreary. 'Here's your key,' and off you go with heavy bag and heart to an unlit cubicle like a million others.

Down the sweeping staircase of the Astoria should have swished fin-de-siècle ladies in long dresses on the arms of distinguished men in tails. Indeed, in the salon on Sunday morning a girl played the grand piano and a tenor sang to an attentive audience backed up by bottles of champagne.

The lift, a cupboard concession to progress, is rightly shoved out of sight. The bar is furnished from the carriages of the old Wagons-Lits, far cosier than the over-vaunted splendours of the Orient Express. Into it one evening incongruously burst a red-sweatered driver looking for the British Embassy. 'S'meant to be on this main drag, ain't it?' But it isn't. This 'main drag' zooms along towards the Palace and the distinguished Place Royale. Here they've constructed an excellent museum of modern art. It contains the usual sufficiency of tortured nonsense – boards of nails, twisted metal, cuckoo colours and comic genitalia disguised as waterpumps – to make the rest of the works seem highly attractive. How our bogus modern artists and sculptors must hoot behind the highbrows' backs when they've just flogged off another lump of rubbish for five years' beer money.

The Astoria, charming, creaking old delight on the Rue Royale is close enough to walk down hill, past the dark, chanting cathedral into the city's hub. 'Nothing to do in Brussels but eat,' sniffed a pseud. 'And the food's just rich and creamy.'

Rubbish, of course. It's only fifteen minutes to the countryside. The Bois on the fringe is huge and pretty with the lake on which, years ago, I used to potter with Béatrice, a rather rich and very beautiful Belgian girl. Her mother, a formidable business lady, decided my prospects were not bright and married off Béatrice to a middle-aged oil-well owner with more acres than I, and in New Jersey, too.

The shopping stretches from elegant 1840 arcades to modern centres like 'City 2'. Round the Sablons, Grand and Petit, are warrens of antique shops. The food, thanks to the Eurocrats on expense accounts, at least rivals Paris, and sometimes surpasses it.

I wanted to see again the first foreign city I ever visited. In the war's wake we would drive there from bombed-out Germany. Until then, I'd never discovered grand restaurants or elegant bordellos.

Brussels had masses of the former and certainly one of the latter, exclusively patronised by the Brigade of Guards, whose armoured division had liberated the city. Madame introduced the young ladies in two's and three's in her drawing-room for social chat over flutes of champagne. She liked us to take them out to smart dinners first.

One girl stirred early. 'I'm off to spend the day with my fiancé by the sea.' When I grumbled she silenced me by saying: 'He's a full colonel in the US Army'.

The Germans had probably been there before us, too. My father, visiting me for a weekend, complained about black stains on his hotel sofa. 'Blasted Prussian jackboots!'

The Grand Place, gothic, spiked and jumbled, is one of Northern Europe's finest mediaeval squares, and the better for being well used by young locals without pompous reverence. Some of the gorgeous merchants' houses are now cheap bars. La Chaloupe d'Or was full on all its three floors until 2 am. Splendid old rooms abuzz with students drinking (yet not drunk) round the long tables and in full flood on *weltpolitik*, poetry, and plans for bed.

Next door is the Maison du Roi, now a small museum showing Brussels' growth from a Roman outpost. It's also got a collection of the uniforms for the city's over-exposed dwarf Mannekin-Pis. Opposite is the tremendous Hôtel de Ville, one of those maddening public places which insist you wait for fretful guided tours.

The famous Vincents was closing but they sent us along to the Armes des Bruxelles which has been open all day long for more than half a century. Mussels in all modes are the thing. A gargantuan bowl of them in wine and cream and greenery cost, with wine and coffee, under £8 each. It stopped me two-thirds through. What stomachs these Bruxellois possess! One such next to me spent lunch trying to make amends to his pouting mistress. He had stood her up to take his wife out to dinner on her birthday. 'Then who is more important?' rose the age-old impassioned, seldom answerable cry.

Writers always eavesdrop. Foreign restaurants are symphonies of plots, for the locals never believe a Brit can understand their language. 'But you made love to the old sack. I know it!' hissed the girl, showing sharp teeth.

Wines are dear. Beers are stupendous in old yellow pubs like La Morte Subite (unfortunate name, but 'Sudden Death' is a card-game students play there). I drank the Brussels beer Chimay and tottered off with my guide, an interesting Hungarian count. A large Chimay plus a *tartine*, a double sandwich of two cheeses and green onions, makes a fair snack.

There are good fish restaurants around the former fish maket on the Quai aux Briques, reminding me of Brussels' close connection with the sea. One called literally 'The Rugby Man' sounds like a clip-joint for singing Welsh tourists, but isn't.

For real style we went to L'Ecailler du Palais Royal off the Grand Sablon. One portion between two all the way through five huge courses is the trick here, recommended by the Magyar aristo. Preprandial snacks in this really pretty restaurant were winkles, eaten with pins, of course, and washed down with champagne. From those we ascended socially to a mousse of different fish. Then sole. Then turbot. Finally, tiny *fraises de bois*.

One evening we nipped out to Essene to eat superb Belgian variations of nouvelle cuisine at the Belle Moulin, a wonderful old mill where Madame Van Ransbeeck also runs a farm. The new Guide Michelin had just removed one of its revered stars and dark tales were whispered about the state of the inspector.

No such anger though in the old orchard and farmyard on the edge of the battlefield of Waterloo. Out in the open countryside where my regiment (with some help from their friends) held off Napoleon through a June day in 1815, the friendly ghosts were busy in the wind.

TRAVEL FACTS

Sabena, 36/37 Piccadilly, London W1 (01–437 6960)
British Airways, PO Box 10, Heathrow Airport, Hounslow, Middx (01–759 2525)
Time Off, 2a Chester Close, Chester St., London SW1 (01–235 8070)
Victor Holidays, 135 High St., Epping, Essex (0378 76451)
Belgium Travel Service, Bridge House, Ware, Herts (0920 61131)
Belgium Tourist Office, 66 Haymarket, London SW1 (01–499 5379)

— CHAMPAGNE —

Champagne has such a naughty sparkle that whenever couples hear I'm going there again, envy is titillated like their taste buds. 'Lord, you're so lucky!'

'Go for a weekend,' I urge, 'illicit or cosy. Even both. So far, it's 50–1 against being spotted. No one goes there. Yet. But they will. And champagne taken in Champagne should beguile most ladies.'

Few know where it is, let alone how close. Fifty minutes by Air France (top class snacks in *classe d'affaires*, as it's suitably known) and then two hours by autoroute east to Reims.

Champagne is Europe's most northerly wine area. One can't count the thin white scentless, senseless stuff earnestly produced in Britain. The Romans in Britain had vineyards and villas in the next valley south of mine at home. They must have had real summers then . . .

People haven't gone to Champagne because, ridiculously, there's been a dearth of good restaurants until recently. The champagne houses, all of which you can visit, entertained their business friends at home.

But for Brits, France means food. Now we can gorge in Champagne. Michelin-starred establishments have leapt up in the last few years like the vine's bright green new shoots in spring. Looked at close to, commercial vines are stark compared with their untrained cousins trailing over arbours. They stand in battalions of strict rows, black in winter, savagely pruned like *mutilés de guerre*, awaiting the greening of the spring. But from Reims south to Épernay are pretty rolling hills combed with vineyards and capped in autumn with golden woods.

The Marne meanders. Grey stone villages snooze. Everything, except at harvest, is at leisure. The ambience is conducive to amour. The unruffled countryside is as alluring as a plump rich widow of pleasing aspect and sparkling pedigree.

This time I'm on my way to something special: a tasting and a lunch given by the House of Bollinger in Christian Bizot's elegant home facing their cellars in Ay.

'I live above the shop,' wonderful old Mme Bollinger used to say as she bicycled about her vineyards.

I'm rolling eastwards with a friend who is Bollinger's British agent – always a bonus to have friends in agreeable jobs.

This luncheon, simply announced as '*Un dégustation de trois grands vins de France*', turns out to be the most memorable of my life. It's prepared by M. Boyer, patron of Michelin's latest three-star restaurant and the wines include – no printer's misprints these – a Château Marbuzet 1875, a Nuits St Georges 1885, and a Bollinger 1914. Bliss.

We travel guided by Michelin, which describes the hotel Le Manoir at Fontenay-Tresigny in red (meaning pretty) as 'belle décoration intérieure!' Another worthy support guide for off-the-main-road stops and stays is the *Chateaux hôtels indépendants et hostelleries d'atmosphère* produced by its own association, free from any of its members and enlivened by colour photographs and helpful chat. Le Manoir, dreadfully hard to find at night, turns out to be a '*belle époque*' hunting lodge.

Here Edward Prince of Wales might well have enjoyed other men's wives and handed out baronetcies as thank-yous after breakfast.

We arrive for dinner at a quarter to ten on a Sunday evening having been delayed *en route*. In England we'd have been told 'Kitchen's closed, you can have a soggy sandwich'.

But here Madame, a former beauty in black leather, sits us down by a log fire to ponder leisurely over a marvellous menu. The other couples are equally unharassed: several sugar papas with lissom blondes.

During dinner Madame enquires: 'Do you lack anything?' Moved by the atmosphere I murmur: '*Une jolie blonde.*' But she roguishly shakes her head.

On the autoroute we proffer our ticket (never get on these speedy but very expensive motorways without plenty of cash – preferably in coins). 'Vierzehn!' snaps the stout cashier glowering at us.

'But we're English, not German', I protest. Broad beam. 'Ah, that's different. *Bonne route!*' she waves us on.

Near here in the grisly war the Germans are said to have shot three RAF men in a cave. And French hostages, too, of course. Memories of the three wars – the Boches came through here in 1870, 1914 and 1940 – are sustained in a commonplace classroom in Reims.

Here, where Germany unconditionally surrendered, is the table round which the generals sat and signed. It was General Eisenhower's forward headquarters. Here the wall maps, pricked out with flags and blackboards showing RAF strikes, are frozen as they were on May 7, 1945, as if those commanders who disposed of millions of lives had just got up.

One point of travel is to tweak memories and the mind. The grey sepulchral cathedral does it too. People like dots murmur beneath not just those glorious old rose windows but the dazzling blues of Chagalls finished by the artist seven and a half centuries later.

Then away up that grand boulevard of champagne houses past Piper-Heidsieck where in the comfortable town house I lunched so well the previous winter with their boss – another steeplechasing contact – the Marquis d'Aulan and his beautiful Austrian wife.

At the top stands a recent three-star Michelin glory, M. Boyer's Les Crayères. The master chef bought this splendid old mansion from the Prince de Polignac but we can't afford to lunch there. In all France Michelin only granted eighteen three-star restaurants that year.

Now the city has two more starred ones, Le Florence and Le Chardonnay. In the tiny village of Châlons-sur-Vesle is a particular favourite of mine, the Assiette-Champenoise, whose young patron once worked for M. Boyer.

Ambling south through the vineyards, we lunch on the hill-top at the Royal Champagne at Champillon.

At Sept-Saulx almost equi-distant about fifteen miles between Reims and Épernay, there's a charming and quiet little hotel in the country, the Cheval Blanc, with a superb restaurant. I still recall the first time ten years ago eating their *écrevisses* in champagne.

We dine and stay at a hamlet, L'Epine, blessed with not only a huge basilica (the virgin appeared here) but a small very simple hotel, the Armes de Champagne, with its starred restaurant. We eat oysters – taken with champagne or even Black Velvet – the best aphrodisiac in the world. At the next table six trade unionists carrying briefcases and fresh from a meeting, wallow over a gargantuan spread of wild duck and listen to the spiel of the local Arthur Scargill.

A good gourmet can never be a Communist. If we all coughed up a few pennies to send our more destructive, malevolent trades unionists for the occasional whirl in Champagne with a bird, would they soften a little? Then comrades might at least see that life's good things are worth climbing up to, not pulling down.

TRAVEL FACTS

Air France, 69 Boston Manor Rd., Brentford, Middx (01–499 6511)
French Leave, 21 Fleet St., London EC4 (01–583 8383)
Sealink Travel, 163–203 Eversholt St., London NW1 (01–388 6798)
Just Motoring, 23 Wrotham Rd., Gravesend, Essex (0474 22243)
French Government Tourist Office, 178 Piccadilly, London W1 (01–499 6911)

— MARBELLA —

Delectable to dart from sunless Britain's leaden November chill at lunch-time (British Airways Club class from Gatwick serves a surprisingly good meal) and land for tea under bright skies in warm sun at Malaga.

A few days off in winter – sun all day from nine to five and a noon temperature of 70° at November's end – is worth two weeks away during one of our summers, when it's often sad to leave the roses.

I scuttle, courtesy of Mr Avis, through the horrors of Torremolinos. Even this looks less vile in winter. The roasting pork herds, Brit and Kraut, and the packs of soccer apes have fled, though the scaffolding for new tower blocks ominously stabs the sky.

I'm bound for southern Spain's most expensive slice of real estate, Marbella, halfway to Gibraltar. In winter's clarity, the old, crouched rock, that bone of contention, stands out plainly. For the expat colony it is still a reassuringly guardian lion, filled with comforting British things like red pillar boxes, Barclays Bank and Cooper's Oxford marmalade. In summer, the haze subdues one's view of it.

'Five-star weather for our five-star hotel,' said the lady at Los Monteros, one of the nicest hotels I've found. Smells of pine and eucalyptus trees, Spanish cigars and expensive scent. The nose is a good initial guide to the quality and class of restaurants, hotels, and private dwellings.

There were a hundred Swedish golfers in the place, making heavy grey jokes and pushing for free drinks. Otherwise, the guests were well brought up and so polite, which makes for a courteous staff.

Los Monteros turns out to be much more than an hotel. It's a complex of quiet, expensive villas, gardens and swimming pools, ponds, streams and little bridges, plus a flock of flamingos vainly stalked by a litter of kittens.

I sit on the balcony of my duplex (prettily decorated rooms) in cotton pants at half-past eight, eating breakfast – never waste a minute of sunshine in our winters – overlooking an unraped belt of woodland. On the other side of the awful main road (which does offend hotel guests with its suppressed racket) are the hotel's stables, run by a Chilean. They, and its own golf course on the same side, have an almost rural feel. But there's a horrible yellow tower on the hill beyond the golf course. Here fat, rich Arabs wobble down corridors in dressing-gowns, getting slimmed down, ready to eat more in Marbella's excellent restaurants. I see few out of doors. But evidence of their golden occupation is everywhere. Arab banks and mosques and palaces, brilliantly lit up at night, glitter along the coast.

I've been to Marbella over the years in most months between May and September but never in winter. 'Is the weather really always like this?'

'My God! No!' exclaimed the Spaniards with whom I dined. They live only twenty minutes from the 'Avenue of Death' as the locals call the dreadful coast road, but up among the mountains you might as well be in the deepest Scottish glen. 'But usually, it only rains four or five days running in November.'

Hotels usually fib about local weather but Los Monteros needn't because it prospers. Locals, however, give one the best advice. Paco said: 'February is very good indeed. January quite good and the light is brilliant. March and April excellent.'

I'd first seen Marbella in May twenty-five years before, after racing two horses in Madrid. Exhausted by Spanish revelry – a grand ball given by the Duke of Alburquerque wound up a non-sleep week – we'd begged: 'Do you know anywhere quiet by the sea?'

'There's a tiny fishing village,' murmured some Spaniards, 'called Marbella. Some sort of German prince has just started a club there.'

We clanked down in an old Dakota, the door of which flew open rather disconcertingly as we banked over Malaga. Prince Hohenlohe's brand new club was already full. So we stayed in the only hotel, the Fuerte, by the then little harbour. Amazingly, it is still there, hemmed in like a little white old lady by stormtrooping high rises. The food then was awful. The loos didn't work, and the place stank of DDT. But a necklet of small boutiques were opening along the single main street, and continental nobs and British nouveaux riches were settling in. When these follow shrewd aristos like Hohenlohe to swoop on a new holiday perch, you need to get in behind them fast. I was offered a sizeable building plot on the main road for £500. I delayed, lost the urge and the name of the lawyer. Today, that part of the High Street is worth half a million pounds.

The next boom in southern Spain could be a place about thirty kilometres the other side of Malaga, where there is, as Marbella was, 'a tiny fishing village ...'

Unlike Scunthorpe and Clacton and other exotica, Marbella doesn't wither in winter. Urban sprawl has at least brought businesses: real life with real people. Tourists in summer flip like sparrows past busy people's windows. In winter in the tourist spots you can see the place at work. Even on a winter's evening on my way to look at the rough cut of a video we're making, I find all the offices open until eight, busy traffic, neons winking, and the pavement cafés chattering in pools of light under a starry sky. Spanish time still runs late.

I lunched in hot sun at three at La Cabana. '*Sol* or *sombre?*' asks the *maitre d'hotel*. 'Oh, *sol*,' I sigh. I stroll, then swim. Groves of pine and eucalyptus rustle. Tennis courts plop and grunt. Lew Hoad appears.

Then I met for an early dinner at 9.45 a Swedish girl friend of a London girl friend. The restaurant was the then 'in' place in Puerto Banus, the Don Leone. It's softly lit with a warm glow and halfway between high falutin' and bistro. Its waiters are in the best Spanish style – which Italians seldom master – attentive without being oily or pushy. Its sporting owner is about to take a holiday in Madeira. 'Will it be quite different from here?' he asks me, 'and will I like Reid's Hotel?'

'Indeed it will, and you will,' I assure him.

Outside the yacht-filled port lies Mr Khashoggi's colossal cruiser, as large as a cross-channel ferry, but gleaming clean. Close by and quite dwarfed is the pleasant yacht of the Spanish king, and several of those of his nobles. Khashoggi's great mountain estates adjoin my friend Paco's. Mr Khashoggi helicopters up to his mountain pad. 'Always some girls kept up there,' said a local Spaniard, laughing, 'just in case he comes. And when there's a big house party, fresh loads of girls are flown up pretty quickly.'

What odd lives they must lead, these blonde playthings of the mega-rich. Like that of soldiers in war, perhaps: long periods of boredom punctuated by bouts of frightening activity.

One day I'm up in Mr Khashoggi's palatial stables with its handy rooms for other mounted entertainments. A Mercedes driven by a delectable blonde in the tightest jodhpurs swishes into the yard. A mare is brought out for her to mount. It doesn't occur to me, foolishly, that this surprising arrival could be one of us and I say something cheeky about her to my companion.

The girl turns in the saddle, smiles whitely and warns in sharpest cockney, 'You wanna watch it, cock!' and rides off.

Puerto Banus is a mix of boutiques and restaurants popping in and out of fashion, and sexy girls in sports cars and men wanted in Britain for various offences swaggering about in natty blazers on the quayside.

The place has a raffish style. It's like St Tropez was halfway between its heyday and the invasion of the packaged trogs. It will be spoilt, too, I expect. 'Sip and buzz on by,' as the flower said to the honey bee, which is not bad advice for the traveller either.

TRAVEL FACTS

Iberia, 130 Regent St., London W1 (01–437 5622)

Air Europe, Europe House, East Pk., Crawley, W. Sussex (01–651 3611)

Mundi Color, 276 Vauxhall Bridge Rd., London SW1 (01–834 3492)

Thomsons Holidays, Greater London House, Hampstead Rd., London NW1 (01–439 2211)

Horizon, Broadway, Edgbaston Five Ways, Birmingham (021–643 2727)

Spanish National Tourist Office, 57–58 St James's Street, London SW1 (01–499 0901)

— BARBIZON —

Within $2\frac{1}{2}$ hours of hellish Heathrow you can, courtesy of Air France and Mr Avis, be rumbling down Barbizon's litle main street and find a place both interesting and soothing, only forty-five minutes south of the buzzing capital. What a place for a weekend.

Overhung by orchards, Barbizon is lined with restaurants, small hotels, antique shops and art galleries, all pleasing ways of losing money and having a naughty dalliance.

The pictures will last longer than the most delicious *nouvelle cuisine* and there is plenty of good food around this artists' village. The pictures by living painters might even appreciate. In any case, they remain the best reminders of a happy stay.

The beamy, beaming village presses like a cat into the ankles of the tremendous Forest of Fontainebleau. It's an undulating mix of oak, russet beech and scented pine. Hilly little tracks explorable by car with the large scale map (Forests of France, no. 401) lead you past rocks, caves and heaths to vast, woody views and to the Jupiter Oak.

This whopper, which must have been around when the Normans conquered us, towers over attendant beech trees and astonishes my American friend. It's bigger than a Californian redwood and she cannot photograph it properly.

Miss Long Island, flying to France to save herself $3000 by buying a duty-free Peugeot, and I both picked Barbizon, haunt of *fin de siècle* artists and writers, for a weekend jaunt.

Robert Louis Stevenson lived in part of our hotel. In another bit lived the first French artist to start the colony, Charles Jacques. Millet lived across the street. In his old home, the caretaker, red-faced and white-haired, tells us bluntly among the paintings: 'The Russians are imperialists. Just like the British. And the Americans.'

Some of those painters' amiable eccentricities, like the scent of an old affair, drift on, part of the charm of Barbizon.

Beyond the forest – and that night we pick up deer, shadowy, alert in the headlights – lies the château of Fontainebleau. I've always preferred it to Versailles. Its gardens, infinitely less grand, are far friendlier. And because it's a hotch-potch inside, grown to fit its kings and emperors, some of its rooms are not just pretty, like Marie Antoinette's games room, but small enough for people like us to live in.

You need to relate to houses, which is why the museum hugeness of places like Blenheim is so depressing, as you file past cordoned-off unused rooms of spotless furniture. Size without people is awesome. I went once to a dance at Blenheim. Full of excitement, movement, chat, the great rooms at last awoke and glowed.

The French have let Fontainebleau get a bit tatty. A shaggy garden's all right. Most of us who live in the country prefer the natural to the regimented look. Neat lines go with garden gnomes. But the interior of Fontainebleau has such a richness of murals, furniture and tapestries that it is ridiculous not to light them better. Moral: go on a sunny day, but they're not so common in misty November.

And their guides ought to learn to smile when they hustle you out of the palace at noon for their enormous Socialist lunches. Certainly not all the French like their old enemy, the English, but in their lovely country they should pretend a welcome. After all, the twin royal passions for which this country palace was built, defined by a po-faced guide as 'Ze chase and ze wimmen', are common to sportsmen both sides of the Channel ('Sleeve', if you're French, of course).

The still privately-owned château Vaux-le-Vicomte, half an hour away, does things much better. Its gardens gloriously uplift hearts, a rare example of great men improving nature. It's the most beautifully balanced mansion I know. It was saved by a sugar tycoon whose granddaughter married its present owner, a French count. Louis XIV so coveted the place that he clapped its owner-builder, M. Fouquet, into jail for life, grabbed his great house and began colossal Versailles.

Mercifully, there's no huge hotel in Barbizon. Most have the aged and tangled warmth of inns. Even the grandest, Le Bas-Breau, where we stayed, calls itself merely an 'hostellerie' (always a good pointer in France) and has the clubbish warmth of a well-run country house of the 1930s.

Brilliant with fuchsias and gladioli scattered round courtyards, it is wincingly expensive at nearly £90 the room and £65 for a wonderful dinner. But we are spoilt rotten by the staff and after all, Thatcher, Mitterand and Co. stayed there – 'whole village shut up for two days!' grumbled a local – for the Fontainebleau Summit.

After our first dinner, warmly welcomed in the courtyard by both the maître d'hotel and the beautiful wife of the owner, we were forced by economics to eat elsewhere. But I treated myself to Calvados and coffee every evening by their log fire and Miss Long Island had raspberries grown in their garden for breakfast. On our last morning, there arrived at breakfast an extremely stylish French lover with his dark and sparkling mistress who ordered the same. Winter breaks like this make naughty weekends bloom.

The Clef d'Or down the street would be a nice place to stay and it offers a good four-course menu at £12, wine included. Eight artists, whose work had just been judged in an exhibition, were lunching there in the sort of dining room – high-beamed ceilings, proper napkins, good cutlery – that so rarely appears in the English countryside.

Fontainebleau has a cheerful Corsican restaurant, the Ile de Beauté, continuing the local link with Corsican Napoleon, who made his throne room in the palace as vulgarly purple and gold as any Hollywood moguls.

We shop along Barbizon's street for better taste. The owner of one antique shop was a wartime American pilot towing the US Airborne Division's gliders into action. He married a Barbizon girl.

While Miss Long Island is getting bargains off him, I'm down the street in the Musée Ganné, haggling with his wife over a snowscape by a living local artist.

The former pilot with a voice from Brooklyn is drowsily content with his lot, like almost everyone in Barbizon, and is therefore an excellent fellow with whom to do a deal.

TRAVEL FACTS

Air France, 69 Boston Manor Rd., Brentford, Middx (01–499 6511)

British Airways, PO Box 10, Heathrow Airport, Hounslow, Middx (01–759 2525)

British Caledonian, Caledonian House, Crawley, W. Sussex (01–688 4222)

Air France Holidays, 69 Boston Manor Rd., Brentford, Middx (01–568 6981)

French Government Tourist Office, 178 Piccadilly, London W1 (01–499 6911)

— BRUGES —

We went to Bruges by way of Brussels – the simplest way to fly, certainly. But we decided to drive first into the crammed capital. We were hungry. There, pressed for time and harassed by lack of parking spaces, we lunched in a real tourists' clip-joint, Maxim's, in the otherwise glorious Grand Place. £85 for two for their 'cheapest' lunch made my hackles rise.

But count early blessings. An early slap in the eye with a foreign bill makes travelling Britons realise we are still Europe's poor relations. But where in London, we consoled ourselves, could we lunch overlooking such a gorgeous mediaeval square?

Travelling angrily, too, can sweeten arrival. The autoroute from Brussels to Bruges is boringly flat and Belgian drivers, butt of French jokes, are as bad as ever.

But Bruges, when you get there, is a soothing balm, I'd bet, for every dented lover's heart. Pink-walled, canal-rimmed, it comes as sweetly healing as a nun, and far more beautiful than I'd expected.

They keep the town, which the locals pronounce 'Bruch-er' (French gets you nowhere fast), heavenly quiet by keeping out trucks. Scarcely a lorry passes down its *pavé* streets between the little old houses lined up like tall, lacy ladies under high-stepped bonnets. Most of the lovely squares are no-go areas for stinking cars. You walk. And love it. You can walk anywhere in Bruges in thirty minutes. Its flatness is a virtue. Crouched in a car, eye level only on people's bellies and the lower halves of shops, you'd miss everything for which you went.

The locals are stout, kindly and Flemish. Even the language is only a Dutch dialect. 'The Belgians aren't exactly sparkling or beautiful,' said my companion. But the place is both. As if cut by a deft film editor, every corner of little cobbled lane, canal, or high-gabled house reveals new views of soaring churches, pillared buildings, tree-guarded squares, and secret, dreaming places like the Béguinage. Lord, what peace lay there!

If you dodge grand places and duck behind the tourist circuit, Bruges isn't dear. Our hotel, the Nôtre Dame, recommended by the thoughtful little travel firm Winter Inn, certainly wasn't expensive. It's down the street past the church from which it takes its name, over a little canal and past a shop which sells excellent coffee pots.

In the church, we adored the magically moving Madonna and Child by Michelangelo, the only sculpture he exported in his life. The marble defeats the centuries. As we walk past, the Madonna's expression changes from divine resignation to human petulence and the boy Jesus, too large for scale, looks as cheeky as any lad off to play football ignorant, like all children, of his real role and future fate.

If you stay at the Nôtre Dame you need to be fit. It has stairs like the Matterhorn and the atmosphere is so 'family' that it would not do for a haughty traveller. We shared one solid supper with the patron and his friends goggling at their telly. 'Sixteen channels', he boasted, lapping up one of those winsome BBC sitcoms on which our licence fees are wasted.

At breakfast – oranges freshly squeezed and the superb coffee which percolates all the Low Countries – we were joined by a stout Frenchman in an exotic kimono and a Jimmy Young wiglet with his even plainer woman in negligée under dyed beribboned hair. I've seen some mutton playing lamb at breakfast and it can often turn the tum. But this couple were Dickensian high comedy. Better still, they weren't married to one another, but enjoying in this tiny hotel in a little town some snatched moments of doubtful bliss.

We stroll to the market and sit in the sun opposite Les Halles to drink Trappist beer with a kick like Scotch. The carillon in the huge belfry plays, on every quarter hour, some booming bars from what sounds like an Edwardian music-hall song. I thought it would drive me mad to live beneath it but, like Londoners with traffic, the locals say they never hear the bells.

We watch the tourists. Here are four Eppings (outer suburbanites) halfway betwixt the strangled affectations of both the Bow Bells and the Absolutely Mirandas. Keen as mustard in the bright autumnal sun, they're scoffing cream cakes. And here strides a crisp Highland lady in sensible tartan skirt, snapping instructions to her docile husband and son who amble in her wake like yellow labradors. Krauts with shaven skulls meticulously study maps. Every visitor to Bruges clutches the city's excellent maps at every corner.

'Zat's Basilica of Holy Blood' the Germans announce, pointing to the wrong corner of another lovely square, the Burg. The same cropped group studied the mock-log gas-fire in the restaurant, the Kastel Minnewater – excellent food on the lip of 'The Lake of Love' – and, after many minutes, asked its host, 'Pliss, where can we too buy wood which so long burns?' The patron, raised in the Belgian Congo, wobbled with laughter. He and our host at the Nôtre Dame were the liveliest Belgians we met. Meeting flippant Brits perhaps rubs off.

The Kastel's former owner, an octogenarian Baroness, had moved into the Béquinage, a dreaming close of white eighteenth century houses tenderly enclosing a green of leaning poplars. It is a home for the elderly. Founded in 1245, it used to be run charitably by the rich daughters of the city. Now Benedictine nuns, who walk briskly but benignly, run the place. I wish something like this existed in Britain, in Bath, let's say, for authors grown ancient and inept.

The darkly primitive Basilica feels like an ancient fort, and was one. On Fridays, the Relic of the Holy Blood, supposedly brought out of Palestine, is on display. A dozing priest kept his hand on the phial which supplicants knelt to kiss.

'On the annual pilgrimage,' said our host at the Nôtre Dame, 'the blood is meant to liquify'. He shrugged, 'Good for business, anyway'.

Looking for two recommended restaurants, De Snippe and De Witte Poort, and for St Jacob's church (luckily closed – you can have too much of good things), we spotted opposite the church a tiny family restaurant, 'T Kluizeken'. It was terrific value at £6 a head for the three-course lunch, wine included. And the walls were hung with pretty watercolours by the owner at £25 each which I now wish I had bought. But I was still wincing after that meal at Maxim's.

We bought lace, as one should, and more intriguingly observed a lace-making class. A cluck of matrons and one sweet young blonde with a neck like a swan, fingers plucking the bobbins like wild guitars, were grouped in a back-street museum, opposite a line of tiny lace shops.

The sun shafted across apple trees, like a peep through a Vermeer window, onto modern metal shelves where the ladies kept their lacework and onto an old wooden crucifix on the wall.

The young girl's shoulders ached from her work and she gently stretched before picking up her bobbins ... image of Bruges.

TRAVEL FACTS

Airline/ferry:

Sabena, 36–37 Piccadilly, London W1 (01–437 6960)

British Airways, PO Box 10, Heathrow Airport, Hounslow, Middx (01–759 2525)

Townsend Thoresen, Enterprise House, Channel View Rd., Dover, Kent (0304 203388)

Packages:

Time Off, 2a Chester Close, Chester St., London SW1 (01–235 8070)

Belgium Travel Service, Bridge House, Ware, Herts (0920 61171)

Winter Inn, Park St., Hovingham, York (065382 425)

Belgium Tourist Office, 66 Haymarket, London SW1 (01–499 5379)

— Part 2 —
European Holidays

— PROVENCE —

Like an old love seen again with a face suddenly stuffed full of tombstone false teeth, most of the sea strip of the south of France is now repellent.

Monaco – ugh! Coachloads of tourists tipping into the once elegant casino to jerk fruit machines and spit gum. Happy memories linger as if from another life. Twenty years ago life was certainly other. Monte Carlo was recherché, rich, grand, when I stayed at the splendid old Hôtel de Paris one November and went to take tea with Princess Grace in her pretty little pink palace on the hill. Up in a tiny lift, then along an outside balcony above La Condamine harbour. With her hands sketching pictures for emphasis, she was suddenly saying that her family had never quite fitted in with the nobs in Philadelphia, and that now in Europe she didn't quite ... 'Here they still think of me as an American.' She'd loved England: 'the cosiness of English villages', (making a nest of her hands).

On another summer holiday we were on one of the most beautiful and luxurious sailing boats afloat, the famous *Blue Leopard*. We were moored in Monte Carlo harbour, porthole to peeping porthole with a gin palace belonging to a then notorious and subsequently bankrupt British tycoon. It was wobbling with tartlets for the delectation of the owner and his guests. Our view of proceedings a few feet away was made even more hilarious when we noticed in another cabin the tycoon's wife being awfully busy with his skipper.

A few green pockets like Cap Martin and Cap Ferrat still resist the concrete onslaught, though close to jostling Antibes there is one nice bay, La Garoupe, with a cheerful restaurant and bathing place called La Joliette. I never, however, allow one drop of the western Mediterranean to pass lips when swimming in it.

My plan was to attack the coast from the west, flying to Marseilles and driving eastwards with my 13-year-old daughter Jane and sleeping in the hills. Real countryside begins only minutes behind the coast's monstrosities.

We made for La Cadière d'Azur above Bandol, using the long but swift three-sided autoroute approach. Only masochists attempt to penetrate the tangled traffic of Marseilles' centre and the autoroutes give you an instant taste of Provence: creamy rocks and tiled roofs. La

Cadière is one of a stony rookery of villages perched on hilltops and pleasantly embraced by excellent vineyards. Drink the local rosé. The famous Moulin des Costes lies within grapeshot of the Hostellerie Bérard, where M. Bérard cooks deliciously and his wife, a fine, striking blonde, runs the restaurant.

From its terrace, the mountains turn rosé, then rouge, as the setting sun flashes back across the valley from the windows of Le Castelle a mediaeval fairy fortress on the next hill north.

Madame shows pleased surprise that I speak French and, looking round the pleasant open dining-room, I hear with initial depression every other table speaking English. To hear your own tongue all round makes abroad seem too much home. It turns out the Beeb's cardigan fellow, Frank Bough, representing Metro-man, has puffed the place on his telly travels. So has my fat friend, 'Arfer' Eperon in his good book, *The French Selection*. But the other Brits are most agreeable and, swimming in the pool before breakfast below our bedroom windows, we're soon actually talking to one another.

Jane and I reconnoitre the beaches, for the slice between Marseilles and Toulon is the only bit of the French Mediterranean coast I've not yet explored. Sadly, they turn out grotty. Writing about this afterwards I'm reprimanded by a sort of English camp-site operator out there. But despite his blusterings I note that he can't even spell Mediterranean. We drop down past country folk in lanes selling strawberries, olive oil, cherries and pottery, into a traffic jam at Les Lecques. We've hit the coast pizza-block.

But in the crowded harbour extraordinary jousting is in full plunge. Poised on the high poops of long diesel-driven fishing boats, local lads grip whacking lances, tilting each other into the greasy water. A squad of holidaying Germans honk with delight at this.

Grieving over the scruffy shores west of Toulon, I supposed that the worst must also have befallen my favourite French beach. With trepidation, we approach Cavalière, never to be confused with boring Cavalaire closer to ghastly St Tropez.

It was eighteen years since I'd last been there. It was blissfully unchanged. At the reception desk of the Hotel Surplage, so correctly named for you walk from the terrace directly on to the sand, a head was bent over a telephone. I asked in French: 'Is it possible the family Engelfred still own this hotel?' 'Is it possible,' replied Mme Engelfred, looking up with a warm smile, 'that I hear the voice of Ivor Herbert?'

I was introduced to the Engelfreds and their hotel by film producer Frank Launder with whom I was scripting in the south of France *The*

Great St Trinian's Train Robbery. All the Surplage's guests seem to come on this sort of introduction from close friends. Rather like the village of Trebetherick in north Cornwall, it's one of those places where, asked where you stay, you answer, 'In a small village – you'd never have heard of it'. And the other person always has.

I loved the Surplage so much that I went back seven years running with a wife, then with a girlfriend, then with my young son. We kept a little water-ski boat out there. We voyaged to the islands. We danced in the disco at Le Rayol. One year, we squatted in the Engelfred's next door empty villa with our boat bobbing at anchor at the foot of the overgrown garden. It is a marvellous place and I wished Jane and I were staying.

Grandfather Engelfred, still hale, was a great resistance fighter who led the French commandos on to Cap Nègre at the bay's eastern end to flush out the Germans. The next-door hotel was then owned by collaborators and its madame had her head shaved after the liberation. Nobody at the Surplage ever mentioned the other hotel. They still don't.

'Can I tell my readers how much I like your hotel?' I asked Mme Engelfred. The writer's dilemma: whether to reveal a pearl. My ears sting from readers lambasting me the summer I wrote about Paxos, their private paradise. 'Bloody press!' wrote a furious man from Henley-on-Thames. 'You'll bring in all the fish-'n'-chippers and ruin our lovely island.'

I wondered what Mme Engelfred would want. She said, 'Of course. We are very full in July and August with our old friends. But other times we would be delighted. The new autoroute keeps people away from this coast road.' Thank goodness, for the next 20 kilometres east are without one whiff of doubt the prettiest on all that coast.

Jane thought she should see St Tropez and she had the good taste to find it tatty and dull. Its glamour died a decade back and it's now a tired old tart of a place.

So we pressed north into the hills west of Grasse to Montauroux (a simple hotel, La Marjolaine) with views so tremendous you could live on them forever. Then to enchanting Fayence, and strange Mons, along little lanes where in an hour we passed just one car.

We had a good lunch for a fiver a head overlooking a little park in beautiful St Cézaire and so via bustling Grasse to stay with Jane's godfather in his handsome old farmhouse in the hills.

Tasteless loonies buy new jerry-built 'villas' in foreign parts. New 'pads' have little charm and, so far from appreciating, your foreign investment often falls apart at the seams.

In Provence, the moral's clear: with one gleaming exception, keep off the coast and stay in the cheap and beautiful hills just a hop behind the sea strip's jangle of false teeth.

TRAVEL FACTS

Air France, 69 Boston Manor Rd., Brentford, Middx (01–499 6511)

Air France Holidays, 69 Boston Manor Rd., Brentford, Middx (01–568 6981)

VFB, 11 St Margaret's Terrace, Cheltenham, Glos (0242 35515)

French Travel Service, Francis House, Francis St., London SW1 (01–828 8131)

French Government Tourist Office, 178 Piccadilly, London W1 (01–499 6911)

— SWITZERLAND (Summer) —

The part-Malaysian actress examined our feet at the foot of the Swiss alp.

'Are you *sure* those old tennis shoes will be OK? And that you want to walk down it, not climb up?'

My thirteen-year-old daughter and I gave nods of confidence. However frail the pound – and it's pretty thin against the fat Swiss franc – one must when abroad maintain an air of war-winning jauntiness. Particularly when amongst the world's professional neutrals ...

Yet the actress and her husband, the dashing Mr Murk, were quite unlike the stolid Swiss who munched in our hotel, the Sunstar, or the pair of baleful Krauts lunching next to us in the excellent restaurant of the Hotel Stern in Chur (pronounced Cockney Coo-er!).

To get to Lenzerheide and the Sunstar, we had flown Dan Air (almost empty) from Gatwick to Zurich, taken a train directly out of the bottom level of the airport and doddled along to Chur with an attendant bringing welcome snacks along the train. The gloomy Krauts in the Hotel Stern must just have received sad tidings from their Zurich gnomes. The pall they cast didn't dilute our enjoyment in lapping up our *capuns*, the local delicacy. Don't leave Chur without tasting. Afterwards, we took the Postbus from the station and went on climbing – the driver stopping at each village to collect mail – up to Lenzerheide.

In winter you can ski to your hotel's front door. In July the fields, flowered like Laura Ashley prints, tip right on to the village's main street.

We could have stayed on the bus to snootier places like Davos and St Moritz. But, as the girl sitting on our sun-terrace said scornfully of nearby St Moritz, 'But that's a *town*. And very ...' she flicked a finger explicitly upwards under her pert nose. 'Lenzerheide's a village in the country.'

Indeed, the fields full of flowers, yellows and reds and blues, lap not only the village but the lake on which windsurfers and little sailing dinghies stitch in and out like dizzy dragonflies. Lower down, anglers, a brooding race, stare mournfully into clear water. Trout plop.

It's a modern place, nothing much older than twenty years and too modern in parts. Why must man erect square blocks among the country's curves? Elsewhere round Lenzerheide they've got it right: paths wander round meadows, in and out of cool pine woods, past neat signs telling you what squirrels look like, and then zig-zag up the mountain's warm flank. Here hosts of cowbells slung under beige-grey necks chime out, a mixture of Caribbean steel bands and Chinese temples.

So on our first day we went up the western slopes of Alp Stätz, an amble first through pines and then the bell-tolling cow fields. But a cold snack and wine on the terrace at the foot of the last ski-lift cost £13! You are paying not only in a rich currency but for the expense of hoisting food up there. And you are paying, as at all restaurants, something for the surroundings. The view was tremendous, the sun dazzling, the air cool.

There wasn't much of a view of anything in the Sunstar and the *table d'hôte* at the otherwise very friendly hotel resembled an MP's speech: long, solid and dull. 'Too much out of tins,' whispered Kate expertly.

The next day, cautioned by the actress about our shoes, we took the cable-car up into the clouds licking the Rothorn, 9,400 feet up, to start our four-hour journey down. 'Follow the white-red-white on the stones. You cannot fail,' murmured the conductor.

No one accompanied us. A girl standing next to us in the cable-car, clutching lupins and lilac (July at Lenzerheide is like May in Britain) turned out to be a waitress in the mountain-top restaurant.

Round the first rocky bend we found ourselves mincing through deep crisp snow in our ridiculous tennis shoes. Clouds whirled coolly. Then the sun sizzled and mountain ridges appeared clutching piercing blue pools. A sun-bathing *chamois* with huge horns calmly regarded us. Two furry beasts with long banded tails scuttled from their watering hole, but I cannot say they were Yeti.

The easy path dropped down into its next phase: a stony and scrubby belt. Then followed pastures with more flowers spurting than grasses. A stream burbled past towards our first goal, the waterfall below Alp Sanaspan.

We ate our hotel's picnic, salami and ham in crisp brown rolls, eggs, apricots and peaches, and then we slept. The air, iced by the height, rinsed by showers, scented by herbs and flowers, was like a decent hock spiked with oxygen.

On the farmhouse below where they later gave us milk and cheese, the solar panels glinted incongruously. Below that spread the belt of dark forest, the pines as neat as toys.

The roar of the falls waxes. Kate gambols blithely on ahead. Edging sideways to cross the torrent on a plank the intrepid author panting after his nimble daughter, slithered and slipped along on the seat of his pants, grabbing at roots. Parental failures are the stuff of children's mirth. 'Daddy panicking in Switzerland' is now part of Herbert history.

As we moved on into the cool pine forest I'm moaning out to Kate: 'Oh, my ankles and my calves, my thighs and bleeding knees ...'

'You wouldn't want to come here just to sit around,' said Kate.

And indeed, when we reach the lake, we find that Mr Murk has organised a *Kinderprogram* – so that children can escape their parents. Mr Murk, husband of the Austro-Malaysian actress, is the dashing Director of Tourism. He whizzes us round in his Audi Quattro and, at his trim home, proudly shows us his nuclear fall-out shelter in the basement. 'All Swiss houses must have bunkers. And here's my machine gun. 200,000 Swiss men are all instantly armed like this.'

But the bunker, like foolhardy British boxrooms, was full of old suitcases and cardboard boxes. 'Still, if the bomb fall on, say, Milan,' says Mr Murk zapping up the hill into Sportz, 'we shall have time ...' He looks sympathetically at us. But Kate, to my relief, bursts out laughing.

The Guarda Val in Sportz, a member of the renowned French Relais et Châteaux association, is a cosily converted complex of old farm buildings with eagle-eye views. It's nice to escape from Lenzerheide's Ruislip-modern houses. The Guarda Val produced for Kate her first experience of *nouvelle cuisine*: seven delicious tiny courses as pretty as paintings and spread out over two hours. Below the windows, an old Swiss farmer solemnly scythed his hay. It was the French Rothschilds, I recalled, who kept servants to row little boats about on their lake just to complete the view from their château ...

'Mountains,' Mr Murk told us, 'are good for making marriage and business troubles feel better.' They certainly make you feel small-fry in a colossal landscape.

Another evening we drive further over the pass and into the next green valley to Muldain to eat *fondue Chinoise* in the Gasthof Junkerhaus. Slivers of smoked raw meat dunked in boiling soup but with such a variety of sauces as to turn Mr Heinz green with envy. The wood-panelled old pub is the haunt of two different types sharing at least one thing in common: the local gypsies and those jet-set wanderers bored of the tinsel glitter of St Moritz.

TRAVEL FACTS

Swissair, 10 Wardour St., London W1 (01–439 4144)
Kuoni, Kuoni House, Dorking, Surrey (0306 885044)
Swiss Travel Service, Bridge House, Ware, Herts (0920 3971)
Thomson Holidays 'Lakes & Mountains', Greater London House,
Hampstead Rd., London NW1 (01–439 2211)
Swiss National Tourist Office, 1 New Coventry St., London W1
(01–734 1921)

— GREECE – THE PELOPONNESE —

Frost in our October fields. Honey sun on the Acropolis at tea-time and 85°F. Red orb diving behind the Corinth Canal and those smelly refineries as I drive west from Athens, then south to explore the Peloponnese. It's a notion of Timothy Timms of Timsway Travel (real name, good firm) because I don't know this mountainous slab of mainland Greece hanging down like four gigantic wrinkled fingers. It's wild, eerie with ancient sites, squiggling with empty shores and still relatively undiscovered.

Like the Loire Valley, the Peloponnese combines culture with beautiful surroundings. Greece certainly doesn't have French food but then the Loire doesn't have the Greek sea.

Three hours from Athens Airport (Lord King and his barons have surely sharpened up BA), I'm in Tolon at the head of the Argolian Gulf, a pleasant seaside village which will be my base camp. In Dolfin Hellas' office opposite the good smells of the bakery, plump Taki, winking, pours me whisky in the warm bustling night.

'So, why not you come here before? Been Athens often, you say, Delphi, islands, islands, you say. All the English want is islands! Why? Here is far more sea!'

It's true. And in the next half-hour, seven English couples ranging from teens to sixties, pop in to book excursions to Mykinae, Tiryns and Epidauros. They tell me they've been coming back to Tolon for the last four, twelve, even seventeen years. Some are *en passage* to the bars (too much like pubs) and the tavernas. Food typically Greek, so generally dull, but the meat is naturally a bit better than the awful stringy stuff you face on the islands.

One bright executive lady (divorced, like so many of her amusing sort) remembered 'when Tolon was all orange groves and olive trees down to the lovely beach on what's now the German end of the village.' Taki interrupts, '*Austrian*! Much nicer than German. We keep them separated.'

The bumpy village street is separated from the sand by lines of shops. Taki's glamorous wife runs a mini-Asprey's. What can she sell to what seem not very well-off tourists? I price some jewellery and retire astonished. The boutique glistens but no-one is in there buying. I can hear the warm sea lapping in the bay. Opposite: cottages, tavernas and small apartment blocks scramble up the mountain. The little road goes nowhere, so even in summer's height it's a pleasantly far cry from Athens' awful outskirts or the raucous hell of Benidorm.

Later in the week in the neighbourhood's best restaurant, the Spilia – tourist-free, fantastic messes, chickens-in-lemon-juice – the advertising lady clasps her neck. 'Tolon drags me back, I love it so.' This, for once, was really good food, though in a bogus cave-like setting. Better in the summer, sitting out, I reckon.

I pad along the narrow sandy beach to breakfast from one of Taki's flats to the Iris, the hotel owned by a Taki cousin. (The family, which settled here from Crete two centuries ago, controls the village.) Old summer houses, Athenian-owned, smothered in bougainvillaea and roses, beam out like dowagers in flowery hats at the boats and the misty islands. They would be charming to rent but even Taki can't help. 'Private people. Rich. Live in Athens. Don't know names.' He needs us in his apartments.

Good place for children, I decide. At the beach's far end past two new nice small hotels I find the harbour. Its water is astonishingly clear and bilgeless. Here flies the Welsh flag. Its young owner, a marathon maniac, runs the wind-surfing school. 'Next three days all protein, look you,' he joined his girlfriend and me for lunch on a seaside terrace crammed with cats, chickens and fishermen. 'Then the next three days all carbohydrates before the Athens marathon.' Really, modern athletes have the most bizarre training ideas! What can their insides make of such treatment?

I drive twenty-five miles north to awesome Mykinae, battlemented fortress palace of a literally golden age, perched like an eagle above its rich plain. Then Tiryns near Nafplion (the 'p' is mute), the closest town to little Tolon. But Tiryns is not much more than a heap of stones and litter. Its photographs mislead. Old sites, like Stonehenge, shouldn't lie too close to main roads, trippers, and dirty passers-by.

Soaringly more impressive, above Nafplion, is the medieval castle built when the Frankish knights ruled Greece. This mass of stairways, ramparts and window-slits glares down on to the bay and its central small sea fort. A German trio are doing the family holiday thing. Teenage daughter not speaking to puffing parents, they all squat in sullen domesticity against the azure sky. They were too old for her, always. Now she, suddenly, is far too old for them.

Argos, great of name, is now a dusty industrial town and should be avoided. The road to it, narrow and serpentine, is foul with diesel trucks, hauling fruit, wine, corn and vegetables to Athens. The Peloponnese prospers. But the traveller fares far better on the eastern coast road: glimpses of dancing sea beneath cliffs and green woods. From this road, too, I visit glorious Epidauros. At one end of this immense site, immaculately tended for a change, stands its perfect amphitheatre, which makes the Albert Hall look hideously ornate and cramped. The acoustics are legendary. One after the other we stand on the worn stone in centre stage and whisper a word. It flies magically up to the towering highest ring of seats on the mountain side.

I stroll almost alone except for lizards over the ancient wrestling grounds, running tracks, bath houses and lodgings for the ancient travellers. Then I stand in reverent silence at the Sanctuary. All this was the great healing centre of Asklepios. The prayers, even the blessed cures perhaps, of thousands come rustling down the milennia like the dust-to-dust.

'Go south to Monemvasia,' Taki urges me. 'Also Sparti, of course. Also most excellent castles of Mystras. Also –'

'I'll be driving all week!' I protest. But I set off southwards along the lonely mountainous road of Arkadia's east coast. Pretty bays, fishing hamlets and tiny beaches start south of Astros. At Tyros – three windmills above orange groves – I drink in a bar above the shushing shingle beach with Greek fishermen. Not a whiff of another tourist. On to Leonidion, squeezing through alleys as squashed and crowded as an Arab quarter.

But going up the great gorge, the light suddenly starts to dim. Hairpins turn into stony tracks. Pebbles shoot from spinning wheels virtiginously into the void below.

No other vehicle. The sun dives finally behind the black mountains. Ahead, even higher, a nunnery clings like a cluster of pinky white bats to the mountain's flank. In pitch dark, cursing Taki's optimism – 'two hour's easy drive to Sparti' – I reach the sparsely lit mountain-top village of Kosmas, 3500 feet up. Rounding a dark blind bend I am nearly turned over by a herd of goats seeking some warmth from the road. Up here, the nights are chill.

Guard dogs fling themselves howling at Mr Avis's door. Braking, an avalanche of stones shoots into the ravine. Cold, hunger and discretion overcome me. Nervously, I manoeuvre round and creep back into Kosmas' tiny square. I park by the church under the impassive silent stares – curious or glaring? – of twenty old men in greasy caps sitting outside the bar. I ask for a bed.

No English. I drag out my thirty words of Greek with ludicrous mimes pointing to head for sleep, to mouth for food. Instantly, all smiles. I'm brought beer and directed to a pork chop supper in the next bar. Here I sit under the neon strips which ruin most of the eastern Mediterranean, drinking ouzo and watching a Western on the black and white telly. The meal costs £2. Then they find me a cot beneath a crucifix in a neat, tiny room which costs the same.

Next morning, I corkscrew on down the stony road in dazzling sun, passing in the first hour only three young Germans camping among the shrubs, one goatherd with his flock, and a minute white chapel. Then I'm into the lovely rich vale of Lakonia, backed by purple mountains.

Ancient Mystras on the mountain slopes behind modern Sparti is indeed marvellous. So much to see, so little time ...

But before I fly home, I rise at dawn to stop again in empty silence at Epidauros and inhale again those faint traces of classicial divinity.

TRAVEL FACTS

Olympic Airways, Trafalgar House, 2 Chalkhill Road, Hammersmith, London W6 (01–846 9080)

British Airways, PO Box 10, Heathrow Airport, Hounslow, Middx (01–759 2525)

Timsway Travel, Penn Place, Rickmansworth, Herts (0923 771266)

Sunmed, 4–6 Manor Mount, London SE23 (01–699 7666)

Freedom Holidays, 224 King St., London W6 (01–741 4471)

National Tourist Organisation of Greece, 197 Regent St., London W1 (01–734 5997)

— PACKAGE TO CLUB
TROPICANA, MAJORCA —

'Everyone is a package,' declared Señor Domingo. His office, bless-edly caressed by fans, was the only cool spot in the hot, narrow Majorcan valley in which Club Tropicana is encamped.

The rift, its flanks dotted by hundreds of little chalets in which we sweated and swatted mosquitoes, was a funnel of heat leading down to 120°F on its bustling little beach. The place could be anywhere rather awful on the coasts of southern Europe or northern Africa. It's part of no village, no community.

It bears no resemblance to Majorca's beautiful and rustic north-west where I spent a glorious rainy week with someone I loved in the country hotel standing alone above Deià, encircled in gardens and terraced olive groves. It has none of the elegance of Formentor nor the local bustle and *vie sportif* of Cala Ratjada on their distinguished north-east capes.

Seven hundred souls fell under Señor Domingo's command and he, a Majorcan himself, was wearied by the heat. 'We have sixty per cent British, then Dutch, French and Belgians. No Germans at all, though this island is very full of them.'

He explained patiently to me: 'You could not come here without you are a package. Not just drive up to come to stay. In any case, we are totally full.' It would be hard, anyway, to find the place on Majorca's south-east shore. It doesn't, like Mr Pontin's other enter-prise, Cala Mesquida, thirty-five miles to the north, bear a local name.

I got lost attempting a short cut back from the ghastly development in the next bay. 'Only place wiv decent shops tho,' two old ex-army Cockneys in khaki shirts confided to me over supper one evening, 'An' you can get aht the camp over them rocks, see!'

A local farm labourer's wife walking with lilies down a dusty goat-track between baking stone walls had been baffled when I asked the way. 'Tropicana? Oh, camp with many tourists! But they are all shut away. No trouble to us, thank goodness.'

In London, I had been sharply corrected twice by Tropicana's representative for calling her precious club a camp. The message had obviously not yet reached the Cockneys. They had a merry disre-

gard for all the free wine, too. 'That white stuff's better mixed wiv the
kids' lemonade! Try it. Better, ain't it?'

As a modest wine dealer myself, the thought of this mixture pained
me. But the old men from the sound of Bow Bells were spot on: the
lemonade certainly improved the wine.

'You a mouse pie?' one asked me. 'All these questions?'

'I'm not a spy,' I said, 'just a writer.'

'Fort so. On your own, see.'

Sadly single I was, since this, my first camp-style package, fell by
ill luck into that half of the holidays when my two young daughters
were with my ex-wife.

'Ah, children,' sighed Señor Domingo, 'we have so many.'

He shook his head. But it was not the children who were to cause the
trouble. They ranged from mewing bundles of fifteen months – 'Do be
careful of the sun on the little ones,' urged our jolly hostesses – up to
adolescents, for whom the joys and tears of puberty were given full
rein in Club Tropicana, spurred by the beat and squeeze of the disco.

This sometimes boomed on till 3 am, occasioning complaints from the
elderly. A children's disco, starting at 6.30 pm, bopped till eight, when
the mites were Pied Pipered off the floor to leave space for parental
convulsions.

I'd been among the happy families embarking at insalubrious
Luton. (Mr Pontin lured us there with cut-price rail and hotel
vouchers.) Due to usual British flight-flap – and the tour operators'
mad wish to get their cattle herded through two hours before take-off,
the departure 'lounge' (what a misnomer) resembled a refugee camp.
Old and young stood doggedly (seats were scarce, refreshment
unreachable), nervously awaiting calls on unknown carriers to every
place I'd ever heard of around the Mediterranean.

We embarked on time. The happy families were feverishly goaded.
'Leave that button alone, Jason! Tracey, don't touch that switch!'

I studied my fellow travellers and my spirits rose. Where were the
threatened yobs, the threatening punks? Everyone was polite, even
friendly. The aircraft buzzed with the good, flat 'at, nasal twangs of the
Midlands and the North-West. And where were those dozens of pairs
of typists, one pearl, one plain, who, I'd been assured, filled every
package tour, seeking sexy satisfaction under the sizzling Spanish sun?

At Palma airport, we broiled at 107° in the shade, waiting in un-air-
conditioned coaches for the tardy Gatwick package to arrive. On this,
the yobs had been at play. Over our first late lunch, the one bad meal
– lukewarm yellow gunge from huge vats, masquerading as 'Spanish

omelette' – one divorced mum with two nice young sons said: 'Sometimes I'm ashamed of being British abroad. On our Gatwick flight, they were chucking cans and all right down the aisles.'

Three of these were probably the charmers who, around two one morning, drunkenly hang-glided the deck-chairs into the swimming pool, smashing the bottom tiles so that the pool leaked, and making the narrow valley hideous with their honkings. More complaints next morning to Reception, where the pretty Belgian hostess said: 'We do have a security guard who goes round during the night. But he is not young. And these three men were young and strong, and very, very drunk.'

On another night, I heard crying near the pool and oaths in coarse French. I pottered out, naked, on to my chalet's little balcony. I observed in the darkness a girl in a white trouser suit, tripping up and down the little road below me, round which the club's mini-bus circles all day moving inmates from point to point. The girl's high heels clacked. She was moaning and whining and sometimes shouting. Two men, French or Belgian, their faces intermittently reddened by the glow of the cigarettes they sucked, crudely taunted the wretch.

'*Viens, p'tit poisson!*' they bellowed.

Rape, it certainly wasn't. She wished to return to her chalet, but not alone. They wished to have her, clothed or naked, in the pool.

Almost everyone else was nice. I did once draw for lunch (you sit wherever there's a gap at the tables for eight) a gargantuan mother from Brum. Her still fluorescent flesh overflowed her black Lurex bathing suit like orange pudding over a dustbin liner. Her vast, hot thighs lapped on to my chair. She and her smug, snivelling, sunburnt child were homeward bound after their fourteen-day stint.

'You only 'ere for the seven?' she shouted into my ear. Sweat drops spun off her hennaed ringlets. 'We allus take the two weeks.' I realised the presence of an expert holiday-maker.

She boomed on: 'Makes no sense to come for one. Save money on two weeks, see.' She was relieved, however, to be 'leavin' this bleedin' heat.'

She machine-gunned my plan to borrow a car to explore the island. 'Waste o' money. Plenty to do 'ere. Ping-pong. That funny golf. And my Doreen 'ere's been learned to swim. Dive, too, she 'as. Pontins, I always like. That's why we come 'ere. I say, "sun first". So that's got to be Spain or Majorca, ain't it? Then I get them brochures. That's 'ow to pick 'olidays, y'know.'

She rose like a whale, discarding Doreen, who picked distastefully at her whopping slice of water melon.

Certainly, there's plenty to do and everything, except for the optional daily excursions and drinks at the bars, is free. Lessons in wind-surfing, sailing, pottering about on a pedallo and snorkelling cost nothing.

As a small substitute for my two daughters, I imported for a day a jet-set friend of mine who was staying privately nearby with her sophisticated eight-year-old daughter. They, I was sure, would find Club Tropicana sheer hell.

'Can't think what you're complaining about!' exclaimed the elegant mother who'd never before seen such a place. 'This lunch is really marvellous. Look at all those salads! And it's all so clean.' Her daughter devoured salami, chips, carrots and went back for more.

We were sharing a table with a five-strong family with broad Lancashire accents, who read the *Daily Telegraph*. Their son told me gleefully he usually had three helpings whenever there was steak at night.

The eight-year-old girl swam in the crowded creek while her mother and I judiciously weighed up the topless. Two good pairs. Sixteen melon monsters. Four fried eggs. Six bee stings.

A package can't make everyone look the same. Nor like the same things either.

TRAVEL FACTS

Air Europe, Europe House, Crawley, W. Sussex (01–651 3611)
Holiday Club International, Broadway, Edgbaston, Five Ways, Birmingham (021–643 2727)
Spanish National Tourist Office, 57–58 St. James's Street, London SW1 (01–499 0901)

Turkey We forget that what's now the Aegean coast of Turkey was once part of ancient Greece. We got a fisherman to ferry us across the gulf to these empty unfenced ruins of a Greek city. The place to ourselves, a swim in the sea, then lunch in a bar above the jetty.

Vienna The Lippizaners are waiting to cross the road into the Spanish Riding School in the Hofburg Palace. You can see more, and without queuing, if you turn up earlier to watch the rehearsals (which last longer) rather than the main show.

Paxos We live in an old olive press in the quiet of the olive groves above Gaios. Jane inspects our landlady's goats and chickens before breakfast.

Anti-Paxos Both daughters in the gin-clear water on Anti-Paxos. We've taken a picnic and buzzed south in the little motorboat.

Jamaica Out of season Jamaica is empty but still warm in our early winter. But it does suddenly rain.

Portugal Sintra, perched on a hill behind Estoril was once the home of kings and nobles. These carriages wait for hire just below the palace.

Portugal, Algarve Except in de luxe restaurants, food other than fish, isn't terrific along the Algarve. But the big sardines caught by these fishermen will be delicious simply grilled with a large tomato and onion salad and lots of potable wine taken on the beach by the clean Atlantic.

Bangkok Boating down the 'klongs' gives you the best feel, sights and smells (typically oriental whiffs) of Bangkok behind the scenes.

Bangkok Glitters with glorious temples and golden gods just round the corner from desperate traffic jams of blue buses bursting at the seams and silk-flagged three-wheeled taxis, and the naughty quarter where I nearly got caught...........

Bangkok My guide made me climb halfway up this pagoda overlooking a monastery while he sensibly took his breakfast from a stall just to the left.

— MAJORCA:
CALA RATJADA —

'Back home, of course,' pronounced the semi-retired English business-man in his cosily converted farmhouse set in the sloping fields and orchards outside Cala Ratjada, 'they'll tell you the whole of Majorca bloody stinks! But look at this!'

Drinks in hand we were wandering through his spreading but kempt garden. Persons, Spanish, resembling the long lost English species 'Gardener' could be seen at work. Our host waved towards neat platoons of orange trees, groves of olives, almonds and carob trees. From the last come the tiny seeds which the ancients called Carats making this common thing the measure of weight for precious gold and diamonds.

Majorca indeed has a rough and common image but many nuggets of quality remain unsullied. You just have to get off the big, bare, boring beaches. Behind Cala Ratjada rear up empty mountains, bristling only with trees and shaped volcanically like old Japanese prints. No houses on them. Not a whiff of a hotel. Little lanes doddle rustically along, following old cart and cattle tracks between stone walls and orchards. A few farm workers phut-phut along on their mopeds. No purple tourist in flashy clothes roars past.

Palma, only an hour's drive to the west, seems a different country. But even that old city has only been ravaged all along its two extending shores. On these strips stand the monstrous developments in stark rows like raddled, hot old tarts.

The old grey core of the city twitches its lacy skirts away from the slabs of concrete, the stink of chips and the menace of drunken British hooligans. The city's ancient parts are worth exploring. You'll see few tourists here: they're crammed like ants on the toasting beaches getting what is likely to be their only dose of sun all summer.

Nor will they waste tanning time by venturing to Cala Ratjada perched on the island's most easterly point. There are no enormous sand beaches. There are no colossal hotels. There are fewer Brits by far and those are more often of the type the Palma packages generally despise or dislike. For Cala Ratjada was discovered in the early 1950s by flying pickets of the upper-middle classes and occupied tenuously by them ever since. Types who take their children bucket-and-spading to Trebethrick in North Cornwall are, both before and after, the *habitués* of Cala Ratjada and of the astonishing Sea Club in particular.

This seedily charming establishment, which would occasion outraged complaints from Thomsons' packaged millions, is still presided over by Mrs Nora Cumberledge, widow of an admiral, once possessor of a well known antique yacht. Mrs Cumberledge, well into her eighties, has reigned over her Sea Club like a faintly muddled, sometimes strict, but always benign and skittish empress.

They say that any Brit of a certain sort weaving his way past the tatty old swimming pool towards the bustling outside bar will be hailed by at least half a dozen friends he didn't know were even on the island. The British bourgeoisie and squirearchy don't need to be upwardly mobile to keep in touch.

It's lively with English off-spring running wild, swimming in the sea, gasping over first cigarettes, chattering of heart-throbs and 'O' levels, all happily unleashed by single mummies and single daddies. 'Anyone here *not* divorced?' cried a sexy woman still just married, moving her brown thighs erotically to the taped music of the Beatles. I had lusted after her strongly the previous night but her husband was both angry and large. Everyone was divorced. But they have brought out their own divorced, deserted or disporting friends for the mutual comfort the one may have of the other and for a lot of laughter.

Twenty years earlier these were themselves the lusty young. Sun, wine, music and bikinis make even the dotards pant. Pairing off from the Club's long single dining table, they made hot sport in the little bedrooms and started holiday things which sometimes lingered longer and sometimes even lasted.

The place is not a club at all. Anyone may stay there. But many mayn't. Applicants for spaces were scrutinised by the redoubtable admiral's widow. If Mrs Cumberledge doesn't know the name already, she 'makes sure the face will fit'.

'How?' I asked of one of her attractive temporary helpers. 'How can she know?'

'She tells by their writing paper,' the girl kindly explained. No-one at the Sea Club would say 'notepaper' any more than 'phone' or 'pardon' (pronounced 'pudd'n'). 'She wouldn't take a booking from someone writing on paper with lines, say, or from an address with a number in somewhere like Wolverhampton, or from a house with its name in inverted commas, or called 'Dunroamin' or 'Jakanjil'. She saw me suppressing an explosion of laughter and ended crossly: 'You know exactly what I mean!'

I resolved immediately to apply the following year from four such contrived addresses. I have yet to stay at the Sea Club and now feel sadly that I never will. I shall go on looking in frequently, however, if Mrs Cumberledge, widow of an admiral, has not had me court-martialled and drummed out.

'Actually, we call the Sea Club "The Compound"' confided one of its denizens to me over a typical supper, clammy schoolroom fare of bulk, not taste, slapped down in front of us by jolly public school children earning pocket money on their holidays, 'Because, you see, we're surrounded now by Germans on all sides.'

I saw, beyond the Club's bedraggled defensive hedge, signs which gutterally clicked their consonants and snapped, 'Frühstuck! Bierkeller! Schweinfleisch!' From somewhere close arose a faint chorus of German singing.

The friendly local shopkeepers (and there are many in the back streets) establish first that you are British before confiding that they warmly prefer you to the Krauts. But they address strangers first in German: such are the odds. I only overheard one butcher saying the opposite to a couple of sweating Germans shoving themselves forward past a snivelling child from Blackpool.

Being addressed in German drives ex-British officer types batty. One crusty cavalry major spotting a Kraut of equal age limping out of the newspaper shop with a soft porn magazine and a very game leg, snapped 'There's one we only winged in the war. More's the pity!'

But the Germans occupying Cala Ratjada are no longer their crack front line tourist troops. The blonde strident Panzer folk have long pressed on into Corfu and Egypt, penetrated the Caribbean and surged victoriously south into Africa. To a German now all the world is cheap. In their wake they leave pale honeymooners, middle-aged couples and lame pensionnaires, for Majorca costs nothing in proud German marks. They are quiet until the evenings when they sing mournfully over their beer. Rather a waste this when excellent wine from Rioja, as good as middle-class French claret, sells at a mere two quid a bottle in the shops.

Shoes at quarter London prices are a regular purchase for me, together with those dead cheap blue-grey cotton slacks which do for gardening when they start in a year to look tatty.

Majorca in September is twice as pleasant as in steaming, cramped July. Storms may break, but thunderclaps rattling round the mountains and the lightning flashing across the night sea beat any man-made *son et lumière*. And how delicious smells the fresh land after rain. The major, spying some young Germans sheltering from a shower surprisingly timorously in a doorway, zapped past them in his old Hillman as close as he could roaring, 'That'll splash you, dam' Krauts.'

The hotel Aguait is probably the best in Cala Ratjada and is usually not Kraut-ridden. Out in the country to the south, Tony's Bar keeps its chicken-scratching rural touch and provides, for Spain, quite good food. The pretentious restaurant in town, noted once by the Guide Michelin, I find disappointing and savagely expensive.

We explored along the coast and into the eerie, spectacular caves of Artà. Nearby we found a surprisingly attractive development by Taylor Woodrow where the better-off *nouveaux riches* Brits have comely villas. Here the houses have been mercifully kept low and crouching, like the huts of mankind should always be in the face of rather splendid nature.

Round the next point lies Costa de los Pinos and the smart manicured summer villas of the seriously rich Spaniards, discreetly removed from British beer and skittles. But there's one good hotel that will let us in, the Europa. Then across the bay another called Port Verde, lying long and low on the rocks. It could have been terrific but lacked a patron, a *maître d'hotel* and good food. The only other lunch guests were two East End villains, aglint with gold and two platinum molls. One sweating through his string vest kept a very heavy plastic suitcase right between his calves all the time he gobbled.

Most evenings we finished dinner at midnight in the long low house on Cala Gat, the eastern finger beyond Cala Ratjada overlooking the crystal clear bay where there's excellent snorkelling. Good to be able to dive, too, when piping hot, slap off the rocks into cold sea water.

Three large sailing boats, all German, bob in the darkness below the terrace where we dine. At an angle on an interesting bluff stand the Goldfinger palaces of the March oligarchy. Señor March's grandfather backed Franco at his start and minted many millions from his bold perspicacity. The March family, which started as the humblest peasants, lives in regal splendour. Great boats come and go at their private rock quay at the touch of buttons. Squads of white-coated servants scuttle all day and evening along the terraces. It is agreeable to watch them across the water. I would like to enter Palacio March but fear he may have sharks trained to snap up uninvited visitors.

As the brandy circulates, a moist-eyed German resident recites Schiller, mournful that his twelve-year-old half-English daughter should be vilified at school in Palma for being German. I take his side. But the major is heard to snort.

And a girl in the house party, who truly has a gift of healing in her hands, asks if my once broken neck which she touched that afternoon, still glows. It does and it is better. She is convinced of reincarnation and receives guidance from what she calls 'Upstairs'. Not fey, let alone loopy, she's a suburbanite worried about her overdraft and her poor old car. But she talks in the oddest idiom. I ponder over this at night and realise at dawn what it is: she speaks exactly as we all did in the 1950s, which is when she was born ...

Odd folk round Cala Ratjada certainly. But that's half its beauty. Strange conversations in beautiful places are an essential part of a holiday.

TRAVEL FACTS

Iberia, 130 Regent St., London W1 (01–437 5622)
Air Europe, Europe House, East Park, Crawley, W. Sussex (01–651 3611)
Mundi Color, 276 Vauxhall Bridge Rd., London SW1 (01–828 6021)
Spanish National Tourist Office, 57–58 St James's St., London SW1 (01–499 0901)

— PAXOS —

The square in Gaios is the real stage of Paxos. Out of it doddle the little island's only two roads. They're tracks, really, rising and rattling through the grey-green ocean of 300,000 olive trees. Even if you're absurd enough to want to bustle through Greece's courteous tranquility, you couldn't. Some pushy Italians get blessedly held up by old ladies riding side-saddle on their tiny donks. Early August is the Wop invasion for it's a short haul by ferry or private yacht from southern Italy. En masse, the Italians off their own ground are noisy and, being basically nervous, become strident and overbearing.

Everybody on Paxos comes into Gaios. With only one and a half hotels, most of us stay in converted cottages, rooms in private houses and a few in rich villas. None of us pant for discos or the sound of the Costa Concreta.

Into Gaios comes the ferry from Corfu Town across the Ionian sea, bringing Mr Hertz's little cars for us and all the food for the island. The caique hired by C.V. Villas docks here, sailing its villas' guests from Corfu's most southerly, least pleasing point: a hot wart which could almost be dreadful Benidorm.

You can only reach Paxos by water. So it's fly first to Corfu airport, then bus down. Try not to be too revolted by Corfu airport which joins Herbert's Horrors together with Agadir and Luton.

But the caique flings tripperdom behind its wash. We look towards hazy mainland Greece to see dolphins leaping. The sea is the colour of the best sapphires – dark and lustrous, like the eyes of a good woman. One should always come seaborne to an island and a caique all the way round and down from Corfu Town would cut out the long, hot, dusty bus ride down the island.

Along the square at Gaios, yachts from Italy, the Channel Islands, Austria, Berlin (yes, truly) and the USA nod grandly at the little shops. Two rival cafés stand side by side. Coffee in the morning, cold beer after a long day out in the boat at heavenly and almost empty Anti-Paxos, forty minutes further south, and a sort of fritter (which they call doughnuts) covered in honey – delicious.

Behind the line of pink oleanders stand the shops in which cosy black-clad Greek ladies squeeze my two young daughters: 'Ver' nice ... bella ...' The girls, twelve and thirteen, have never been anywhere like this. 'Everybody's so kind to us,' they keep murmuring, blushing over the hugs, as I cluck about buying straw hats and sun filters for them lest they burn in the heat.

We're charmed, too, by Corfu Villa's very English double-barrelled gentleman in his long khaki shorts. He cossets clients like a kindly harassed hare. He came to Paxos fourteen years ago and, with actors Peter Bull and Albert Finney, was one of the first Brits to find the island. Intending a short break at a cross-roads in his life (small islands ease contemplation), he stayed on. His small children, prattling a mixture of Greek and English, play hide-and-seek with mine in and out of the covey of the three cheerfully competing restaurants on our road homewards up the western hill. Take your pick from menus and clientele which vary evening to evening. Late-comers stand gossiping in the road, the Brits polite, the Wops surprisingly thrustful for a nation regularly defeated.

We stay in an old, converted olive press up a tiny, stony path. Its pink bathroom is much more Eaton Square than barren island but there's precious little water which has to come in by lorry. A book lists twenty useful telephone numbers. But there isn't a telephone. However, the sweet widow next door who 'does for us' and whose hens cluck and goats bleat all around, knows someone with a neighbour who might have a telephone if needs arise. Joy to be without the thing, anyway. Who but the love-lorn or the work-besotted (often the same thing) need telephones on holidays?

As country dwellers, we're not disturbed by the rustic music of the night. The bleating goats, the honks of donkeys, and the dawn tirade – like bingo boosters – of cocks crowing at each other across the miles of olives, myrtles and cypresses in a rosy haze.

We stroll down to dinner in the dusk, and puff back in the velvet dark, crackling with cicadas and tolling with goats' bells through the ghostly olive groves. The girls have never seen the stars and moon so clear. I weave with much Greek wine in a body dried out all day by sparkling sun and the clear sea's salt.

We alternate between the three restaurants at the foot of the hill, the girls correcting me, 'the food isn't dreadful at all, like you said it'd be.' Who goes to Greece for *haute cuisine*, anyway? And the girls, kind to my pocket if harsh on my sensibilities, were then almost as happy with fish fingers and tomato ketchup as with sole *bonne femme* from La Gavroche.

Greek salads are fine. So are the chips. Some kebabs are passable but the meat is leathery. The meals are ludicrously cheap. Eight or nine pounds buys three courses for the three of us, with plenty of wine for me and Coke for the girls.

Pizzas are safe. Sometimes we carry them off piping hot to eat in our cottage. And sometimes with colossal tomatoes, sweet as plums, we take them to picnic in the little boat along the east coast in tiny, empty bays. The sea is vodka clear, shading from translucent aquamarine to emerald to sapphire. The scent of thyme wafts out of the woods across the lapping of the waves. 'We thought you were dead, Daddy. Till you snored!' I've flaked out on smooth, warm rocks, uncoiling in empty coves.

A boat is even more vital round Paxos than a small, tough car. There are two other tiny ports: Longos (now generally called Loggos) is almost too pretty to be true. Its middle taverna of three on the quayside is the best. It's run by a Cretan who left that large island 'because too many tourists there now'.

One Englishwoman found her room by the tavernas noisy at night. But she has been coming for ten years and wouldn't go anywhere else. She prefers it to 'up in them woods' as she put it. But an English family staying up there in another C.V. cottage deep among the olive groves, and picking oranges from their bedrooms, adored it.

Only dumb sheep travellers stick to marked roads on holiday. We jolt down tracks steeper and narrower pursuing flashes of azure sea glimpsed through the tangle of olive boughs and trunks. A bearded Triton walking in the grove with a blonde nymph calls out, 'You won't get down there!' But we just do. Swimming in the bay we see the pair again rowing out to their white leased sailing cruiser and we laugh. 'You won't get up the hill, anyway!' they call back cheerfully. Stones fly. Wheels whizz. Desperately closely we just crawl up the hill. A pinch of fear adds salt to holidays and merits the wine needed to recover.

With a boat you can go almost anywhere. We get ours from cheerful Spiro and his sister, next to the 'mini-market' (more a dark Dickensian shop) by the quay at Gaios. But you mustn't miss, along the spine of the island, the track to the magical little Church of the Apostles. 'Down there,' pointed an old Greek sitting on a chair in the middle of the road at Magazia. He talked of brothers in Michigan and Wimbledon. But he himself had only been as far as Athens.

There is an astonishing view from the churchyard over the sheer white-cream western cliffs. My daughters, sun hats nodding, skipped hand-in-hand away from the church down the dappled tracks, singing. The old Greek gods would have liked that, I thought.

On the morning we had to leave, Kate and Jane sat dolefully in the square saying, 'We *love* this place.' We were thanking Spiro and his sister who, typically Greek, had scurried off with a flock of neighbours to help us find Jane when she had wandered off buying our lunch-time pizzas.

'Why go?' they ask. 'Come back.'

'Next year,' we call, 'next year ...'

TRAVEL FACTS

Olympic Airways, Trafalgar House, 2 Chalkhill Rd., London W6 (01–846 9080)

C.V. Villas, 43 Cheval Pl., London SW7 (01–581 0851)

Greek Islands Club, 66 High St., Walton-on-Thames, Surrey (09322 20477)

National Tourist Organisation of Greece, 197 Regent St., London W1 (01–734 5997)

— MENORCA —

As a team we kept our peckers up over early disappointments. (Never use this phrase in America – it means something quite else!) But sharp hors d'oeuvres can enhance the main entrée on holidays. Rain sluiced on the tiny airport of Menorca. A very dull road ran through stone-walled, brown-grass country like a burnt-out Ireland. Menorca, unlike its sister isle Majorca, possesses no big mountains, no forests. We had yet to discover its great delight: its secret beaches.

The taxi driver represents the general Menorcan type. They have the yellow pallor and withdrawn mien of Welshmen or Sardinians, two other small nations knocked about by occupations and disease.

Nor were we pleased by our first glimpse of the San Jaime 'urbanisation' (hideous word for usually hideous places). We came through a tunnel in a high cliff percolated by the caves of troglodytes – one with a TV aerial. It should have been a fine curtain-raiser to a view of beauty. But twin tower hotels erectly defiled the wide blue skirt of sea. Unease stirred in the steamy taxi, mollified slightly by the driver's gleeful, 'They full of cracks. One not used. Both can fall down.' Later we discovered he was right.

But then – 'This *can't* be our villa!' The team gazed upwards at the villa, wide-eyed as Christmas children uncovering from dull wrappings a fabulous gift. Villa Seekers had indeed sought well in Menorca. Enormous Sunningdale or even Beverley Hills, our villa basked halfway up a hillside spiked with pines richly scented after the downpour. It never rains but gardens improve. Our own swimming pool jutting out over beds of roses – 'Look! they've all been weeded! Hey! someone's put some in the rooms!'

Everywhere around was neat. In late September all but three of the twenty villas in close sight were empty. Voices floated across from one. 'Say bye bye to Auntie, darling.' In holiday peaks might these heights be too clamorous, I wondered.

We dashed through our rooms like hounds on a breast-high scent: 'This dining room has its own terrace. And a barbecue. Two bathrooms. Get this kitchen! See this view! The pool's *sparkling!*' Tremendous cleanliness isn't a Spanish thing. 'And it's so quiet.' Horrendous reports of muggings on the mainland had hammered tourism on this distant, quiet island.

I've lodged in digs from Kentucky to Thailand, South Africa to Turkey and the Isles of Greece. But this was real de luxe.

The local rep bustled up to deliver our hire car – Jap, I fear, but damned good, for it was going to get severely tested down the tracks we intrepidly explored. The rep was a bonny Scots girl, like so many I meet worldwide. When there were Nannies, they were usually Scots, too. Caring for fractious, frightened, greedy, grizzling and inept children is much like coping for packaged tourists. 'They only call us up,' said the girl cheerfully, 'when there's something wrong.' In a rep's world, silence is golden.

'Just showing old Fred the ropes,' explained a kindly Midlander in the urbanisation's single supermarket. These uncompetitive places are always far more expensive than the real shops used by the locals in the nearest town. A large part of the cost of a hire car may be offset by judicious shopping, a task which the ladies in the group seemed fortunately to enjoy. Wheels plus enterprise make shopping far less boring for everyone.

'Fred's just got off the Bristol flight,' said the Midlander, 'so he's feelin' pretty groggy.'

Fred, queuing in the *supermercado*, nodded dumbly. He was not quite a heroic pilot returning from combat but at least I realised quickly the fraternity of Brits on Menorca: clubs, gatherings, English newspapers. But this polarisation is heightened by these clumpings into urbanisations. These I deplore. To be abroad means foreigners for good or ill. We can see plenty of our own lot at home – and often far too many.

Menorca, bar these new clumpings and Mahon's old waterfront, is not tourist inclined. The locals genuinely farm or make shoes and gin. So the visitor lives at least on the fringe of real life, which you cannot say of most of the mainland's ghastly costas.

Alayor, our nearest town, sombre with some good buildings, lies self-sufficiently off the tourist highway. Menorcan roads aren't bright with jaunty kerbside cafés. It has a good restaurant, 'Bennetts', in a strange house with Georgian windows, a fine hall and staircase with an odd feel about them, and a pretty garden courtyard. Here we ate chicken cooked in lemons beneath a lemon tree twittering with birds. Behind our backs stood huge fading hydrangeas.

Mr Bennett, a former Birmingham speedway rider, and his tiny Italian opera singer wife had been powerfully drawn to Menorca sixteen years earlier. 'I've been trying to leave,' he groaned, 'it's The Force that keeps me here.'

He felt he'd been mysteriously lured to the Island. His home outside Birmingham had been imposing. 'We had an "in-and-out" drive,' he told us, singularly impressing us, for we could think of no friends who had such a thing. 'Then one day someone left these brochures on Menorca. I felt compelled to read them.' Clapping his hip pocket, he cried: 'I feel those brochures here now, still pulling me out here.'

'I cried for the first fourteen days,' his wife added morosely.

He talks of the strange Taulas, which stand about the Island like elements of Stonehenge, and of 'lay-lines' radiating spookily from India. 'Haven't you seen the piles of stones the farmers build in their fields to keep The Force away?' he asked. We had indeed, without knowing what they were, and we decided to investigate and photograph some.

In an upstairs room of the house above the restaurant, their son had seen the ghost husband of a newly widowed friend 'who was sitting right there', he pointed across the courtyard.

As we were leaving, he remarked, 'Behind the closed shutters of this town there's black magic and sexual orgies ...'

We looked and listened earnestly for these. But in vain. We got caught up only in a rural carnival and decorous dancing in the street. But out on the farmland and close to, the Taulas do give off potent vibes. Inland the Island emits a powerful brooding character in the quiet fields which lie behind the pretty hidden necklace of tiny beaches.

The ladies of our team hearing of the fabled potency of the 'ginger-haired men of Ferrerías made us sweep through that rather dull place whenever we drove to or from Ciudadela, but had no joy.

We had a marvellous lunch under blue awnings on the harbour's edge and opposite the Yacht Club in Ciudadela – mullet, langoustes, good Menorcan cheese and Marques de Riscal to drink. The old capital is easily Menorca's most stylish place. On its outskirts in a sort of factory we bought quite good shoes at half British prices.

We rattle down tracks to the sea guided by *Meon's Book of Beaches* – an essential companion for the traveller on this island. The true countryside – how its habitués will curse me for revealing this – is as quietly rural as Western Scotland or Ireland. We climb locked gates (cars are blessedly banned in certain places), avoid grazing Friesians and their cow pats, climb a brow beneath wheeling buzzards and wow! – what a perfect sandy bay at Cala Pregonda. We swim out towards its rocky islets. On the beach stand just two dwellings and one person: a slim topless girl throwing sticks for her dog.

At Reclau in the north – 'Follow the signs to the Menorca Country Club' – we ate piles of gambas and a huge salad on the edge of what looked distantly like a Scottish sea-loch but basking in the sun. Behind us stood a pleasant new development, and the comely proprietress sitting on a high stool swinging her delicious legs.

On the north west we find a pair of strange red-sanded, wood-fringed beaches at Algaiarens. Dozing on the deserted sand, I'm startled awake by a jeep slithering urgently over the dunes. It's meeting a motor boat which has silently slipped through the rocks. Two men and a girl speaking no language known to me – Menorquin, perhaps? – winch the boat in and dash off with lots of wheel-spin. Smugglers? Spies? The men, one bearded, lean and smoke. It's the girl who twirls the handle of the winch.

We explore up the broad valley behind and find a strange stone 'bee hive' like a prehistoric tomb. Here the feeling of The Force is powerful. Beyond broods a great white shuttered house. This so vividly resembles at first sight the setting of my last novel (a half-ruined great house placed in the future) that I feel compelled to trespass forward. Nothing stirs down tracks steeply banked like Devon lanes. We creep nervously about the place and dash away at a rustle. Mr Bennett, we agree, wasn't exaggerating about The Force.

Nor can I exaggerate the beauty of the beaches for the bold traveller. It is a very long stony haul to our favourite through farmland then a wooded gorge like something out of Africa to the perfection of Turqueta. In this horseshoe bay girdled by cliff and woodland Prospero would have been content; as we were, gorging gambas, swigging wine and plunging into the unusual surf.

TRAVEL FACTS

Iberia, 130 Regent St., London W1 (01–437 5622)
Villaseekers, Holiday House, Domestic Rd., Leeds (0532 434652)
OSL Villas, Travel House, Broxbourne, Herts (0992 87211)
Thomsons Holidays, Greater London House, Hampstead Rd., London NW1 (01–439 2211)
Spanish National Tourist Office, 57–58 St James's St., London SW1 (01–499 0901)

— PORTUGAL —
The Coast of Estoril

Style you're born with. Or it takes, like good taste, ages growing. The coast of Estoril, thirty minutes west of the city port of Lisbon, has both.

Lisbon is old and dusty, like most of its inhabitants. Its best buildings went up soon after the 1755 earthquake, so are in the finest period of European architecture; some are pock-marked, many need a scrub. But even the lettering of the shops' names looks as if it hasn't been altered since the 1920s.

The place seems ready to wake up but in no great hurry – except along its roads – to do so. Portugal, like a once rich old man long fallen upon hard times, seems reconciled to its unimportant lot. This philosophical humility (utterly opposite to that of Britain) makes it an extremely likeable country.

The Portuguese, unlike the Spaniards (whom they find arrogant) are quietly dignified, as good family butlers used to be. Yet they drive like maniacs, sniffing your exhaust pipe, leaning on their horns. They go top of Herbert's list of the world's worst drivers, easily overtaking the Belgians and the New Zealanders. What's more, their swarms of mopeds rip your eardrums.

It being six centuries since we signed our oldest alliance with Portugal, I thought it high time I flew down for a weekend.

Evicted European royals settled round Estoril like disrupted starlings out of gilded woods. They added their own style like antique furniture. But they came with good taste. The town is pretty, clean and full of courteous people. Here, under seagulls and swallows swooping, among pines and palms along quiet roads, stand the exiles' villas. A touch of Sunningdale rises to face the clean, cold Atlantic.

Rumania's garden is overgrown round its empty house. But the home of the Spanish king's father is spruce and guarded. The last home of the Italian royals looks good too, facing the bracing sea, and it was here that the poor Windsors perched. Those who had known good things and gentle living liked this coast. The taste continues.

I stay in the fine Hotel Palacio, overlooking its own large pool, the casino and the elegant public gardens. It's the sort of old hotel I love: marbled bathrooms, gurgling plumbing, bells for maid and valet, and a man in a green baize apron to clean my shoes. It was a very long time and hundreds of modern chain hotels ago since I'd last enjoyed such care.

Up in its golf club-house, the stern guardian lady at reception has been fifty-seven years with the club. She recalls, with wild green finches flying round her head indoors, 'the little Duke – your ex-king but we call them Windsor – playing golf quite good. The Duchess she drinks the cocktails on the terrace there and watches close over him'. The golf course at Estoril seemed suitable for our brief king for, though outwardly attractive, it is short and trappy having more snares than fairways. Was there, I wondered, a bunker called Baldwin?

On the verandah where we lunch overlooking the bright greens and the azure sea in early May every voice is British. But none nowadays speaks English like the Queen. 'Crossroads' up here: down on the beaches some 'East Enders'.

A few gentry, retired Brigadiers in tropical suits, and a spruce ex-RAF wingco with bristly white moustache, patronise the bar in the Palacio proper, attended by fearfully smart wives dressed almost for Ascot, and adding to the cocktail of mixed English.

The coast is hilly, tree-capped, with nice coves. Only the girls are plain, plump and dark, and the men resemble squat Welsh miners. They sing, too, their sad fados, wonderfully. Once, like us, a tiny maritime nation which girdled the globe with its empire, it has accepted, which we haven't, its new role.

In the Palacio's elegant bar, with the air of a St James' club to which women are surprisingly admitted, German spies and British spies played cards and other things with one another, standing each other drinks and swapping 'chicken-feed' intelligence for what they hoped would not prove dummy. Estoril was the light which drew the moths when the lights went out all over Europe.

Sintra, on its enchanting hill skirted with a deep green forest, was where the Portuguese kings kept their summer palace. Two offspring of the last exiled king, who scuttled to England in 1910, still live up there and farm.

The nobles followed the kings so that the winding lanes are clustered with baroque mini-palaces and one heavenly mid-eighteenth century château, now a hotel furnished in discreet taste and commanding a great view across the plain. Obviously expensive, its guests were naturally American but of that nice sort who wear quiet British tweeds.

On the very peak stands the craziest castle I ever saw, built by a German prince (cousin to our Albert) who married the Portuguese queen. It's a hotch-potch of Moorish, mad Gothic and cuckoo rococo. But it's jam-full of splendid things – not all in bad taste – and well worth a climb to the top through preserved woodlands. 'Wunderbar!' exclaimed a group of Krauts at some hideous German furniture, as dark and convoluted as their national character.

The lesser gentry's castle-style summer houses spike the seafront's wide, clean beaches, which run north from the Tagus mouth past Estoril and its extension, the most attractive little port of Cascais. A touch of Biarritz, with its villas of the rich and faded glories, and like that city's neighbour, St Jean de Luz, a collection of pretty streets, good shops, a host of restaurants and several lovely houses. I returned to stare at two stunning ones in the Rua Valbom being very ornately re-painted in Portuguese scroll-work style.

We dine one night at the João Padeiro ('John the Bakers'), old-fashioned, stained glass and leather: fish soup, an enormous sole, a bottle of Portuguese wine (you will not go far wrong to ask for Dão), and fierce brandy like a French marc followed by the Turkish-type coffee, and the bill is £18 for two.

You should really stick to fish and crustaceans in Portugal, plus an occasional grilled chicken. Good meals like this cost less than £5. In a week I ate no meat and began to wonder if I would give it up entirely.

One evening I had a superb meal in the Hotel Albatroz, perched over the sea and extended from a pleasing eighteenth century private house. A delicious crab purée was followed by a fine turbot. Below us, rusty working fishing boats daily chug in and out, selling on the quayside and in the fish market. This genuine activity of real life in Cascais gives the place something to bite on, which playboy marinas never can.

Estoril's new casino, handsome to look at, offered a floor show so awful, recalling a wartime Workers' Playtime after the only moderate meal I had, that I scuttled off pleading an early start. Be brave on holidays for time is short. Faced with rubbish, stand up, cut and run.

Best by far for lunch is by the great beach of Guincho (the name means a horse's whinny). On it appears a group of shacks which have grown over years of dramas into a famed hotel, the Muchaxo. The curving restaurant looks down on to a vivid sea with white spume breaking onto sand as golden as egg-yolks.

Its owner, a splendid snob since he cultivates interesting people and cuts bores, whips out his red leather visitors' books. What an assortment! Walt Disney and Diana Dors, Patrick Lichfield and his ilk, a fleet of American admirals, unknown British Ambassadors, long forgotten pop singers, and the pearly kings and queens of abandoned thrones, sprawl across the pages with well-oiled comments.

Tiny villages, with white walls and red roofs, stretch northwards in little bays extending from farmland and forest, with simple cottages for sale at £30,000 upwards. A multiplicity of 'For Sale' signs always signals a struggling economy but it means a buyers' market. I can think of many less pleasant, less friendly places in which to settle, and there is a large and happy British colony.

Compared with much of southern Europe, central Portugal remains unspoilt, undeveloped and gently snoozing. I paused often by the cliffs to watch the great Atlantic rolling in, and most times comfortable middle-aged 'Coronation Street' ladies appeared in cosy couples and cardigans, praising the stylish coast of Estoril.

'The Portuguese are so polite. So quiet, kind. We'd not go elsewhere now, would we, Mabel?'

TRAVEL FACTS

Air Portugal, 38–44 Gillingham St., London SW1 (01–828 0262)
Caravela, 38–44 Gillingham St., London SW1 (01–630 9223/4)
Sovereign, 17–27 High St., Hounslow, Middx (01–897 4545)
Suntours of Witney, 37–39 Corn St., Whitney, Oxon (0993 76969)
Portuguese National Tourist Office, 1–5 New Bond St., London W1 (01–493 3873)

— HUNGARY —

Four years since I was last in Hungary, and then I was riding through the Mátra mountains. I'd liked the taste of the place then: warm, frivolous, and apparently quite unawed by Big Ivan next door. I wanted to see if it had changed.

I admire Hungarian film makers and musicians and enjoy the definition of my Austrian friends (Austria under the old Empire used Hungary as its granary): 'Only a Hungarian can go into a revolving door behind you and come out in front!'

Travelling is looking into strangers' lives. And the back of a horse is a good way to do it. You're high up, moving not too quickly, so you can pry.

I'd liked the flowery villages and the pretty English model who was part of our group. She's now a TV actress, Tracy Ward, who resolutely refused to buy our poncey Riding Master with his silly waxed moustache the statutory round of drinks for overtaking him. 'Don't have to do it with the Heythrop, so shan't pay the Commies!' laughed Tracy in the semi-Cockney accent our aristos then affected.

So I jetted to Budapest by Malev Airlines, in a Russian TU. This provided an adequate lunch with as much deliciously fiery Baracks (Barack-Palinka is a good make of apricot brandy) and local wine as we wanted. Bull's Blood, which comes from near Eger, and Tokay are the best known Hungarian wines. I find the latter too sweet. But when some of my father's hundred-year-old Imperial Tokay was sold at Christie's, it made a then world record price. 'Is £5 for a teaspoon of it too much for the Elixir of Eternal Life?' the millionaire buyer from Hampstead asked the press. I could find no Imperial Tokay this time in Hungary. But it's plainly a good long term buy.

I prefer the Hungarian Pinot Noir and the Rieslings from the north shore of Lake Balaton. On this freshwater sea, the bourgeoisie of Budapest keep their holiday homes. Exactly! This is *not* a ground-down, sullen grey slave state like next-door Czechoslovakia, a country not much liked by the Hungarians.

That evening Rita, a bubbling Magyar lady (she and her husband, a professor, share six jobs) took me to the gorgeously baroque Opera House: golds, purples, marble columns, and ornately painted ceilings all recently refurbished. My good fortune continued. I was not subjected to an opera. My old major in the Army used to snort 'Loathe havin' to look at fat foreigners' tonsils while they're bawlin' out their fri'ful lingo at me'. I took his point. Instead, we saw my favourite ballet, Prokofiev's Romeo and Juliet, choreographed by the local maestro, Seregi, and theatrically based on Zeffirelli's sumptuous film. Stupendous stuff: a cast of a hundred dressed like lords and unaffordable in poor old capitalist Britain.

Our best centre stalls cost £3. Snacks in the intervals were free in palatial withdrawing rooms. Glasses of wine cost 30p. This isn't just reserved for foreigners, like those sad stores in China. There are plenty of Hungarians in the audience, including children, and all far more smartly dressed than our usual Sadler's Wells scruffy turnout. A buzz of Austrians who daily nip across the frontier to shop, Germans of the quiet kind, and just in front of us four Americans in full evening fig. It was a celebration for one of their women, clutching a bouquet.

Then, as the curtain rose, enter Seregi down our aisle with two gilt chairs and a man of lofty brow and grey-haired distinction. 'That's Arkady Raikin,' whispered Rita excitedly. 'He's the famous muppeteer – I mean puppet director – who runs the Moscow Miniature Theatre.'

On each lapel medals glinted as the old man keenly clapped. Orders of Lenin, I supposed, as the top Communist settled down within handshaking distance of the rich and happy group from Washington, DC.

I took Rita to dinner in the Vigadó in the Redoubt, another concert hall facing the Danube on the Pest side. It's close to the line of three new de luxe hotels. Mine was the Forum: top class service, with a view across the river over the cruise boats and the commercial barges up to the Palace on the Buda side. American efficiency coupled with European charm and no obvious KGB agents, or their lively lures, lurking round the bar or grill. There was the odd hooker or two about on the streets. 'Polish tarts,' said Rita crisply. The Hungarians do not think much of the Poles.

Reared on Le Carré, penetrating the Iron Curtain has a certain frisson of trepidation. So it makes the jolly Magyars even more enjoyable when you get to know them.

Rita and I rattled off by Metro – 'The second oldest in Europe after London's, though my Parisian friends won't believe it,' she said.

We ate – pancakes, stuffed, with a cream sauce – and drank extremely well for £8.65 the pair.

Pest ('s' sounds 'sh'), the lower, flat, eastern half of the double city, had been dreary four years earlier. Wide, late nineteenth century boulevards had then stretched grimly. Trams were grubby and crowded. Now there were traffic jams of newish private cars made in Russia or East Germany (the latter much despised). The Magyars drive like Jehu.

Shops then were as sparse as in the old industrial districts of Paris. Now they had multiplied like daffodils. They certainly weren't Bond Street or Fauborg St Honoré; more Kettering or Mullingar. But they were well stocked and busy. A queue of young men waited to buy spring flowers for their girl friends from a street stall. 'Americans would say that was a bread line!' giggled Rita.

The warm spring (75°F in mid-April) surprised the citizens. They sat about gossiping, gorging cream cakes and ices, Viennese fashion, at bustling pavement cafés in pedestrian precincts. Snugly clothed, elderly ladies walked large, fat dogs, a certain indicator of national prosperity.

The food, stodgy, dull and mostly porky in 1982, was much improved. The Karpatia was a good draw for my favourite mincemeat pancakes, salty with hot onion, much paprika and sour cream, and delicate enough to mouth-melt.

But I still greatly prefer Buda, perched on the western bank: picture-book seventeenth- and eighteenth-century houses in pinks, greens, orange and strawberry colours; cobbled alleys and the superb 'Coronation' church on Castle Hill. Now that most of these houses are again privately owned, they're kept bright and polished. State tenants on either side of the Curtain are less fussy about other people's property.

The Hilton up there, which could easily have been an eyesore, has been deftly grafted into old cloister walls. It droned with respectable Americans, who inflated the prices in the nearby cluster of private enterprise boutiques.

The church is smaller, more humane, than the large Basilica down in Pest. Both flicker with Catholics nipping in to pray and cross themselves. On Sundays and saints' days, Hungary's churches are full.

I saw no Russian soldiers. 'Any trouble with them?' I asked a man in my favourite Hungarian village, Szentendre (St Andrew).

'They get sent home if there is,' said he brightly, 'like your American bomber men in England, I expect!'

Szentendre is multi-coloured baroque like the best bits of Buda and is the home of writers, artists, sculptors, small museums, craft shops and a dozen excellent privately-run small restaurants.

I thought I'd like to take rooms there one summer to finish the present novel. IBUSZ, whose London agents are Danube Travel, tell me they can easily fix this. It's only half an hour north of the city on the Danube's bank, with lovely forests, rustling with deer and wild boar, rolling westwards across the Danube Bend, where there are two good castles at Visegrád.

I liked Eger also, two hours east, at the foot of the Mátra and the Bükk mountains, an ecclesiastical town with good houses, two splendidly ornate churches and a grand teachers' college built during the French and American Revolutions. There is also an excellent restaurant connected to the Park Hotel. From the old castle, the dreaded Turks were kept at bay for years by local Hungarian heroes.

We drove out to a lonely Romanesque church at the foot of the hills and then on to see the famous Lippizaner horses at their stud at Szilvásvárad. The Hungarians always win all the world's carriage driving competitions, thwacking Prince Philip and co., for they are master horsemen.

So we, too, drove behind a spanking pair of greys through the national park past trout pools and wild deer and strolling Hungarian families. 'Look! Living horses!' cried out a city child.

Six months earlier, I'd been perched by another coachman's side on the banks of the Ohio, in Kentucky. It isn't just jet travel which shrinks the world, but shared interests.

East and west, like the two greys below us, trotted happily along together. The two Magyar words I remember are 'egan' and 'jo'. They mean, significantly, 'yes' and 'good'.

TRAVEL FACTS

Malev, 9 Vigo St., London W1 (01–439 0577)
Danube Travel, 6 Conduit St., London W1 (01–493 0263)
Sovereign, 17–27 High St., Hounslow, Middx (01–897 4545)
Travelscene, 94 Baker St., London W1 (01–935 1025)
Hungarian Tourist Office, 6 Conduit St., London W1 (01–493 0263)

— THE CAMARGUE —

A fence of lawyers were arguing across my dinner table about the wild Camargue:

'Flat and flies,' snapped one.

'Magic and mysterious,' retorted another's more romantic wife.

But, like most Brits, none of us had really penetrated that weird delta glittering with its shallow lakes across the sleepy mouth of the Rhône. I went to see for myself.

The lakes are called 'étangs' pronouncing the 'g' heavily for Provence has an old language of its own. The biggest, the Etang de Vaccarès, is so broad you cannot see its furthest side. Alistair Maclean used the name in his novel, filmed by a friend of mine, about the gipsies. Their caravans of today, unromantic and hideously modern, still clutter the outskirts of that strange sea village, Les-Saintes-Maries-de-la-Mer, with its grim fortress of a church.

'You're the first English writer I've ever met,' said the *gardien* there accusingly. He helps control the Camargue's regional and national parks which blessedly bar all high-rise horrors and ticky-tacky strip building.

The *gardien* is as whiskery and naughty-eyed as a Marx brother. His more serious wife, an ardent ornithologist, leads me down private tracks to watch the pale pink flamingo flocks, the ducks and gulls and the scurrying, piping waders.

'Swiss, Swedes, Dutch – even the Germans – come here,' goes on the *gardien*, but the English,' he concludes dismissively, 'only like terrible St Tropez.'

Here I protest, for no-one of sensibility can walk along that place's Tahiti Plage, past that shelf of monstrous, wrinkled, hairy, naked apes without wanting to chuck up.

Nîmes and Arles, the two civilized Roman cities, sit on the Camargue's rim. Nîmes, for all its splendid amphitheatre and temples, is for me too much a modern city and garrison town. The hotel Cheval Blanc is your best base, opposite the gigantic Roman arena. Now they fight bulls and hold concerts where the gladiators died.

One winter's night there, I'd suffered the first intimation of the end of an affair. My nose was bleeding like a gladiator's. I glanced up from the basin into the mirror and caught the lady observing me from our bed, not with concern but with a rejection as plain as any Roman thumbs-down. Mirrors are life's great give-aways. Use them to dodge the stab in the back.

I took the *gardien* and his wife to a jollier place, Le Courbet. The *panache de fruits de mer* – everything from winkles via shrimps to oysters, piled on a tiered tray – makes an entire meal for a tenner a head. At the next table, a woman, once sharply beautiful, croaks across to me like Edith Piaf: 'I guess you are a man of affairs. No? Then a professor?'

'Well,' I begin, for I have been a professor in America.

'If not, you are a priest!' she cackles and, on leaving, insists on kissing me thrice.

Eight young shaven Foreign Legionnaires, white, brown and black, grouped womanless at the table beyond, regard me enviously. But, outside on the pavement, plump girls in mini-skirts wait to pick them up.

Arles is one of my favourite French cities. It gloriously mixes antiquity (its central mediaeval warren of tiny streets is something like Oxford) with sun-warmed boulevards and cafés thrumming with the Provençal life which so bewitches artists and writers. The restaurant of the hotel Jules César there serves magnificent nouvelle cuisine with courtesy in a classy room. How marvellously France does these things.

But only thirty minutes south lie the plains and the herds of white horses and black fighting bulls. There are the clouds of flamingos which should sing melodiously as we ride past them but who sadly croak like frogs. Vineyards stretch – the local wine, Costières du Gard, is excellent – and silvery waves of spring asparagus under their ribbons of plastic duvets. Few trees, bar umbrella pines crouched over the huge farmhouses called mas (again in Provence you pronounce the 's') which look out at you slit-eyed, wary, grim.

'Those big farmers keep themselves apart,' says the *gardien*. 'They never enter Les-Saintes-Maries when the tourists come in droves in July and August. And then, too, the mosquitoes are troublesome.'

The Camargue is as flat as Norfolk and an equally acquired taste. The wind here is the steely Mistral, the name of their famed Provençal poet, which sandpapers the sky from azure down to silver on the horizon and makes me want my water colours.

A picture of the Camargue would be seven-eighths sky in a wash on wet paper and then the bottom brilliantly sharp, for the light is dazzling in April.

We ride white horses across the whistling, empty beach which seems to stretch almost to Marseilles. The horses splash through the étangs, knowing the deep holes. We hoist our feet up to keep them dry, and that's hard enough to do in the deep Western-type saddle.

'Not Western! Camarguaise,' corrected the proud man who owns the horses. But only the mediaeval stirrups differ from the saddles in which I once loped across the purple Catalina Mountains in Arizona.

The dark girl in charge of us is tanned like all the locals by the Mistral. She rides well, leaning back as you must in those saddles (particularly if you're a normally equipped male) to avoid the high pommel used to anchor the wild bulls. *'Promenade á cheval'*, is advertised all along the roads. Children and total duffers can easily ride the dozy mokes.

'You go to the bullfight?' I was asked on Sunday.

'Certainly not!' I'd loathed what I'd seen years ago in Spain, particularly the cruelty to the picador's wretched old horses. And I still remember one English racehorse trainer's wife in our party, panting excitedly that 'bullfights are one of the few things which turn me on'. I've viewed her oddly ever since.

'They can't hurt the bulls in these Courses', explained the *gardien*. 'Your hotel, Le Sanglier, is named after a famous fighting bull from here, who lived till he was sixteen in happy retirement.'

The hotel, outside Le Cailar, is clean and friendly, but too motelishly modern for me. The Michelin Guide lists half a dozen quiet country hotels round Les-Saintes-Maries which must have more character.

Aigues-Mortes, the strange walled city, has two good restaurants, Les Remparts (splendid old furniture) and the Camargue. The old port part of Le Grau-du-Roi, whence the doomed French king set forth to die upon a Crusade, is attractive, too.

Half a dozen fighting bulls are being dashed through the streets of Les Saintes Maries on Sunday morning, enclosed by a tight posse of *gardiens*. A photographer from Paris, who was captivated by the Camargue seven years ago and now spends every holiday there, smuggles me on to the balcony of a café for a better view.

A basic traveller's trick is to find locals with access to angles. The *gardien* also knows the town's best restaurant, the Brûleur de Loupes. It is packed, as most French eating places always are for Sunday lunch. Without our guide, arriving after 12.30 would have proved in vain.

The arena where the bulls will be chased has the atmosphere of an English village gymkhana. Half a dozen young men clad in cricket whites and shirts, and armed only with a sort of little comb, have to nip either the red rosette perched between the bull's high vertical horns or one of the two white 'acorns' stitched at the horns' base. They lounged about till the bull dashed at them. Then they sprang, one-footed, on to the wooden barrier and thence on to the bottom step of the stands. The bull smartly ripped the wooden planks apart.

To exhort the youths, and advertise themselves, local tradesmen offer incentives. 'Petrol station Elf,' shouts the commentator, 'offers 450 francs for the red cockade!' One lad nips across, clawing behind him at the small rosette as the bull's horns whistle past his pants.

After twenty minutes, the bull swaggers out, tail high, back to his paddocks.

'These are third division youths,' mutters the *gardien* scornfully. 'They look windy,' I agree. 'You come down then,' says the *gardien* swiftly, 'into that passage.'

I nod and swallow nervously. At that instant, the next bull smashes through the barrier and hurtles round the passage like a furiously steaming express. But the good lunch has made me bold. Squeezing through a bolthole in the concrete (my travels have dangerously widened the girth), I gaze eyeball to eyeball with the bull. He looks as surprised as I do and smells like a very high pheasant. I feel retreat will not do and am delighted when one of the youths teases the big black bruiser away.

'Horses,' I said to the dark girl galloping across the sand dunes with the Mistral making our eyes weep, 'are more my thing.'

But the Camargue itself is a powerful thing. Not for cosiness, not for honeymoons, not in high summer. But either side of those, it is slightly magical, mysterious and exciting.

TRAVEL FACTS

Air France, 69 Boston Manor Rd., Brentford, Middx (01–499 6511)
Air France Holidays, 69 Boston Manor Rd., Brentford, Middx (01–568 6981)
French Leave, 21 Fleet St., London EC4 (01–583 8383)
VFB, 1 St Margaret's Terrace, Cheltenham, Glos (0242 35515)
French Government Tourist Office, 178 Piccadilly, London W1 (01–499 6911)

— MADEIRA —

'Two strange things about the British,' remarks the beady-eyed agreeable manager of Reid's, Madeira. The world-famous hotel was founded in 1891, and the Swiss manager seems to like us warmly.

'First, my Portuguese staff will never call you "foreigners". They say, "there are forty per cent foreigners here and sixty per cent British". It's your old friendships, I suppose. But, for me, a Swiss, it's strange. The other thing is that the English never complain until twenty minutes before they leave after their two-weeks holiday! Germans, French, say immediately, "This bowl of orchids is not quite correct." We put it right at once. But the English always complain too late. Is it that you are too polite? Too shy?'

Except, perhaps, for a marginally misplaced orchid in a suite full of sunshine, opening on to those palm-studded lawns, I could see nothing but bliss.

We sat in his grill room over an enormous, delicious lunch. Below us, two young, but mostly senior, couples lay about in the warm March sun or swam slowly in sea pools heated to 80°F.

'Average 68' read a sign. One of the younger couples naughtily enquired: 'Average air temperature or age of guests?'

We ate smoked ham from the island and the fabulous Estrada fish, black-skinned from the very depths of the ocean's pit. It's the very reverse of British Rail cod: it melts like butter in the mouth.

Veal in Madeira wine is another local speciality. But I forswore veal years ago when a woman I knew dreadfully kept and named and petted calves at home to fatten up, slaughter and devour. Incipient schizophrenia, this nasty cut from kindliness to callousness, is particularly dangerous in females.

All round spread the manager's happy family of guests: the Brits awaiting afternoon tea in flowery bowers, gently perusing yesterday's *Times* to see which of their friends had died back there in chilly Britain.

All spoke English which the Queen would recognise. Down in my quiet, comfortable and wonderfully serviced hotel, the Savoy, a merry-eyed East-ender confided: 'We went up to Reid's, but it was, y'know, *smart* for us. Happier here. Service smashing, ain't it?' So it is throughout the island.

I asked Reid's manager if it were true that all his guests wore dinner-jackets each evening in his lovely dining room. 'Oh, no. Only eighty per cent,' he said.

'And tiaras?'

'Now you joke!'

Breakfast comes at the Savoy with a smiling waiter even before you have time to brush your teeth after ringing for it. As I was pocketing the notice 'Please do not feed seagulls', one dive-bombed the marmalade on my balcony, where I sat above the glittering sea.

Two friends of mine recently survived a Force 7 matrimonial gale. They chose Madeira in general, Reid's in particular, 'because we needed pampering', said the wife. It worked.

But I needed to explore. Mr Avis took me over the hairpins through the volcanic mountains. The flower-hemmed roads are bumpy *pavé*. Children and old men saunter about in the middle.

Madeira's south side is softer than the north and, west of Funchal, prettier: a confection of white-walled, red-roofed and green-shuttered cottages, perched on minute terraces of sugar cane, bananas, sweet potatoes, peas, beans and lucerne.

The north is violent: towering great cliffs, waterfalls spuming down and a dark tunnel bored through for the narrow, rattling road to Porto Moniz. Here there's a tangle of ledged rock pools. Foaming breakers smash at the island's ankles like leisurely giants. There's a cluster of good fish restaurants. I chose the Cachalote, crammed when the package coaches munch, empty otherwise. Germans crunch carefully, French chatter, arms flailing. Wood floors, bamboo roof, perched like a gull's nest over the surging Atlantic. We are three hundred and forty miles off Africa, six hundred miles south-west of Lisbon.

Waitresses dash about dressed up like sailors. Madeiran ladies tend to be very small, stout and, sadly, seem to cease being pretty immediately they leave school. Only one here speaks English. Spanish I find almost useless here, except as a base for reading the road signs.

One huge sole, crisp-skinned with firm flesh on the bone, plus local rice flavoured with winkles, and a garlicky mayonaise for the salad, plus a bottle of Dão 'grey' costs £3.

By Seixal's vineyards I pick up a bearded Madeiran, hitch-hiking to football over the cloud-capped mountains, five thousand feet high and wildly Landseer.

'Any stags?' I ask. 'No, but they grow some hash.'

Tracks wind, sweetly smelling, through forests of pine and eucalyptus. But all I see are black goats with tinkling bells wandering about in the soothing stillness which is Madeira's strength.

Below in the sunlight appear a host of allotment sheds but they turn out to be cow byres, often thatched. I inspect one. Its contented beast and its curious owner, a peasant lady, black garbed with shawl but wearing modern black wellies and cutting grasses with her sickle, inspect me back.

Beard halloos every girl we overtake. Madeirans have to walk almost everywhere. 'Why every walking girl,' he asks 'never so pretty when you see face?' But we pick one up trekking from her father's tiny vineyard to seek summer work along the coast.

Beard wants to stop for a drink by the sea at Ribeira Brava but it's a dreary spot. Madeira really doesn't possess beaches. The cliffs are far too steep. For sands you must nip to the next island, Porto Santo, where Columbus once lived.

I prefer Camara de Lobos, a higgledy-piggledy fishing village where we drink poncha in a bar overlooking a cliff-top square with a tiny bandstand. Poncha, sugar-cane spirit and pineapple juice, is madly drinkable. So, after several, attempting a short-cut through a precipitous banana grove, I get Mr Avis stuck in the soft red soil. Tweed-capped peasants emerge smoking the strong local tobacco and push us out.

'How much should I give them?' I whisper to Beard.

'Fifty escudos for a drink.' That's 27p – Madeira is certainly cheap.

But the Savoy's restaurant breaks all rules of good design: it's far too vast – 'I can seat twelve hundred persons,' says the proud maître d'hôtel, so it's less than half full. It's too low and garishly overlit by neon strips, cruelly recalling an awful Chinese hotel in Canton. Windows which could overlook the Atlantic are clogged by curtains. Good restaurants need pools of warm light per table – which is why candles shine – against murmuring shadowy backgrounds.

Most of the guests are quiet, grey contented couples, several lame. But here's one fellow in too bright a pinstripe (suits are almost obligatory). He has the highly manicured hands which boast of executive success and certain conquests. One of these he is sliding up his young secretary's inner thigh. She, affecting disregard, nibbles her pink steak (the food is excellent) with maddening slowness, aiming to postpone singing for her supper with her office boss.

Life is a cabaret, old chum, but you need to watch it.

Embroidered linen is the great buy in Funchal and the Casa do Turista is the place to go. It sounds dreary but it's an attractive former private house where all the goods are laid out in different rooms.

In the neat city's east end beyond the port are a cluster of restaurants. Golfino – pretentious, haughty and expensive; Romana, sensible, recommended, and often full; and Le Jardin which, if you can bear its décor which is Habitat pseudo-garden junk gone mad, serves fat gambas in a spicy sauce and slabs of that wonderful espada fish.

Would I go back to 'Madeira m'deah' as the nobs call it? Flowers, peace, service, and winter warm at 65° and summer cool at 75°? If I were weary, broken hearted, old or lame, I'd zoom back there like one of those seagulls – if Reid's had one of their garden rooms to spare.

TRAVEL FACTS

Air Portugal, 38–44 Gillingham St., London SW1 (01–828 0262)
Caravela, 38–44 Gillingham St., London SW1 (01–630 9223/4)
Thomsons, Greater London House, Hampstead Rd., London NW1 (01–439 2211)
Suntours of Witney, 37–39 Corn St., Witney, Oxon (0993 76969)
Portuguese National Tourist Office, 1–5 New Bond St., London W1 (01–493 3873)

— RHINE CRUISE —

Love seeds were sown before our good ship *France* had left Rotterdam (that displeasing Dutch port) for her six-day cruise up the Rhine to Basle.

With both elbows on the bar on the starboard side was the American schoolboy trying to explain to the Tunisian barman that his home, Wyoming, was not a town but a state.

'Bigger than Holland,' I interjected from the next bar stool. Ships encourage chat.

On the deck below, the last passengers from fourteen different countries were still embarking.

'Bigger than *Great* Britain', retorted the lad tartly.

The only other single Briton on board then introduced himself. He was a diffident bachelor with tombstone but smiling teeth, a partner in a firm of auctioneers. 'I always take cruises for my holidays,' he said. 'This'll be my sixth trip on the Köln-Düsseldorfer Line up the Rhine'.

'You make friends quickly on a cruise,' he assured me. 'Quite unlike hotels. And I'm so shy I might not speak to anyone all week in a hotel. There's something different about boats: they make people so friendly'.

He was to prove so right.

The Wyoming schoolboy announced firmly: 'I'm travelling with my mother'. But his delectable, red-haired mother was about to start travelling with someone else. Soon, a gold wrist-watched, mature and portly American from Baltimore heavily materialised. (The cruise is very much de-luxe and far from cheap.) Baltimore man also had a son in tow, an uneasy college youth whom the father aggravated with a bossy paternalism.

At my table in the airy dining-room – large windows on both sides (I cannot call them portholes) – appeared a busy, funny Australian lady of uncertain age, with the lovable air of an animated penguin. She spoke, mysteriously, fluent German. I discovered as the cosy boat slid smoothly up the great river towards its source that the Australian lady, too – and not alone among the 147 passengers – was in search of her roots.

My preconceptions had been entirely wrong. I'd supposed a Rhine cruise would be on a vessel as cramped and noisy as those that ply the

Thames between Maidenhead and Marlow. I'd also feared squadrons of *lederhosen* Germans bellowing songs alternately lachrymose and bellicose. I'd dreaded Teutonic discipline and dull, heavy food. But there were no impassioned Krauts and everything was easy, and the menus were quite delicious.

Only a dozen passengers were German and these were serious middle-aged. Seventy-four Americans, many on leave from highly-paid but unsocial, unpleasant jobs in the Middle East, comprised the bulk. There were French, Brits, and Canadians (at great pains as usual to mark their differences from the Americans). There were couples from Switzerland, Holland, New Zealand and Australia (the Kiwis as usual making sure we knew they were different from Aussies), Italy, Spain, Israel and South Africa. Finally, there was a shy Argentinian family whom I had taken to be Spanish. It was the year of the regrettable Falklands escapade.

The boat stops daily or nightly for jaunts ashore and on top of Düsseldorf's gigantic new tower the Argentine parents asked me if I could lend them some coins to buy their children a drink from a cola machine. When they realised I was English, they looked at first appalled, then ashamed, and finally rather frightened. Guilt overtook us all. A common wish to make amends for countrymen lost struggled under the handcuffs of different languages.

I shook their hands warmly, struggling with Spanish. 'Argentinians always friendly with England till ...' they began. 'I know, I know', I said remorsefully.

When I awoke that first morning, the countryside was already creeping slowly backwards. Friesians scarcely moved. Cyclists only crawled through the hot, flat, green land. The boat was a constant somnambulist.

Cars, coaches, even planes are jerking, shrieking mayhem compared with the lovely languor of a large river cruiser.

The art auctioneer pointed out: 'Unlike a sea cruise, we not only get landscapes all the time, but different ones on either side.'

We glided beneath the bridge at Nijmegen. Was this spick city once that battlefield where boys from school got killed? Here by this bridge a friend of mine won a Military Cross and another died.

Xanten slid past, with its Roman amphitheatre, relic of another earlier pre-Reich empire on the Rhine.

On the top sun deck, aft of the swimming pool, I observed the nubile lady from Wyoming. She was seductively reclined in a cyclamen one-piece in a blue chair on the hot green deck. She knew her legs were excellent: she moved them voluptuously about, keeping her knees raised so that her thighs retained their slimness.

Her teeth and eyes were assets, too, so she smiled a great deal and kept her sunglasses pushed back on to her auburn hair. I told my Australian friend that I thought Mrs Wyoming was thirty-three at most. 'Forty-three', said 'Aussie'.

Mrs Wyoming was being thunderously courted by fat Mr Baltimore. Crouching forward over her out of his blue deck-chair, he was delivering a powerful spiel. Their respective sons, like dogs impatiently awaiting the outcome of their owners' meeting, watched each other with surly wariness. The fat man, peeling off wads of Deutschmarks, continually dispatched his grumpy lad down to the bar to buy drinks for the boy from Wyoming.

The chief steward, Mr Mustapha, was an Egyptian, ever smiling, with a grey crest peaking his frizzy hair. He was also the ship's matchmaker.

'Where you want to sit, Mr Herbert?' he asked, deflecting me away from the English auctioneer. 'Why you speak so very good German?'

I muttered embarrassedly that I had been out in Germany at the end of the war for some years. 'Part of the Occupation', I murmured. Mr Mustapha grinned happily. But I thought, with a sudden chill, what a child I had been then as a young officer, a schoolboy in new khaki uniform, believing that the peace would be won just as we had won the war, that Britain was still supreme and that the Welfare State was feasible.

Mr Mustapha placed me at a table with the American couple who were going to be close observers of the Wyoming-Baltimore *entente*. This American was tremendously fit and had been eight years a Marine, ending up a major. He was working as 'an adviser' in the Gulf and did not smile when I made a joke about the CIA.

His wife, pregnant for the first time, hailed grandly from Virginia and was not only a Daughter of the Revolution but a Colonial Matron, which she assured me proved an even longer lineage. Americans from our former colonies are just as snobbish as us. Her family, she said bluntly, had not been pleased when she married this tough, clever husband from beyond the Virginian pale but whom she had met at college. He had German and Swiss roots and, in true American fashion, was in earnest pursuit of them.

So, too, was 'Aussie', placed at my side by the naughty Mr Mustapha and soon my friend. 'Oh, a woman never forgets a man who makes her laugh,' she said, squeezing me, as we sat at two o'clock in a hot Düsseldorf night, downing the powerful local beer, surrounded by a thousand singing students in the city's streets.

'Aussie's' background emerged as we pottered together about the grey splendour of Cologne cathedral. I had first seen the Dom, the miraculous survivor in a rocky sea of stinking rubble, when I first crossed the Rhine thirty-eight years earlier. Then I had also seen the vast Ford factory pumping out trucks for the Wehrmacht. It had been an obvious target a few miles downstream. Yet, like the cathedral, it had been miraculously spared. So came my first example of the wartime powers not only of God but of international Mammon. 'Aussie' told me that she had been born a German – had we bombed or shelled her? – leaving that country as a two-year-old to emigrate with her parents to Australia. She, too, was back here for the first time since the war. But she wanted to test whether she still felt German beneath her Australian skin.

Her father, not then naturalised, had been interned by the Australians for six years and became, without bitterness, the camp tailor. Her subsequent husband – 'such a funny, such a clever man' – was also German-born. He, too, had been interned in Australia as an alien. But for him that wound of apparent unjust cruelty never healed. Drink, then divorce, then death. 'An accident?'

'No, something worse, something horrible,' 'Aussie' said, crying. Like most funny people, misery lurked beneath her laughter. There had been a murder.

'If I didn't look outwards, if I didn't laugh with people, I couldn't take it,' she said later on the cruise. This time we were sitting in the little mountain railway winching its way up the Drachenfels above pretty Königswinter. Below us on the opposite bank of the Rhine lies Bad Godesberg where poor, grey Chamberlain had thought he'd done a deal with Hitler. We reached the summit. It was loud with stout, sweating Germans admiring their Seven Hills and sluicing down the beer.

As our boat drifted away from Königswinter sharp cries shook off our gurgling river torpor. The sons of the Baltimore businessman and the nubile Mrs Wyoming were leaping from the jetty at the boat. The hooter signalled hard astern. For their respective parents hurried into sight down the street aglow with embarrassment and the smiting sun and probably something else. They re-embarked beneath our curious eyes.

Heat haze. The river smells of Eton and Cambridge, a battery of ancient castles crouched on peak after peak, as the boat wends south-wards. Vineyards begin, combed in strict rows almost vertically upwards. Refreshed by all this languorous travel, we went ashore at sleepy Koblenz one night, leaving a feeble dance on board, as soon as we saw Mrs Wyoming scampering cabinwards off the floor lustily pursued by a sweating Mr Baltimore.

Sitting much later in the ship's bar, 'Aussie' told me her husband had been killed in 'a sort of accident involving our son. My son is still detained in a state institution. I shouldn't have told you.' Her face crumpled but she didn't weep. 'But I'm glad I did,' she said.

The boat moves leisurely on between the once warring castles along the Rhine. We pass the Rock of the Loreley and sing in German of that temptress who lured sailors to destruction. All men desire to be tempted. And many, like the genuine gamblers, wish to crash.

The next night, bottles of champagne are suddenly ordered in the bar for a certain cabin. Mr Mustapha, with a smile like a Cheshire cat, whispers to me that they are for Mr Baltimore and Mrs Wyoming, now happily conjoined and sharing all.

The couple do not surface again all next day. The boat slips southwards between the famous vineyards. Nierstein in a heatglow rises up, then falls away. 'I *knew* that woman would catch a rich man on this trip,' snaps the Daughter of the American Revolution, 'I heard her say to him this morning outside their cabin that now she could throw her vibrator overboard.'

TRAVEL FACTS

Lufthansa, 23–28 Piccadilly, London W1 (01–408 0442)

KD Rhine Cruise, 80–81 St Martin's Lane, London WC2 (01–836 1876)

National Holidays, George House, George St., Wakefield, W. Yorks (0924 387387)

Anglia Holidays, Norwich Airport, Norwich, Norfolk (0603 43764)

German Tourist Office, 61 Conduit St., London W1 (01–734 2600)

— CYPRUS —

The dusty road to the bay where Aphrodite was born of Zeus and out of foam, swoops down to a sea so brilliant blue in late October that I thought the love goddess had ordered it specially touched up.

The milk white cliffs, flecked with shrubs like huge cream cheese, start soon after you leave Limassol driving west to Paphos along the southern coast of Cyprus.

Limassol is a dullish town but with good hotels like the Churchill on the sea front, and an expanding commercial port. On the hill just behind it I was taken by a local to dinner in an excellent fish restaurant. Too brightly lit (a common Greek failing) it was full of Greek-Cypriot families down to two-year-olds toddling round the tables. But though the name blazes over the town in garish yellow neon, not a tourist had made the journey up there. It was run, like much else in southern Cyprus, by an emigré from the Turkish-occupied north.

Routes into cities from international airports are usually dire — don't, for example, be put off Cyprus by the environs of Larnaca. I asked the friendly girl behind Reception in the Churchill the best way west. I'd swum, even waded about, in the sea before breakfast that autumn morning.

'Go out past the old port through the lovely Phassouri plantations,' she advised me, 'then stop at the Roman amphitheatre at Curium.'

I drive through a tunnel of pine trees, vineyards, groves of green lemons. But here's a track to a tiny tortoise-backed Greek church under a clump of eucalyptus. Then the shore with two tavernas, three cars and, on his phut-phut moped, one old Cypriot, all on a Saturday morning. Curium is perched above us on the cliff-top. First settled by the Greeks thirty-three centuries ago, the whole city is being excavated and you can potter where you will, inhaling the past.

Columns are re-erected, a great basilica revealed. Bright mosaics gleam. The amphitheatre, scalloped like a vast radar disc, listens on the cliff edge over the twinkling sea. I test the accoustics by whispering from the stage up to the top-most ring of stone seats. No-one regiments you at Curium. There are no ropes to hem you in. Looking to the east I think about those other more modern listening posts picking up whatever's interesting in the airwaves over the furious Middle East.

Highbrow classicists abhor reconstructions of old places. I prefer them. Scholars damn what Evans did rebuilding the amazing palace of Knossos on Crete. But I'm grateful to any archaeologist who shows us how our ancestors really lived: not roofless between stone stumps and broken bits.

Sustained by ancient civilisations (Apollo's Sanctuary a mile on is beautiful, too) and hungry for my lunch, I press on through the spick Sovereign Base at Episkopi. I plan to eat at the Bunch of Grapes in the hill village of Pissouri.

The army's signs, strings of bright red initials on hugh white boards, whisk me back to my military years. What heaven this brightly-scrubbed slab of Aldershot set in Cyprus' antiquity must seem to troops after accursed Ulster.

At the Base's end, past the polo ground, the main road soon starts to crumble. I pass signs to seaside hotels, then see Pissouri clinging to a hillside and turn left. But village streets here are tracks for mules not motors. I shunt about, asking help of a priest, bearded and bunned under his black chimney hat, squatting outside a bar.

Faint arrows on white-washed walls lead to a mulberry tree, a vine-latticed roof, red-checked table cloths and too much good dry wine (asinou) with my moussaka (all for a fiver).

Dreading crowds and commercialism on Aphrodite's landing-beach (for development threatens on the hills behind), I find it empty, bar two couples. The Tourist Pavilion is hidden behind the hill. There's one ice cream van on the road labelled, like a pop group, Venus Rock.

I dare say there's a boring geographical reason but the only sea's edge I found in Cyprus with white foam frothing on it was this one where Zeus' heavenly but tricksome daughter arose.

A blonde, probably Swedish (for pockets of these beauties nest in Cyprus) is swimming in the aquamarine water, carefully keeping her hair dry and shouting to a couple of Germans poking cameras at her. Then, like the goddess, but in a not totally transparent mauve bikini, she steps out of the buoyant water on to the harsh grey stones of reality.

The beach suddenly fills with people. I spot the English couple I saw that morning, he pale and faintly sweating, she pretty and blushing pink, trying to book a double room at my hotel. On the beach these two, magicked by Aphrodite's kiss, move away from the crowd and walk, arms entwined, to where the white foam hisses.

Paphos harbour with its old Turkish fort and two outdoor restaurants on the water's brink remains unspoilt, a fishing port still. I marvel at the mosaics in the House of Dionysus, twenty-two rooms of a Roman villa. Expat Brits in their cottage cleverly converted from cow-byres in the pretty village of Maroni (one telephone only, in a box outside the taverna) had pressed me to go. They were right.

Then on to the west past the Coral Bay development (not too bad) through olive groves, carob trees, and banana plantations to reach a headland with just one old church, Ayios Yeorgios and a plain restaurant where I lunch on red mullet and salad.

Cypriot goodwill rubs off on visitors. My car, bundling down a rocky track by the coast, blew a tyre. As I wrestled, two mopeds, German-ridden, then two with Brits aboard, then a British Mini, and finally an old Cypriot goatherd wrinkled as an olive tree, all materialised out of the scrub to offer aid.

I cut across the north western spur of hills to Fontana Amorosa and the Bath of Aphrodite (that girl was everywhere) which is a grey-green grotto continuously filled by tinkling water. At the Tourist Pavilion nearby (a dreary place, alas) I split a bottle of wine as the sun sank flaming across the bay. There's a clump of tavernas near the army post of Latchi. One of these might have fed me better. From there to Polis, up and over two valleys of vineyards and so serpentinely back to Paphos.

I found one of the prettiest villages, Lania, on my way up to the Troodos Mountains. There the artist whose watercolours I had come to buy, pointed me on the road to Troodhitissa monastery – neat, dark, with lame ladies in black kissing the icons and a priest with a bottle nose on whom I practised faint traces of my classical Greek.

The artist had called after me as I walked off: 'You like strange places, odd people? Visit that weird collapsing Hotel Berengaria on top of Prodromos – if it's still there!'

It just was – a huge stone-winged castle, its tower roof agape, its windows broken. I, the only guest, am welcomed by father and son, who are struggling to survive. They lead me through empty ballrooms as creepy as a Hammer film.

For seven thousand years Cyprus has been invaded, hammered, occupied, knocked down and built up. So how can they love foreigners so? But they do. And they keep seeking signs of hope. The old man in his wreck of an hotel pointed out a modern building arising on the next ridge. 'Owned by a once penniless dancer in a third class nightclub. She was watched and watched by a rich American from

Cyprus Mining Corporation. He fell in love. Then one night a drunk man attacks him with a bottle. He bleeds badly. He is unconscious. She rescues him, takes him home, nurses him. Then she married him. But he was sad always from the blows to his head. When he died, she was rich. She helps everyone around. She is too kind. People prey on her. She offered to help us. But we were too proud. A big mistake ... She is a princess now – she found an Italian title – and lives in Nicosia. A wonderful woman. Go to see her. Say we sent you.'

The old hotelier with his grey artistic locks loaded me with bunches of grapes and red apples from the overgrown tennis court and warned me in a whisper about Larnaca. 'Be careful there. It is full of spies.'

Waiting for my plane, I sat beneath the palms along Larnaca's promenade. I was joined by what seemed a wretchedly poor old peasant lady who came to me across the sand clad all in black and smelling of her beloved cats. She was quite certainly no peasant. She said she was yet another refugee from Famagusta. She spoke to me first in fluent French about theology – 'How many gods are there now, do you think?' – and then in German about Communism as a religion.

Cyprus, island of love, they say. What a place for meeting strange people.

TRAVEL FACTS

Cyprus Airways, 29–31 Hampstead Rd., London NW1 (01–388 5411)

Thomas Cook, PO Box 36, Thorpe Wood, Peterborough (01–437 9080)

Timsway Travel, Penn Place, Rickmansworth, Herts (0923 775349)

Thomsons Holidays, Greater London House, Hampstead Rd., London NW1 (01–439 2211)

Cyprus Tourist Office, 213 Regent St., London W1 (01–734 9822)

— PORTUGAL: ALGARVE —

Portugal's southern shore was 'in' twenty-five years ago, 'out' when the Commies briefly displaced another dictatorship, and 'in' again now. Drives of golfers thwack round its array of courses. Eastenders of a quiet sort suck up the undoubted sun. No other Mediterranean resort area has so far disputed the Algarve's oft-repeated claim to have more sun hours per year than anywhere else in Europe.

To explore the unexploited country between the Algarve and Lisbon I drove south from the capital. You can easily fly TAP (an agreeable airline with slightly above average food) to Faro in the Algarve but no-one can get the feel of a country simply by flying over it. I was in Estoril so, on the advice of the Portuguese Tourist Office – a great deal more helpful than some of their competitors – I set off to explore.

'Take the Atlantic coast road,' advised my friends in Estoril, 'not the one down the middle.' It's far prettier along the coast. Over the dizzily high suspension bridge over the Tagus, I went. 'Stop for lunch at Santiago,' the friends had said. 'It's half-way there. Look in at Milfontes Vila Nova at the mouth of the Rio Mira, that might be a coming place in the future. And you *must* go to the south-west tip of all Europe. But the Algarve to the east you will find rather crowded and a bit spoilt.'

And so it mostly was. Its development, though nothing like as appalling as the brutalities committed on Spain's Mediterranean coast, does come as a shock after the quiet countryside you enjoy driving down.

Santiago, perched in a dazzle of white ancient houses up on a hill, is topped by a castle, now enclosing a peaceful cemetery. The high family tombs, some as big as beach huts, stand inside the old ramparts. From these, there are bold defenders' views across the plain to the sea. On the coast I spotted something looking in the distance like a refinery. I resolved not to try it.

But I endured a dreary lunch on Santiago's outskirts in a dark poussada, (a government-owned restaurant equivalent in part to Spain's paradors). I had committed the basic traveller's error of not asking a local the name of a restaurant. The poussada seemed shut though a timid maid finally unlocked the front door. Had the place been sold, I wondered. But no, I could eat. The place was empty and I should have left at once, like the sensible Brits who peered in later, said clearly, 'No, thank you', and hurried away. Half an hour later, surrounded by screeching peacocks, only one other table was occupied by two Portuguese travellers talking business.

There looked to be quite a few little eating places in the pretty town. But too late.

The Vila Nova parts of Milfontes are too Nova by far for me. A clucking coach-load of elderly Midlanders were stepping upon the sand below the bizarre moated castle as nervous as chickens. But further on, boys in a battered French van rolled up with six wind-surfing boards. A Portuguese couple sported intimately on the sand beneath the cliffs on the way out to the northern point of the Mira estuary. Not much else pulsed. But I could see that one day it might. Like much of Portugal it seemed asleep and not too keen on waking.

South of the wide and almost empty estuary (I saw three boats) shone great golden bays with no-one on them. With time I would have explored them for there was something looking like an out-of-use beach restaurant. Had the place tried and failed?

Driving south through forests of eucalyptus and fields of fat cattle, I saw lane after little lane leading Atlantic-wards to Praia this and that. Men in the black 'baddie' hats of Westerns, and women draped in perpetual mourning, rode donkeys and drove mule carts along the road which wound sinuously through pretty farmland and small woods. Little traffic else. One day, I am sure, this will be the next sea coast to find in Europe. And if any reader already has, they will not be pleased by my saying so.

Cape St Vincent is indeed magnificent. This was the last land Prince Henry and the other great navigators saw as they rocked forth in cockleshells as puny as our capsules into space to open up Brazil, the Cape of Good Hope, India and far distant China.

Running out to the Cape west of dreary Lagos (pronounced Largosh) the land is high, wild and handsome. It has a Celtic feel of North Cornwall or Brittany. I lunched at a pleasant hotel with a pool, the Baleeira, high on the cliff's edge at Sagres. But the sun was scorching to purple a gaggle of Brits as ugly and querulous as Giles' Grandma's family.

The young waiter with whom the girls were flirting watched me watching them. 'What you write in that little book?'

'Good grilled sardines, nice hot bread, and well dressed salad,' I read out, 'and good dry white wine and a friendly waiter. But six repellant Brits with shrieking kids both spoilt and neglected. How awful we are abroad!'

Given good beaches plus hot sun, every coast road of southern Europe has become abominable. Driving east along Portugal's dreaded 125 reminded me with horror of Spain's even worse 'Avenue of Death', the terrifying artery littered with dead animals and crumpled cars along the Costa del Sol, France's murderous N7 in the bad old days, and the road west of Athens to Corinth.

I didn't take much to hot, grimy and narrow Portimao nor the latter's famous and therefore jostlingly crowded Praia da Rocha. Buzzed by mad Portuguese drivers up my exhaust pipe, I reached Portugal's largest modern development, Vilamoura, with increasing gloom, wishing I'd stayed north near Estoril.

Soaring yellow cranes, ranges of eyeless buildings, two tower block hotels and empty apartment slabs scarred the great plain of former farmland.

But my hotel, the Dom Pedro, though huge, brimmed with happy people and a staff helpful, unrushed and jolly. Surly foreign waiters are made so only by rude, shouting, non-foreign-speaking Brits. The visitors here were polite and cheerful. They smiled at strangers and made polite conversation in the lifts.

The land around, instead of being the creation of one hand, has been sold off to different developers, always a dangerous dodge. It demonstrated, like a sort of Milton Keynes in the sunshine, wildly different tastes and costs. Shining out like a good deed among tenements and other grotties was one exception and this by a British company, hooray! It is Montpellier's charming cluster of 'town houses' built like a stage set for a Chelsea musical – but so far without any dancing girls. How much do pretty women improve drab scenery. But how few pretty women there are in Portugal!

The next large development east of Vilamoura is Vale do Lobo – a very different kettle of fish. It has a classy, established feel with trees and flowery gardens. There is an obvious pride in the place shown by owners, tenants and staff which you normally find only in very pretty English villages. Even Roger Taylor's battery of tennis courts, and its pools and golf courses, are nicely hidden away in woody folds. A good spot for my teenage daughters, I thought, wondering how they'd compare it with La Manga Club, south of Alicante in Spain.

The most expensive development I visited on the Algarve was Quinta do Lago. It has little to show. 'Only seven per cent of our estate is developed,' said my guide proudly. I soon saw why, for he went on, 'You must pay £60,000 up to £250,000', pausing for emphasis, 'and that is for the plots alone.' I did not rush to pay a deposit. Even if I had that sort of money to spend on a foreign field, I would be uneasy with such mega-rich neighbours. I made my excuses and left.

The Algarve's eastern frontier with Spain is Vila Real, a flat and dull town on a handsome river neatly laid out on a grid. Like a husband with adulterous thoughts I saw on a signpost that Spain's beautiful city of Seville was only 100 miles away and wished I were there.

The great white beach nearby at Monte Gordo is a bit bleak, too. Lots of room. Inexpensive snack bars. Quiet local people. But bleak. I dozed under a palm by the tiny closed casino.

Instead of driving back along the noisy coast road, I took the hilly way, the 270, through rolling beautiful countryside via São Bras and Loulé. What a lovely change! Now, if I found a small farmhouse up there ... There are still nice places left.

To other travellers' surprise – 'How *can* you like it? Crowded, full of bloody trippers' – I really liked the core of Albufeira, with its pretty walking streets, steps, slopes, flowers, restaurants and shops. It is probably crowded for swimming but what an improvement on the generally grim Quarteira just east of Vilamoura. For the best bit of the sea turn south from Lagoa to Carvoeiro, and find your way along that exciting coast (its residents will kill me for this) and you will come across a necklace of quiet, golden coves bright with brisk, clean surf.

TRAVEL FACTS

Air Portugal, 38–44 Gillingham St., London SW1 (01–828 0262)

Travel Club of Upminster, Station Rd., Upminster, Essex (04022 24000)

Meon, Meon House, Petersfield, Hants (0730 68411)

Arrow Holidays, Alban Row, 27–31 Verulam Rd., St Albans, Herts (0727 66200)

Portuguese National Tourist Office, 1–5 New Bond St., London W1 (01–493 3873)

— BIARRITZ AND THE
BASQUE COUNTRY —

'Half Devon, half Switzerland.' My fourteen-year-old daughter points across the foothills of the Pyrenees behind Biarritz. She's right. The land is rich and curvaceous and the earth is red. Lanes meander between banks. Cows are plump. Their bells toll even more melodiously than the Swiss. Trout glide in streams. White farms bask under red roofs, red beams and balconies bedecked with flowers. The Swiss feel grows as we gaze up behind Ascain.

This is an ideal French village with a pretty square, a few essential shops and whiffs of bread baking, coffee, garlic and Gitanes. Being in the heartland of the mysterious Basques, it has one of their great black-timbered churches with galleries segregated for the sexes. And prayer-books in their own untraceable tongue. Did it, did the Basques, come mysteriously from the East like the Hungarians? Here's the ubiquitous pelota court, the fronton. Whoosh! go arms and balls. Click-clack: they hit the wall, smack back. Wine glasses clink as we watch outside golden-haired Madame Aspirot's Hotel de la Rhune, which borders the fronton. An author of a famous Basque novel lived here. But I think I'd either be distracted by the pelota, or nod off.

We sleep in the annexe of Mme Aspirot's hotel up a lane of working farms and rich men's summer houses. My daughters are delighted because we have a bungalow in the garden. Here they can femininely unpack, hang up clothes. I travel so much I leave everything, but a coat and a better pair of trousers, still in the suitcase. When Mills & Boon pall, they trip across the lawn to swim in the annexe's private pool. 'It's like our private house,' says Jane. Behind stands the 2700 foot high hill of Rhune, its funicular railway hidden. Climbing it is one of the things we never get round to doing.

Westwards, misty, purple and snow-capped in July stand the intimidating Pyrenees. And the locals all ask me: 'Why do the English no longer come to Biarritz? Are you all poor now because you don't work?'

It's ridiculously cheap. Five super courses for a fiver in our simple hotel, the Marbella, down a narrow Biarritz street. And in the furniture-making village of Came, we dine with the farmer for £3 a head at his 'Ferme-auberge' (a sign worth spotting as you swan around this part of France). You can stay at the farm for little more.

One day we lunched at St Pée – a delicious meal at the Hotel de la Nivelle, run by a former pelota champion, and afterwards watched a chistera match played by six men (sashes showed their sides) on the fronton next to the ivy-hung ruined castle.

French aristos still summer in Biarritz, in their tall, grey, empty-looking houses. The young, tanned and shaggy swarm in for surfing in battered old vans. Biarritz has two quite different types of visitor. The elegant elderlies primly walking their poodles frown at the zapping motor scooters, the unsweet birds of youth.

Past quiet Jermyn Street-type shops named after the old Prince of Wales or Napoleon III or the Duke of Westminster who all made Biarritz *the* place, the untidy young jostle to and from all-night discos.

Like a decent dish, the area is a blend of tastes. Over all broods the proud, rebellious Basque spirit. A touch of menace sharpens holiday wits.

An intelligent and pretty French girl, Claire, takes us round Bayonne, a splendid city of ramparts, arcades and a great river. 'Down there,' she points into a dark mediaeval alley, 'a friend of my brother's was assassinated.' We gape, for she is taking us round the good Basque museum next door.

'We Basques are like the Jews,' says an old master-craftsman in Larressore. He has typical Basque looks: squat, immensely strong shoulders, a very broad brow, contemplative eyes. He travels the world and makes his exquisite Makhila walking sticks (some cost £75) for the Pope and the Presidents of France and of the USA. 'We're a people of three million at home here, with ten million spread through the world. But Basque still. In some American towns they still speak Basque and play pelota.' We sit and drink outside his simple workroom. He looks shrewdly at me. 'You and I are lucky. Our work is our pleasure.'

The joys of driving through France shouldn't be hurried. Biarritz is too far, though, from the Channel ports for just one week's holiday. So we loaded the car on to the Mototrain at Boulogne, a far nicer entry into France than ghastly Calais or hideous Le Havre. The special station for the Mototrain makes things easy. I drive the car up its ramp on one side of the platform. Our Wagons-lits await us on the other. Between there's a buffet selling *pique-niques*, for there's no dining-car (bad marks) for our twelve hour journey through the night. But our *conducteur* brings me pâté, biscuits and a bottle of Bordeaux. The girls

are asleep on the two top bunks before I slip into mine and can disturb
them with my snoring.

French railways give all travellers with cars a good breakfast at
Biarritz station. By the time we've finished our *chocolat* and *croissants*,
not only are all the cars unloaded for us and waiting but a man is
actually washing the windscreens.

A car and Michelin map no. 78 are musts in the Pays Basque. Little
roads are smooth, empty and sinuous with 'oh, look' views. Stopping
at Ainhoa, just inside the Spanish frontier, we have our best dinner at
the Ithurria.

We drive into Spain down a track, for most of the Basque country
lies there. We go to San Sebastián and its pretty horseshoe beach
where I once, under the dreaded Franco rule, got struck by a
policeman for wearing too-short bum-bags. No bikinis were permitted
then; some women are topless now. But it is a dull place with mostly
pensioners or rich brats tended by nanny. So we scuttle back into
lovely France where we have a marvellous fishy lunch in the sort of
white shack overlooking a beach car-park which, in Britain, would
offer only oily ice-creams, stale biscuits and weak tea-bag tea.

Flushed with Listel rosé, we argue about careers. 'Do have one', I
beg my daughters, 'so you'll be free and won't need to marry for
money!'

For it was to Biarritz that middle-class British girls, who would have
screamed if you had called them hookers, used to have themselves
flown for the weekend's pleasure of rich yachtsmen whom they
vainly hoped to marry.

We, too, sailed (£12 for all day, including lunch) from the neat
marina of Capbreton across this rolling corner of the Bay of Biscay to
pretty St Jean-de-Luz. It's bright with boutiques but French clothes
cost twice as much as ours, just as their food costs half.

We pass the beaches where the world surfing championships swoop
and see our favourite beach – just at the southern edge of Biarritz – the
sign to it reads 'Hot Sea Baths'. But park in the cul-de-sac and walk
down.

Then we sailed back to dine in the Capbreton Marina (plenty of little
restaurants) just as the sun set behind the forest of rocking masts.

TRAVEL FACTS

French Rail SNCF, 179 Piccadilly, London W1 (01–493 4421)
French Travel Service, Francis House, Francis St., London SW1 (01–828 8131)
French Leave, 21 Fleet St., London EC4 (01–583 8383)
Brittany Ferries, Brittany Centre, Wharf Rd., Portsmouth (0705 751833)
French Government Tourist Office, 178 Piccadilly, London W1 (01–499 6911)

— SPAIN: ANDALUCIA'S
WHITE VILLAGES —

Is there really a Spain, fresh, wild and natural behind the monstrosities of the Costa Concreta y Chippa? 'But naturally,' says José Ignacio Domecq the Younger, on his white chalk hillside, west of Jerez where his family owns 5,800 acres of vineyards. This chalk makes the dazzling whitewashed villages in the mountains of Andalucia where tourists never go.

José Ignacio goes frequently. This sophisticated man with the long Domecq nose, bright eyes and busy walk, speaks five languages but hates cities. He prefers to ride through his countryside. He spent a month on horseback, sleeping out under his poncho beneath the stars and the eagles and among the deer, the jackals and the snakes. He travels with his own Sancho Panza on a mule all the way down the Guadalquivir, the Moors' 'great river' (from which Columbus sailed for America and Magellan to circumnavigate the globe).

'Follow the road of the white towns' says José Ignacio over lunch in the bustling roadside taverna among his vineyards. 'The best shrimps in all Spain' he says, sucking the pink shells. 'Jerez, there on its hill, is a white town. They're all on hills. But start on the Atlantic. Tourists don't go there either, thank God! There's a wonderful nature reserve and at Sanlúcar we race horses on the beach.'

Sanlúcar with its rows of striped beach huts has been in a siesta for some thirty years. You could shoot a fifties film there. No tourist disturbs the peace of Puerto de Santa María either, the fishing port on the cold Atlantic whence come the good fish you get in this south-west corner of Spain compared with the usual Mediterranean muck.

Much, mercifully, has changed in the twenty years since I spent regular family holidays in southern Spain. Gone are the filthy garbage-strewn potholed roads. Gone the stink of open sewage. Gone the Fascist brutality of Franco's police and less obvious is the common cruelty then meted out to horses, donkeys, cats and dogs. Spaniards are proud Europeans but in their blood lies the alien streak of the Moors who occupied them for centuries and bred with their women.

The food is transformed, too. No longer, even in little country inns like the government-sponsored Hostal at El Bosqué, are you offered those flyblown messes fried in crude and stinking oil. At El Bosque, pretty as a tourist picture postcard, with dazzling flowers tumbling down white walls, even the Hostal's floor is clean enough to eat off. No other foreign tourist has come east this weekend down the winding roads through the cork forests. The young manager, not yet acquainted with the workings of a Visacard ('Though I have the máquina!' he says proudly) recommends the Atlantic soles he bought that morning on the sea. The chef steps past our table out on to the rose-covered terrace to pick herbs for the fish.

We tried to stay at incredible Arcos, perched like a fairy city on a mountain spike above a vertical ravine. But no-one told us that the government Parador, an elegant Georgian building in English terms, was closed because it was slowly sliding over the cliff.

I nearly got our car stuck fast in Arcos. The white houses with their wrought-iron window grids are crammed so closely together along the little streets that there is only room for a Don to ride by on his thin war-horse. In the old fortress castle lives the English widow of a Spanish duke. Plump and popular, she gives huge English tea-parties up in her eyrie.

'They say the Duquesa Inglesa eats vultures!' muttered a Spanish peasant, crossing himself. He wore a typical battered black trilby of the type favoured by Chicago gangsters of the twenties.

Along the green river below the 300 foot cliff of Arcos a bee-eater, brilliant as a kingfisher, flashes past. Frogs croak. Cicadas click. In some specially double-fenced fields (enforced by law) graze the fighting bulls, wedge-shaped like black tanks on light, quick legs. Otherwise the land is open. A huge white bird with black tail feathers, an Egyptian stork, stands by the bulls then slowly flaps away.

Vast acres of golden sunflowers turn their drooping heads like a million pilgrims awaiting a solar blessing from the Pope. The road grows wilder, zig-zagging between the cork trees. Their bark has been stripped off and their trunks painted brown, making them look like old grey men wearing chocolate beach towels.

After El Bosque, the road soars over a mountain pass. Parked on it under the wheeling ravens and overlooking the green valleys either side, are two of only four cars seen all day on the road to Grazalema, prettiest of all the White Towns.

Women whitewash their cottage walls, scrub pavements and even their bit of road. They water their bougainvillaeas, roses and geraniums. No tourists here either, though there were two tents pitched outside the town by a spring under the trees. But another excellent Hostal overlooks the cascade of white houses and the jumble of their old, flaking russet roofs.

Ubrique, once pretty, is now industrialised with its leather factories, but you can find bargains here. We lunch in a bar by the small town's swimming pool for a fiver with a bottle of wine. The waiter can't remember when last he saw 'English peoples'.

Silence in the oak forests full of fritillaries on the winding way to Jimena. Goat bells toll below. We are above the old smugglers' route. A local murmurs, 'Sometimes you see lines of lean, fit mules moving very rapidly up these valleys from the sea, with fit, lithe men running alongside who don't stop to say "Buenos"! They've carrier dogs, too, trained to spot a Guarda Civil at a distance and to cower the instant they spot him. The smugglers dress up in police uniforms to beat the dogs to teach them this. That's where they go.'

Below the hilltop village and ruined castle of Jimena run green valleys and streams where the deer come out to drink, lined with pink oleander bushes and eucalyptus trees. Beyond, the cork tree forests stretch almost to Gibraltar. An old man in the usual trilby chivvies goats down through the ruins of the castle into the town. Mules graze on weeds between the cobbles.

Castellar, another citadel village, was partly refurbished. Then money ran out and now it's partly occupied by surly hippies. The one crammed bar is dank with greasy locks and marijuana. One German dropout offers us 'chocolate', the hippy word for something harder than Moroccan hash.

Ronda is last. Still the same feeling of finding a Shangri-La when you reach that fertile upland plain suddenly revealed after climbing so long through the bare mountains. Still the gaping gorge below the garden of the old Reina Victoria hotel where twenty years earlier we sat talking with the famous Peralta, who'd been fighting bulls off his dashing grey horse in Spain's oldest bull ring. But Ronda has swollen and spread. Highrise blocks shaft cruelly into the sky.

Yet they are nothing to the horrors of that stretch of dire coast road, the N340, which we must use to reach Malaga airport. It screams with maniac drivers behind the hideous developments of the Costa del Sol. 'Fred's Pub', 'Steak 'n' Chips' bellow the signs. Scarlet broiled Brits in nervous battalions try to cross the rushing road from their crowded lodgings to the filthy beaches which even the Spanish newspapers now condemn.

A gentler scene lingers in my mind. Pedro, the barrel-chested forester, naked from the waist up – unusual among Spaniards –

padding down the dusty country road from Jimena to San Roque. He is on his daily twenty kilometre hike to the railway station. He has done this every day these last four years to see if his absent wife has yet returned from a visit on the train to Madrid.

'Did she die?' I ask, staring back at the small marching man struggling on beneath the gum trees.

'No, she came back years ago. But she lives with another richer woodman in another part of the forest.'

TRAVEL FACTS

Iberia, 130 Regent St., London W1 (01–437 5622)

Mundi Color, 276 Vauxhall Bridge Rd., London SW1 (01–834 3492)

Hayes & Jarvis, 200 Sloane St., London SW3 (01–235 0901)

Andalucian Express Train, Marsans Travel Ltd., 7a Henrietta Place, London W1 (01–493 4934)

Spanish National Tourist Office, 57–58 St James's St., London SW1 (01–499 0901)

— CORFU —

Jolting in my jeep down the steep, stony flanks of Mount Pantokrator – all mountains should have names as fierce as Corfu's highest – I nearly struck two friends slithering up the track on their hired scooter.

Corfu town hospital is crammed with scooter casualties; not surprisingly, as things were to turn out. These little buzzing beasts, a pain in the ear for others, are often physical pains for those who ride them. Beware, share a more companionable bone-shaking Japanese jeep.

Meon Villas, the travel company, had warned me strongly against bestriding one of these wobbling hornets whose blasted noise, like that of the water-ski speedboats, rips through the silence of the northern half of this lovely island. The south has sadly turned grotty.

We were above the grey-green sea of the olive groves and the dark green cypress fingers jabbing up to the sky. A last farm crouched where a spring emerged from the rocks. Goats, whose milk makes feta cheese, panted under the shade of fig trees. Tiny fields like stepped pocket handkerchiefs marked the course of the plunging winter rains which keep Corfu green, unlike most of Greece's other islands.

Years ago, when I was writing a book about diamonds in South Africa, my girl friend and I had yearned out in that brutish land for a taste of Europe's classic civilisation. We jumped on a plane to Athens.

The Greek captain advised us: 'You must go to Corfu because it is full of English'.

We grimaced. 'How about Crete?' we asked. 'No English there,' he said. So we went to Crete and loved it.

This time friends in London warned me, 'Corfu has been ruined. It's crucified by trippers!' It isn't. Get beyond the cheap chippy strips which belch out north and south on the east coast from Corfu Town and the land is beautiful, almost empty, deliciously silent and friendlier than anywhere in Europe except Portugal and, ironically, Greece's eternal enemy, Turkey.

But the face of a portly, polished German lumbering incongruously up this goat track at the wheel of his squat, black Mercedes limousine is neither beautiful, silent, nor friendly. My friends and I spring aside to let the Fourth Reich pass. I give him a not absolutely respectful salute. On Corfu, countrymen everywhere raise their hands to you in quiet greetings, mornings or evenings: *'Kalimera, kalispera'.*

Then, hacking off hunks of my picnic salami for my friends, we planned a dinner date in Kassiopi, the little port on the island's pretty north east corner. They went on upwards. I bumped on down into the olive groves.

Little stirred in the siesta. At a taverna in the tiny huddle of white cottages which Greeks call villages, some tourists drank wine in the sun. Old Corfeotes in faded groups sat in the shade earnestly discoursing. Greek men read little but talk much. Their old black-shawled ladies, side-saddle on sleek little donkeys, rode in from the fields with olive loads in sacks for the village oil press.

Long views of glades like the backgrounds of Renaissance landscapes opened at every corner. Nymphs and shepherds should have still been bounding about. The azure sea suddenly appeared miles below. Corfu's interior doesn't feel like an island and that's an added bonus.

I parked the jeep up a stony track, devoured salami rolls, tomatoes sweeter than plums, and drank powerful wine. I re-read Gerald Durrell on a rock. Shakespeare's *Tempest* and Homer's *Odyssey* both use this island's setting but Durrell is much more fun for holiday reading.

I dozed beneath some writhing olive trees, full of holes. 'You mustn't,' a Greek friend had instructed me, 'ever sleep beneath a cypress tree. It will steal your spirit away.' Like the occasional damned woman, I thought, and so steered clear.

Then a girl's cries shrilly split the dreaming olives. I thought someone was being urgently satisfied by Pan or Dick or Harry up there among the myrtle bushes on the banks of thyme, crushing the blue and yellow flowers and the blood-bright poppies.

When the startled cicadas had resumed their ticking and the sheep their bleating, a sorry cavalcade appeared below me. Three London fellas and one girl with long red shanks slowly scootered past. But there followed a sobbing girl pushing her crashed scooter. Her gashed leg bled freely.

I caught them up in a farm's green shade where tethered nanny goats like wet school teachers anxiously bleated after their kids who were larking about over the terraces. A thin cat crouched, then sprang and caught a lizard. I offered the wounded girl a lift.

The girl's eyes were still wet with tears: 'Oh,' she burst out, 'you're my guardian angel!' No-one had ever called me that, though I'd like to believe my children might sometimes think it. 'And I'm the only trained one,' she went on, 'in our lot, you see. I've been a nurse two years and I'm the one who's fallen.' Her scooter, like they always do, had skidded.

Relief from the shock made her babble. 'But everyone on Corfu is so kind. They taught me Greek dancing up there in that taverna. And everyone waves and smiles. They are lovely, lovely people and that makes all of us feel better.'

At long last, for all Corfu's maps are crazy, we reached a main road and a taverna under a spreading vine where she could wait for her friends. They were camping on that displeasing strip of Corfu behind the jerry-built-up, scooter-zapping beaches of Damia and Ipsos. Pass by these in blinkers until, twelve miles north where the hills start, a chain of delicious, rocky inlets begin and you can dip into Arcadia.

My scootering English friends had also crashed that day. The girl showed her wound as we sat drinking in the little square of Kassiopi. The village was jumping. Flocks of children darted about like swallows in the dusk. In my hillside villa above the sea the swallows had been disturbed by my arrival and I'd left them chittering like mothers-in-law beginning, with mud spatters under the eaves like an artist's first blobs on white canvas, to start their nests.

The English couple finding the German's great Mercedes stalled on a hairpin near the top of the mountain had slithered past and crashed. The Führer overtook them without a word or glance.

The German hordes consolidate on Corfu's north coast. Sidari is their awesome headquarters. Keep away. But there were only two couples of them at Arilas on the north west where I found a good beach taverna down the dusty track with views of dreaming islands. While we ate, a fisherman, sun-black and bent like a seal, brought in his catch to plop into the taverna's fish tank.

Corfu's loveliest *sandy* bay lies remotely at Ag. Georgios (St George) south of Cape Arila. It's as empty and wild as the southern rim of County Kerry but four times warmer.

Don't confuse this St George's bay, north of the amazing but tourist-ruined Paleokastritsa under its hilltop white monastery with the flat and boring St George's *beach* down in the dreary south.

Brits were thick and jolly at Kassiopi. At the next table near the harbour – £3 a head for baby octopus, red mullet, Greek salad, cheese and wine – sat a totally middling English lady: Midlands, mid-thirties, and middle class. She was escorted by a young, dark, curly-headed Greek. One of the girls in our party whispered 'typical English virgin'. But her man and I disagreed.

The odd couple dined surprisingly on only Greek salad and Coca-cola not, in my experience, famous aphrodisiacs. But none, under the starry night by the water's lap in the dark bay, might be needed. The middling lady in her crisp, clean pink Courtelle dress had a face as eager and pinched as a Corfu cat. The couple were absolutely silent. Language was not what they shared. Suddenly she slid him green pound notes under the table. He rose to pay the bill in drachma.

'That's not very nice,' whispered a girl to me.

But I don't see why there should be that difference between the sexes. If some men have to buy tarts why is it so bad that some women need to buy a foreign stud?

As the couple left the restaurant the woman ruffled and caressed the curls at the back of the Greek's neck, as girls do when men have made them happy. '*Not* virginal!' I remarked, as the couple with a lively rhythm in their step were sucked into the ebbing crowd of night.

I drove home in the open jeep along the lonely winding north-east coast road past all the pretty villas and the tiny inlets where you can swim off the stones almost alone in crystal water. Lightning suddenly flashed and the thunder rumbled like warfare over close Albania. Fat rain slapped on the taverna roof where I sheltered. There was a wizened Greek teacher of windsurfing – a sport silent, undisturbing, graceful when done well and quietly comic otherwise. He said to me: 'Look always at the wind as if he was a strong man. Put no trust in him. But above all never show him that you are afraid. Or he will destroy you.'

Refreshed by this philosophy and strong red wine I drove home, soaked by the storm and illuminated by the lightning flashes sent down by that old lover Zeus.

TRAVEL FACTS

Olympic Airways, Trafalgar House, 2 Chalkhill Rd.,
Hammersmith, London W6 (01–846 9080)
Air Europe, Europe House, East Park, Crawley, W. Sussex (01–651 3611)
C.V. Villas, 43 Cheval Place, London SW7 (01–581 0851)
Thomson Holidays, Greater London House, Hampstead Rd.,
London NW1 (01–439 2211)
Sunmed, 4–6 Manor Mount, London SE23 (01–699 7666)
National Greek Tourist Office, 197 Regent St., London W1 (01–734 5997)

— MOROCCO —

It had been thirteen, mostly lucky, years since I had last visited Morocco. My then pregnant companion had been nauseated by the poverty, the beggars and the stench.

Magic carpets wafting us back four centuries are like everything: pricey in their way. Filthy smells and filthy hawkers are two prices of the Arab world. Squeezing mint leaves beneath her nose she had gamely staggered on past tanneries and drains, wincing when mutilated creatures groped for alms outside a pseudo-nightclub in Marrakesh.

But friends kept recommending a Thomson winter break in Agadir.

I had been disappointed in a filming trip to India where I had hoped to watch Geoffrey Reeve producing *The Far Pavilions* in Jaipur. And February is England's foulest month and I urgently needed the sun.

So off I went to look at the far west of the Arab empire. The Berbers of Morocco have as little to do with the rich men from the Middle East as Irish peasants from County Mayo with Italian motor magnates from Turino.

There have been drastic changes.

Agadir, eradicated by its earthquake, has been rebuilt at a respectable distance from the hill on which thousands were buried. The mound crouches ominously.

There were other warnings, too.

'Don't ever go out on the beach at night, ladies,' advised the jolly Thomson rep from the stage of the nightclub on our first morning, 'unless you want to get raped or sold for camels.'

A frisson of part-fear, part-sexual fantasy shivered through the latest draft of pale, fresh-landed British holidaymakers. Arabs and sex couple in Western minds reared on tales of harems, sheikhs, Rudolf Valentino and the £300 an afternoon suburban housewives earn for the best of three throws with Arab businessmen in West End hotels.

An American girl warned me in Paris: 'In Morocco they snatch white girls in shops and put them in brothels.' The only whores I saw in Agadir were Arab, fat, plain and smelly, slinking along the dusty street outside the huge Hotel Europa.

Inside, by the poolside, is another group as markedly unlovable. An encampment of middle-class, braying, golf-club English are already entrenched in their defensive positions under their special palm tree.

Like most of their ilk, they detest all foreigners, who should be subservient yet, these days, by luck and trickery have grown richer and uppity.

They also loathe the cheerful, high-spending working-class Brits. There are some very merry dockers from Felixstowe out on the jaunt. The German guests, who at forty per cent equal the British regiment in size, are all literally glitteringly rich and regard us Brits as poor white trash.

The golf-club platoon under the palms scorn, (but secretly envy) the new majority of Brits who don't believe in saving up for anything, let alone a private education. Having observed me closely, they seek to speak. The loudest female of them shrieks out as I pass: 'Do tell me, are you English or French? We're having a bet on it. We heard you speaking French but you have an English book.'

'English,' I grunt. 'Ah. And what's that?' demands this abomination, jabbing my sheets of foolscap.

'I'm a writer,' I mutter. 'He's an English writer!' bellows back Madam to her goggling friends. 'And I'm also a very nasty journalist,' I add. This dread threat reduces them to angry whispers.

Middle-class Brits abroad are frantic buyers of English newspapers. 'After you with the *Telegraph*, Daphne,' shouts one. 'Ghastly Nigel Dempster!' shrieks her friend.

I walk out on to the beach. The Atlantic surf roars along the great bay. The distant sand dunes merge this hot February morning into a dazzle of sunlit spray.

I have to dodge matchstick Moroccan figures booting footballs with hard brown feet and shrill Berber cries. Others, less poor, canter Arab steeds.

Old men squatting on their dromedaries offer me rides. Pedlars badger me ridiculously with carpets. 'How can I carry that home?' I protest. 'Pretty silk scarf for girlfriend, then, no?' Others of particularly evil mien extend doughnuts, digital watches and their repulsive selves.

No other race begs so vilely as Arabs, though millions on the Indian sub-continent are infinitely poorer, and thousands of oil-fat Arabs are stinking rich.

The triple banes of southern Morocco are these poxy hawkers, the vile roadside rubbish, and the offensively Fascist airport officials. Pederasty also prevails. I find revolting the sight of soldiers in khaki strolling palm in palm, and fishermen linking their scaly fingers along the busy quayside. Who minds homosexuals? Some lesbians are lovely. But these squint-eyed hideous lovers are like warped survivors from a medieval plague.

An Arab entrepreneur falls into conversation with me in the bar of the luxury Europa Hotel. 'You want pretty local girls for the evening?' Having seen the form, I shake my head. But he takes me to dinner in the excellent à la carte restaurant of the hotel. Fish is the best food in southern Morocco: sole, turbot, whiting, and mackerel all caught fresh each day. The French, fortunately, left behind not only their language but remnants of their cuisine. The Europa's inner restaurant is superb but expensive. The pension menus in the ordinary eating place were as dull as one expects of these places but buffet lunches snacked up poolside on hot February days were pleasing.

Next to us in the dark à la carte restaurant sit a distinguished German couple with, I supposed, their lithe, sun-tanned twenty-five-year-old daughter. 'Bah! She is forty plus. Wife of rich Ruhr industrialist who is too busy to take holidays. But she comes every February and March like all your poor, cold north Europe ladies, for bang-bang in the sun. Do you have no sex up there in winter? Last year this one was tireless. She exhausts me. She is like riding a bicycle up the Atlas mountains,' groans the Moroccan.

Later we spot her watching a fashion show and sipping *crème de menthe*. But she is now with a white silk-suited, golden-jewelled German who (one of two such) minces about the hotel twirling a glittering handbag.

'New tricks for old bicycle,' sighs the Moroccan, 'better you go up to Atlas mountains by motor bus.'

There's an excursion on offer every day, with guides who talk too much and boast of their poor country's riches in public and then tell you secretly afterwards that they are longing to escape to universities in Europe.

I gaze out of our space craft coach as we swish along. Men and boys in jellabas and turbans loll by the roadside in piles like dreaming puppies, watching their women work.

Tiny donkeys in pairs tug crude wood ploughs through stony terraced strips. Veiled Berber ladies in long robes winch water up from scarce wells, hump firewood and hoe weeds.

Our coach is luckily too polyglot to be hearty. But camera clicking is universal. Do all my travelling companions, I wonder, laboriously paste up all these photographs in albums to bore their friends through winter evenings?

My drawers at home are full of old forgotten stuff. You cannot snap and look around you. Isn't it better sometimes to stand and stare, then buy a few good postcards?

The place is picturesque all right. Our coach climbs on beneath the soaring purple ridges, past tiny pink houses lop-sided like children's drawings. Fences are cactus, eucalyptus or dead thorn branches. Loose red rocks prop up terraces intended to catch the rain which so seldom falls. Where a precious stream does trickle, the green is dazzling.

Tiny boys tend goats who crazily climb twenty feet up thorn trees. The kernels of the fruit they crunch are passed through, then gathered up to be ground into cooking oil on donkey-powered millstones.

Tafroute is sweet with the scent of pale pink almond blossom under a sky of piercing blue. Children proffer porcupine quills as pens.

As usual for lunch we eat a tolerable chicken stew then, for a pleasant change, oranges laced with cinnamon and honey. But to what sort of food are these little children, with their huge dark eyes, returning?

At Goulimine, the camel-market gateway to the vast Sahara desert, the vendors shriek, preachers bellow to the converted and the camels honk out their protests. Just beyond lie the first sand waves of that cruel sea. On its fringe I spot a huddle of evil black tents.

Morocco is nothing like southern Africa where you are aware all the time of nature's savagery and the insignificance of man. Here, there is little animal life and it is mankind which is savage.

'Don't go close to those nomads!' warns our guide. 'Tough, angry desert people.' The black figures stalk sternly towards us and we scuttle back into the safety of our coach.

One day I go to Tiznit, the best centre for the delicately crafted local silverware. Bidding one quarter of the asking price in the *souk*, I finally get two bracelets for only £12 plus a dirty look from the seller. Silver, hand-painted pottery, and leather are best buys, found in the shadowy menacing mazes of the *souks*.

On my last night I'm in an old white-washed casbah stuck away down winding agricultural tracks. Squatting Berber-style over a low table in what seems a lowly cattle shed but is, in fact, a human dwelling, I'm struggling as an interpreter. I am asked to translate for a shouting fat family from West Berlin into French to a white-robed Arab who is trying vainly to sell them dreadful garish belts.

'Tell the creature it's too "kitsch",' shouts the Frau to me in German.

Musicians wail and clank iron castanets, thumping bare feet on the courtyard's earth. Sticky-fingered, I wrestle with the couscous, as dull as always, and the slightly better chicken stew.

'Last dance now is for visitors!' shouts our guide. Then, to much British merriment, he bellows, 'Dance of the Pouf. All be dancing now, please!' Circulating with a cushion, we place it at the feet of any other tourist who faintly appeals.

Selected by a friendly young Swedish girl who kneels before me on the cushion, I, too, kneel down face to face with her and we kiss. Now I must dance on, pouffe on head, to find another appealing lady when the music stops.

Good, here's a bold beauty from Wigan. 'And another kiss for luck, love,' she breathes, giving me two smacking good ones.

The music dies. Above us, in the indigo sky, a plane for Europe and the twentieth century crawls across the stars like a glittering scarab. From a distant mosque another call to prayer howls like a dog in the darkness.

TRAVEL FACTS

Royal Air Maroc, 174 Regent St., London W1 (01–439 4361)
Thomson Holidays, Greater London House, Hampstead Rd.,
London NW1 (01–439 2211)
OSL Villas/Wings, Travel House, Broxbourne, Herts (0992 87211)
Cadogan, 9–10 Portland St., Southampton (0703 332551)
Moroccan Tourist Office, 174 Regent St., London W1 (01–437 0074)

— GOZO —

You get to Gozo from Malta on a clanking ferry. It's only twenty minutes across a sapphire sleeve of sea, past the even tinier island of Comino (which has just one hotel and the best sandy beach of the three islands). But Gozo to Malta is like Cornwall to Cardiff.

Air Malta flies remarkably punctually direct from Heathrow. But the good service is ruined by ludicrous immigration delays. I waited fifty-five minutes in a queue with just two out of six immigration desks manned. Behind us, three more flights crammed into the small hall. 'You were lucky,' said some Maltese friends, 'in summer you can wait three hours!'

Such first impressions do Malta much harm, particularly as most Maltese and Gozitans yearn to recapture 'our best guests', the lost British tourists.

The Phoenicia is a beautiful hotel just outside the gates of Valetta, with service as swift and kind as anywhere I met that year. The more modern Corinthia Palace, overlooking the Presidential Gardens, is pretty good, too.

Gozitans generally dislike their bigger, bossier neighbour and a number, too, lowering their voices and glancing behind them in bars (which have splendidly brave old names like 'England for Ever!') spoke harshly about their government which has seemed to prefer Libyans to Brits and North Koreans to Americans. No accounting for taste these days.

The Maltese respond by viewing Gozitans as rustics. They pour across there for weekends. 'Nice for holidays,' drawl the Maltese haughtily. I declare it warmly, for I loved the little seven mile by five mile island. It's domed with hundreds of churches, latticed by collapsing roads leading to cliffs which grip slim beaches and tiny harbours. Terraced fields step down, bright with fruit and almond blossom and spring vegetables. Gozo is Malta's kitchen garden.

The eastern side, below Xaghra ('x's are pronounced 'sh') is easily the prettiest. The hilltops are sliced off like ancient fortresses and, indeed, there's a large temple just outside the village where gods were worshipped and people sacrificed to them 2,500 years before Christ's apostle Paul was shipwrecked on Malta.

I stayed at the Cornucopia, owned by dark, lean ambitious Mr

Victor Borg ('g' is soft as in large). He turns out to be 'Mr Gozo' for he also owns the Eclipse Restaurant on the road from Victoria (the very grand little capital) to Mgarr (M-e-g-a-r) the ferry's harbour. He also owns Gozo Travel and the Gozo Garage where I hired a car very cheaply, and he also bosses the Gozo Tourist Board. His two brothers-in-law help him run the hotel and the garage. 'Vic' – Gozitans prune every name – can fix anything. He contradicts the Maltese view of Gozitans and our view of the Maltese; that they are just amiable incompetent mañana people like the equally Catholic-dominated Irish.

Vic heaves golden, porous stone blocks along the new wall above the Cornucopia's swimming pool and urges on his workers. He is adding another suite for Easter. 'It's already booked for this weekend, so must be ready! Otherwise, I show you all over the island myself. Everyone look after you, though, you'll see.'

They do. It's good to fall among so many friendly strangers, reminding me of the northern heart of Corfu and fragments of Cyprus.

The Cornucopia's bar is like an English backwoods pub, where people leave messages, car keys and invitations, and the locals, like jolly labradors, long for you to like them and their ancient island.

Gutteral Maltese sounds to me like Arabic but they firmly disown any Arab connection. These small islands, occupied down the centuries by dozens of different invaders, have somehow against all the currents kept their own language alive.

I set off down donkey tracks through orchards to find Calypso's Cove where the nymph so enchanted the journeying Odysseus. Even nymphless, it's an attractive place, perched above Gozo's best beach, the red-sanded Ramla.

A contemporary nymph, who kindly acted as my guide, had happily converted a farmhouse and made a dazzling garden at the top of the valley pitching down to Ramla. 'Even in summer,' she said, 'the beach there is almost empty every weekday.'

Old farmhouses were once dirt cheap and bright Brits then snapped them up to live with little tax. A tiny colony of English writers which started with Monsarrat still exists, and a number of British citizens (some of dubious backgrounds with sleazy Soho links) still have holiday homes. But the Maltese government has reduced the earlier attractions. Anxiety fretted among the expats.

Walking down a steep, tiny path, I encountered what seemed to be an ancient peasant. Squat, dark and wearing, like most Gozitans, a very old tweed cap, he hailed me: ''ow yer doin', mite?' Startled, I supposed him to be a Cockney relict of the decades of British forces quartered here. Occasional blue eyes and fair skins among the Maltese recall close manoeuvres with the local ladies.

'Will it rain?' I ask him, pointing beyond Marsalforn Bay, the prettiest harbour with a decent restaurant, Il-Kartell.

'Rain?' the old gentleman mockingly mimicks my accent. 'It won't rine, mite, that's bleedin' mist. Sun'll shine.'

He's an Australian Gozitan, one of 330,000 Maltese (far more than all the islands' populations) who settled on that vast distant continent, made money and then returned to build bizarre mini-palazzo's on the outskirts of their original villages. Imposing balconies and carved stone balustrades of several new villas around Xaghra are surmounted by leaping effigies of kangaroos.

I disturb the wheezing old priest in his braces and carpet slippers, so as to inspect the grotto of stalictites and stalagmites below his kitchen, which his father unearthed sixty years ago digging for a well. Outside his house is a huge carving of the Archangel having a brisk set-to with Lucifer, so we discuss sin and blame. Next to the sculpture in the wall stands a firm prayer ornately carved: 'God bless Australia!'

'I have relations out there,' says the priest, and I suppose fat cheques come whizzing back to impoverished Gozo.

As in Ireland, the power of the church, if not faith in it – two very different things – is mighty. Church bells ring all the time. The nymph tells me that coming home from parties at 5 am she meets the early worshippers going off. 'Good night' she calls, 'Good morning,' they smile back.

Gozitans are batty about English football. In the Eclipse Restaurant, the Dutch manager introduces me to a man: 'This is the local Mafia head'. I hesitate, remembering that at least one Soho porn king keeps a pad out here.

'No, I joke. He is only trades union boss.'

And the man adds fervently: 'I am head of Manchester United Fan Club here. I publish monthly paper here called *Echoes of Old Trafford*.'

I laugh so much that I nearly choke over the excellent firm white fish and strong white wine Cittadella. It's named after the Citadel which crowns Victoria, well worth a visit with good museums. The red Gozitan wine ensures a hangover and much of the food is lower-middle Italian pasta.

A golden exception is the de-luxe hotel at Ta'Cenc (Chench). It has private rooms in courtyards full of flowers and it's run by an elegant, sad-eyed Italian who gives me lunch on Vic's introduction. Ta'Cenc would be *the* place on Gozo for a loving stay and, sure enough, I discover when I get home that several sprightly couples of my acquaintance know the place well.

Calypso leads me to the Gleneagles Bar overlooking Mgarr Harbour. 'Not very elegant, but in the end you meet everyone on Gozo here.'

And, indeed, after thirty minutes and several good Maltese beers I meet an Irish foxhunting lady, a Canadian driller of oil-wells, a net of local fishermen, a mew of English mums and kids, and a lofty old salt with grimy bare feet, grey hair tufting out of his greasy yachting cap, and piercing blue eyes in a face as wrinkled as a rejected boot. He turns out to have been an officer in the Household Cavalry and is now a self-employed sailor on what he calls 'my tub out there under the Red Duster'. He is just back from bringing out from Britain an enormous old British yacht for an American millionairess.

The nymph and I take him out for a good lunch at Il-Kartell on the sea's edge at Marsalforn, a much nicer village than the too fish-and-chippy Xlendi on the west side. We eat langoustes and down three bottles of Cittadella, while he greets every passing Gozitan by name.

Odysseus was bewitched by his Calypso for seven years. I wasn't quite so deeply smitten but, as the nymph drove me to the ferry, I said to the old salt, 'I badly want to kiss her. Do you mind staring at the horizon for a bit?' And I, too, was disinclined to leave.

TRAVEL FACTS

Air Malta, St James's House, 13 Kensington Square, London W8 (01–937 7181)

Meon, Meon House, Petersfield, Hants (0730 68411)

Gozo Holidays, Dunny Lane, Chipperfield, Kings Langley, Herts (092 7762059)

Bonaventure, 5 Kensington Church St., London W8 (01–938 3671)

Maltese Tourist Office, College House, Suite 207, Wrights Lane, London W8 (01–938 2668)

— CAMPING IN BRITTANY —

'Le Camping!' chortled my more sophisticated friends, rocking on bespoke heels. 'Absolutely not your thing!' I replied that this would be in the grounds of a château in Brittany and that I would be taking my two young daughters.

'Well, that may be different.' So it was. We went to an Inn-Tent and Eurocamp site at the Château des Ormes, south of Dol-de-Bretagne, taking Brittany Ferries overnight from Portsmouth to St Malo. This route has three boons: it saves the dreary drive south from the Pas-de-Calais, (another, next best, new way to Brittany, and best into Normandy, is the same line's latest route to Ouistreham); it's a French boat, so you're half abroad when you get on board and they serve you a gargantuan dinner, for normal unstretched British tummies, for about £12 a head in a quite attractive restaurant; the third advantage is that you sleep your way for ten hours and arrive in a very pretty port. Dull Calais and hideous Le Havre, like a woman with a sullen scowl, cast gloom on the keenest explorer.

Petit déjeuner by the water's edge at attractive St Servan, just outside St Malo, looking towards the dam where the go-ahead French have harnessed tidal power. It's fifty years since a series of unenterprising British governments started limply thinking about doing this on the Severn. We put our heads together over the red Guide Michelin which we need to pick restaurants, their green Brittany Guide (for what to look at), and then we studied the yellow Michelin Map (no. 59 for this area). It's essential reading if you are to avoid the main road mayhem. Without the local Michelin, the driver in France either travels blind or becomes an *autoroute cochon*. With it you can shun the noisy, buzzing red roads, picking instead the 'yellows' and, better still, the tiny 'whites' where only a few farmers trundle and barely a Brit dares. The girls pick the D.201 out of St Malo because it's edged in green on the map signifying pretty views. 'Let's go the squiggly way all along the coast!' How nice to have travelling companions whose tastes coincide.

So at Rothéneuf, where an old priest has carved a host of figures into the stoney headland, we got our first gaze of the emerald sea. 'It's like Cornwall!' said the girls delightedly. This is high praise for we all used to love staying at Trebetherick on the North Cornish coast when my daughters were still at the village school and could escape for two weeks in mid-summer.

Brittany's a contrast between mixed granite walls of greys and pinks, dark blue slate roofs (rather stern) but with sprightly shutters and snug cultivated fields flowing right up to the cliff edges and onto the tongues of so many sandy coves.

Warmer though by far: it's a long way further south than Jersey, let alone Cornwall, and it's infinitely emptier even at the height of the French holiday season at the end of July.

A smudged sign points down a dusty track: *'Plage du Petit Port'*. It's a sandy bay between two pine-crested promontories and one of the prettiest beaches we discover in our four-day stay. Yet only a dozen people are there.

On to Cancale, a white fishing village, slipping down its slopes like *Under Milk Wood*, and most attractively approached down the steep hill from the south east. Past the lighthouse, along the seafront, past the harbour and we park easily in the little square, where the girls practise the art of menu-picking from a line of small competing restaurants. 'Maximum 65 franc menu!' I ordain, knowing that, for about a fiver, we'll get a delicious four-course meal. Only the ignorant pick à la carte in France where one item can cost as much as the whole 'menu'.

We select Le Galion, and the girls bravely attack fish soup and a whole crab which seems, at Kate's first blink, to be alive. My daughters are watched by an amused French woman and her pipe-smoking companion, both devouring piles of local oysters, though we are weeks away from an 'R' in the month.

Britain beats France in at least three things – oysters, asparagus and girls with long legs. There is probably a Freudian connection. But I won't eat French oysters in summer, even though all Brittany's north coast offers them at knock-down prices from road-side stalls. I have suffered grievous bodily harm from them twice.

The coast road to Le Vivier, where we turned south towards Dol and Le Camping, is boringly flat and it pongs – typical oyster country. So we find instead a pretty cove on the other side of Cancale. The green sea bobs with two hundred white sailing boats, some of them very ritzy.

Le Camping is signalled by a battery of foreign flags. Down a lane, through a wood and we glimpse the substantial grey château beyond its lake where the girls are soon whirring a pedallo incompetently through flotillas of ducks and fits of giggles.

Most of the cars are British. Lovingly polished, they gleam on guard at each tent's flank in the Comte's paddocks and woods. They reassure nervous Brits who fear assassination by wily foreigners and give the impression of a British task force about to liberate the Continent. They also reduce the scale of Le Camping because, as the girls exclaim: 'These aren't really tents! They're Wendy houses!'

Eurocamps have plastic windows with simulated white framed panes, furnished 'living room', three separate 'bedrooms' with comfy camp beds, and a gas-burning fridge, cooker and lamp.

The girls are thrilled to be home makers and quickly make the beds before we dash into Dol for breakfast supplies. For £10 for the three of us for three days, we load up with croissants, butter, orange juice, jam solid with tiny strawberries, bottles of vin rosé, Perrier and beer, bags of cherries and nectarines.

People play bad tennis on the Comte's court and worse ping pong on his tables. But it's warming in a new place to watch strangers performing more feebly than one does oneself. I drowse by the lake. The girls pedallo away up the shaded river. In three swimming pools behind the old stable block pink Scottish children splash, shrieking as loudly as the black swifts darting over their heads.

Later we eat rather expensively in the camp's own restaurant in a pleasant farm barn. This is operated on that good old maxim: 'When you've got monkeys stuck out on a limb you can really squeeze their pips!'

So we make daily sweeps to the beaches west of St Malo, either side of the peninsular of St-Jacut-de-la-Mer and the magnificent sweep of Sables-d'Or-les-Pins, where the sea is so dazzlingly emerald and cobalt that you can't believe it's true. Don't eat at Le Terrier in St Hacut, even Michelin sometimes nods. And don't try to swim to its west: lovely sand for sunning but the water's as weedy and muddy as a Tory Wet.

'Let's go home across country,' said Jane, meaning to our Wendy house in the bird-loud glade. So Kate, for our last night, map-read through the hinterland, through immense forests gliding with deer to Le Tronchet. Here we dined in a room full of French doing themselves well at the old Hostellerie l'Abbatiale. A fine grey courtyard. Dinner overlooking the lake for £6.50. A nice place to stay and eat well as a change from the polite camaraderie of our wooded campsite.

In the Comte's grounds, where he originally kept cattle till he found that campers pay better than cows, the first birds twitter at five, cocks crow at six, the Dutch in our neighbouring Wendy house grunt at seven, and at eight – as I pad back from shaving in the sanitary block freshly reminding me of some of the rougher parts of army life – I hear our Scots neighbour on the other side bellowing to his dozy, idle family: 'Rise and shine! Let's have yer!'

And that, having safely ducked the oysters, was almost the only note which jarred.

TRAVEL FACTS

Brittany Ferries, Brittany Centre, Wharf Rd., Portsmouth (0705 751833)
Brittany Ferries Camping, *address as above*
Canvas, Bull Plain, Hertford, Herts (0992 59933)
Eurocamp, Edmundson House, Tatton St., Knutsford, Cheshire (0565 52444)
French Government Tourist Office, 178 Piccadilly, London W1 (01–499 6911)

— TURKEY —

Enchanted for thirty years or more by Greece, I'd always felt – like hearing but one side of a quarrel – hostile to Turkey. I expected the Turks to be fearsome, their country filthy, and their food foul. I was wrong in every respect. To travel gloomily – like going to a dreaded party – is often to end up delighted.

We drive west from Dalaman's new airport in the south-west of the country. The setting's wild, the airport itself still stark, and the armed soldiers patrolling its perimeters are menacing or reassuring, depending on whether you're a pessimist or an optimist. We find our helpful rep from Aegean Turkish Holidays and she shows us our dusty but stout hire care just outside. The advantage of small new airports is that everything, even if muddled, is close at hand.

We are driving to Bodrum where the Aegean and Mediterranean mix. Some of the isles of Greece lie immediately off shore. For all this gorgeous coast was settled by the ancient Greeks, as we discovered in the classical temple and town across the Gulf of Güllük, and – outstandingly our favourite place – in the little amphitheatre and ruined palace on Cleopatra's Island off Sedir.

I liked this last so much that I'm reluctant to reveal it. But if you buy a good large scale map and turn west off the main road north, you'll find your way along a back-of-beyond dusty track leading through a prosperous agricultural valley. Push on past a jetty where you see the gulf and finally, on your right, you'll see a singularly undistinguished little 'Motel' (the Turks love this awful word). At it, we lunched under a shade of bamboo on the edge of the sea and then hired a boat, winding over a footpath on the headland to find it waiting in a creek still lined with the stones and graves of ancient Greece. And from there we launched off to the blissful little island where Cleopatra stayed.

The swift main road from Dalaman to Bodrum is a very different thing. The traffic is mostly trucks hauling timber, fruit and tomatoes. Turkey is very poor by European standards. Private cars are the exception and usually old, battered and expensive.

Bent women in long dresses and scarves hoe the cotton fields in the fat flat valleys. In the shaded corner bars their gossiping men sip coffee.

Reaped corn stands in stooks. Minarets stab the sky. Around a mountain pass the sea flashes deep blue, boatless, lapping empty shores. Greece was this peaceful before its tourist hordes swept down.

The road grows emptier and clings to the southern coast. Where are the villages, the resorts, the 'campings'? Miles and miles are uninhabited, though the main road is smooth and easy. We stop anywhere, walk down empty slopes, strip off beneath the olives and the pines and swim in sea as clean and bright as that surrounding Paxos, my favourite Greek island.

Restaurant ritual and the best Turkish food is quickly learned. You step into the kitchen and point out which *mese* you want: aubergines stuffed every way, scores of salads, liver and spring onions, squids, yoghurts of every sort, calamari, peppers, vine leaves, rolls of nasturtium flowers ... We seldom, during our whole stay, ate a main course, sharing instead half a dozen of these starters at about £2 a head including beer at roadside tavernas.

But 'you paid too much!' declared Elizabeth, the red-haired girl from Edinburgh reputed to be Bodrum's disco queen. Bodrum swings. The harbour, which held half a dozen yachts ten years ago, now jostles with hundreds beneath its towering Frankish castle, red with Turkish flags by day and floodlit nightly in silver and gold. Bodrum has a touch of sophistication. Some elegant Europeans have been long established there but it is richly mixed, with the hub-bub of a country market. Driving in it is like being set about by honking dodgem cars.

Boutiques beckon the travelling companion. Restaurants fill narrow streets in solid lines, a Turkish trait, and an amusing one for you can not only see just what's on offer and how it's going down, but who's eating where.

Carpet vendors ply us with *raki* as we haggle. 'Twelve hundred pounds!' I repeat incredulously and turn to leave the shop by the port.

'Ah, I meant eight hundred, sir. A little more raki?'

'Ridiculous.'

Outside yachts bob. Caiques, like the one we'll sail on, nod. Echoes of the old St Tropez crowd float past.

'I've only one hundred and fifty pounds to spend.'

'Ah, sir, a little more. These carpets – see the fine double-stitching, see the fine work – take years to make. Two hundred pounds surely? Good. Visacard most certainly. More *raki*, Sir and Miss.'

We pant up the steep stone stairways of the castle, home once of those romantic multi-national crusaders, the Knights of St John. A present leading light of the Order in Britain has introduced me to the

Governor, a lean khaki-clad figure looking like one of Monty's desert generals. He is engaged in earnest chat with an American professor, for the castle has a wonderful museum of old Greek treasures salvaged from ships sunk off these shores long before Christ.

The Governor leaps to his feet – Turks are tremendously polite even to their former long lost foes. 'Friend of Sir Hamish Forbes? Welcome! 'Hamishforbes' (as he pronounces it) 'Good friend of Turkey.'

I had met with Forbes some Turks planning two hotels along the coast. I urge him on my return, 'Let them be in the old Turkish style. Please no Costa Concreta horrors!'

A powerful lobby in Bodrum fights to preserve its charms. 'No house allowed higher than two floors,' says Fatma, long-term leader of local Turkish society as we sit on her terrace drinking *raki* overlooking the bay behind the castle.

A four-master lilts on the indigo waters. She talks in perfect English, French or German about our own books, about Tolstoy and Ibsen. I hand her a packet of Welsh Guards' brass buttons for her brother's blazer. At least the Welsh motto will fox her. But she translates it instantly, rocking with pleasure in her voluminous long grey dress. Such charm and probably naughty, I thought. Bodrum has its slice of Bohemia.

And Arcadia, too. The local agent for Aegean Turkish is Annie, an attractive English archaeologist, married to a handsome Turk engaged in yacht chartering. They live in a gardener's cottage in the midst of the mandarin groves which sweep down to the sea just west of Bodrum. Their loo is outside in the orchard's centre, doorless, and peered into by cows. Before her parents first came to visit, she tried to hammer up a bamboo door. 'For the first time I wondered if I was mad living out here, like this!'

We dine with them at Bitez by the seashore in a restaurant presided over by huge bearded Osman, close to the Falcon Sailing School. Down go the squids and calamari and *mese*, and the *raki* flows.

At the peninsular's western tip – weeds in the sea, sadly – there's an old fort, a ruined Byzantine church and a beach quite empty save a beagle, and a duck and her drake waking us with quacking from our sleep under a thorn tree below the fields of green peppers.

Next day we sail in a caique called *Maya*, built of sweet smelling wood in the shipyard just beyond our tiny charming hotel, the Villa Bergamut. The Turkish skipper, almost naked, looks like a pot-bellied Sinbad. His wife, tall and distinguished, is a well-known Dutch concert flautist.

Driving west, we explore a plain dotted with fig trees and find a deserted restaurant on its lonely beach and a cluster of half-finished houses. Soaring inflation means many Turkish plans collapse. But it makes living wonderfully – embarrassingly – cheap for British travellers.

On the far north shore of the Bodrum peninsular we shun an awful fenced-in holiday camp orange with Austrians. 'Have you tickets?' demands the guard on the gate. But it is, so far, the only horror there. And just a mile past it, down a track is a tiny harbour and rich Turks' pretty holiday houses, their children with nannies on sailing boats – it's a sort of pre-war Bembridge in the sun. Yet in the open-air restaurant at the roadside Vivaldi is being played.

We reach Tarkbuku by a track past veiled, robed women herding black goats and find a sandy bay with jetties into the shallow sea. Nothing stirs but three children with whom the travelling companion rashly plays. Giggling, they won't leave us. But otherwise the place has an unusual sullen air.

We press on to Kalikavak and find in its harbour, among fishing craft and the sponge boats, a most unlikely vessel: a huge Austrian catamaran, up for sale.

A courtly Turk on a bicycle greets me in German: 'Can I help you in any way?' So after drinking with him in the bar, he takes us home to see the five bungalows he wishes to let to tourists. We meet his German wife and son and then he takes us out to dinner. Marvellous fish and good wine at £3 a head in a tiny café perched over the slapping water as the scarlet sun superbly sets behind the flashing sea.

TRAVEL FACTS

Turkish Airlines, 11–12 Hanover Sq., London W1 (01–499 9247)
British Airways, PO Box 10, Heathrow Airport, Hounslow, Middx (01–759 2525)
Aegean Turkish Holidays, 10 South Molton St., London W1 (01–499 9641)
Falcon, 33 Notting Hill Gate, London W11 (01–221 6298)
Sunmed, 4–6 Manor Mount, London SE23 (01–699 7666)
Turkish Tourist Office, 170 Piccadilly, London W1 (01–734 8681)

— Part 3 —
Long Haul

— NEW ORLEANS AND
THE MISSISSIPPI CRUISE —

The *Delta Queen* looms over the mud like a five-floor white hotel. Her top-deck calliope honks out 'Dixie' in farts of steam against December's lemon setting sun.

We must run to catch her. Down past the one-time brothels and clip-joints of Natchez-under-the-Hill. Past the dark saloon where we've been drinking, stomping to jazz.

The *Queen*'s crew unleash her hawsers and we cruise away with a gaggle of Californians, strangers in these parts, northwards up the mile-wide ochre Mississippi. Surging logs menace the flailing red paddle-wheel astern.

Winter evenings here in the Deep South have the translucence and blandness of English Junes.

I have driven three and a half hours north from New Orleans (say it Noo Orlins or you sound barbarian here) up this enormous swampy valley – flat to the far horizons, a forest of spindly trees and slippery alligators – to dine in Natchez proper.

And it is so proper, too, with its two hundred grand pre-Civil War homes perched on the very first hill you come to from New Orleans. That city's French Quarter is fairer than any traveller's tale. It is like Seville – squiggly wrought iron balconies, inner courtyards with fountains and orange trees, eighteenth century streets called Toulouse and Chartres, down which a dark confetti of mixed races drift all night like Mediterranean *flâneurs*.

Jazz pumps, trumpets squeal from bars and cafés. In one a jockey-sized old negro, with powder-blue coat hanging over his hands and down to his quivering knees, tap-dances under an enormous trilby, while a pretty girl in black braces over a white shirt plays her sweet trombone.

We stroll all night, loath to waste a minute.

Preservation Hall: octogenarian negroes with proud resigned faces under short grizzled hair, weary like old elephants, belt out the old favourites for us. The one white man in the group, a clean-cut college guy, sits deferentially to one side in the white stage lighting, eyeing the great old men of jazz with reverence.

Ancient hats and dead flowers blanketed with dust are the spotlit backcloth of the famous tiny hall.

Next day, brunch in a corner café, then Jackson Square, as French as a city in Provence, but whizzing with fire-eaters and trick cyclists, and aglow with pavement artists.

The Deep South is eccentric, therefore memorable, like holiday places should be, and like the strange spicy shrimpy Creole food which we enjoy in the *Delta Queen*'s fine fern-hung dining-room. Only an unadventurous dolt eats boring food abroad. Telly-snacks and baked beans are for home.

Our fellow travellers are odd, too. Here in the vast saloon in the bright morning light, antique American couples mince about like garish transvestites in gold lamé and powder-blue and glittering slippers, practising Country Dancing dead seriously.

In the paddle-wheel bar (a marvellous place to drink at night with the great blades flashing floodlit astern) a sharp-nosed gentleman from Brooklyn is giving his morning bridge lesson. Middle-aged ladies hang on his stern words, 'No, Myrtle! You would not bid "two clubs"!' he snaps.

Upriver at Natchez (named after a long-lost Indian tribe no one seems to care about), the rich plantation owners built their elegant white-pillared mansions. This spry town stands above the floodable, good-for-cotton plains where their slaves sweated, drowned and died.

Members of their high society clubs now open their doors in startling crinolines to bug-eyed tourists in the mornings. Their forefathers swiftly surrendered Natchez to the North lest the dam' Yankee gunboats (looking like black spacecraft on the Mississippi below) should shell their precious homes.

The Deep South is so foreign to other Americans, including the big party of sun-brown, bright-eyed Californians on board, that I feel more at home than they do.

In the grand houses there are grand European things: Chippendale, Sèvres, Meissen, good Dutch School paintings. The Californians, scorned by many older-established Americans, gape at these things bemused.

Who says Americans aren't snobby? They split themselves, just like the Soviets or the dying British aristocracy, into tiers of common interests. Special packs exclude other packs. But their legendary hospitality to the passing stranger is immense and genuine. The father of my very best Kentuckian friend, an actress born here in Natchez, asks me to dinner. I expect, English-fashion, perhaps two other couples as guests. We are to dine Southern-style early at 7 pm (New Yorkers dine at 9 or later). I am admitted by the black butler and warmly greeted by Jane's father, the local patriarch, hugely distinguished with a dashing black patch over one eye. He has the slyest sense of humour and ribs me gently as he and his second wife introduce me to sixteen assembled local friends. They have come early, as one must do in England when a Royal has been invited. But this is to await my arrival. I'm overwhelmed, and mumble. 'But you're our guest of honour,' declaims the great man in his deep southern drawl.

An Englishman down here is something from another world, for here even the north is strange and generally nasty. As for Europe ... well, many take holidays there but ... I am examined and cross-examined over delicious southern food: beef with a local rice and green-bean mix; then the famed pecan pie (the nuts come from the spindly pecan trees around), and French champagne.

I'm taken through the green baize door to meet their old black nanny who raised her beloved 'Miss Jane' and her brothers, and now – like nannies once did in Britain – lives out her cosy retirement. Here's the black cook busy over her stove and a black maid ironing. My host puts his arm around my shoulders and says in his rum and honey Mississippi voice, 'They were sure glad to see you but they couldn't understand *one* word y'all were sayin'!'

Britain, whence many of these southern families originally sprang, puzzles and disappoints them. Still cold about the Yankees, they're not exactly – in this most isolationist area of the States – exactly warm about us. They don't like us even talking to the Soviets. They feel we should show constant gratitude for Cruise. Outside the pleasant old hotel where I'm spending the night off the boat, a friendly couple startlingly adjure me, 'We want you Europeans to understand this: we don't *need* to defend you. If you don't want us over there – those women of yours squawking away round our bases – we sure as hell will pull out and leave you to it.' This is delivered, not in anger but with such force, I sit silent in the car. The man adds, 'We never meet any English. We think you should know how we feel here. Tell your friends back home.'

Shaken by this warning, I repeated this conversation in Kentucky, originally a semi-neutral state during the War Between the Nations, as the South still calls the American Civil War. My Kentuckian friends were appalled. But the message lingers.

The Deep South has none of the great American virtues of zeal, efficiency and planning. Renting a car is more shambolic even than in

Britain. Wake-up calls don't happen. Other people's breakfasts arrive by accident.

'Yes, it's got charm,' Mrs Lurton Scott, wife of the hero who walked on the moon, agrees. She was raised in Alabama but is glad she left for California. She wouldn't want her southern-born children raised in the South. 'It looks back.'

In the paddle-wheel bar of the *Queen* is a tall, thin man from the opposite side of everything. The pale, high-cheekboned Polish count with mournful grey eyes is now, like Mrs Scott, a travel agent in California. In 1944, having lost his relations, friends, and vast estates to 'Zoze blutty Russians', he walked across embattled Germany to try to join the British Army. 'May I speak frankly?' he leans forward. 'I respect your Enoch Powell. But what power has he? Nothing.' He clicks his long white fingers. 'The American government – and yours, too – are so liberal. Ours lets in millions of Chinese. Yours lets in millions of blacks. Is crazy, no?' He adds, 'Let me say I respected the Germans. Without to be snobbish, many were gentlemen.'

Up river at Vicksburg, a splendid southern lady, Mrs Amelia, seventy-plus, magpie-bright under white woolly Tam o'Shanter, shows us round the battlefield, the second of the South's fatal defeats.

'Where y'all from?' she drawls as we board her coach, shepherded as always by our bright and sparkling blonde from Kuoni Travel. 'La Hoja, California,' intones the Polish count. 'San Something, California,' says Mrs Lurton Scott.

'England, England,' I say cheekily. 'First time a-visitin' the United States?' asks Mrs Amelia. 'Twenty-seventh time,' I say.

'Shure, ya'll must love it.' 'Ah surely do, ma'am,' I say, attempting her Southern drawl. The Californians applaud.

Mrs Amelia re-fights the siege of Vicksburg as we circle the green undulations outside the town-park, cemetery and war games all combined. Monuments bristle greyly to states, colonels, captains, and baffled soldiers all of whom were here only one hundred and twenty years earlier, bayonetting and cannonballing kith and kin from the same towns, even the same families in border states.

'By this stream,' cried Mrs Amelia, 'the Missouri men from either side would meet by night to drink the water and exchange news from their home.'

'Y'all too warm there?' called Mrs Amelia. 'I'm not. I'm still a-fightin'! And some say if we'd got those provisions from Jackson, the South'd still be a-fightin'. And some say we still are anyways!'

The little British contingent, led by our delectable shepherdess, roundly cheer Mrs Amelia, but the Californians mumble uncomfortably together, having less common history and nothing to do with the War Between the States.

The caliope honks out 'Dixie' once again. We sip the first whiskies of the evening as the *Queen* slips downstream, and dream of Noo Orlins once again.

TRAVEL FACTS

Pan Am, 14 Old Park Lane, London W1 (01–409 0688)
British Airways, PO Box 10, Heathrow Airport, Hounslow, Middx (01–759 2525)
Kuoni, Kuoni House, Dorking, Surrey (0306 885044)
Speedbird, 152 King St., London W6 (01–741 8041)
Trekamerica, 62 Kenway Rd., London SW5 (01–373 5085)
United States Travel & Tourism Administration, 22 Sackville St., London W1 (01–439 7433)

— EGYPT & THE NILE —

'What do you see?' whispered the explorers in the dark dusty tomb beneath the soaring mountains in the Valley of the Kings.

Howard Carter shone the first light for three thousand two hundred years on to the still-glittering glories of King Tutankhamun. 'Wonderful things,' he breathed back.

I, too, saw wonderful things voyaging up the grey-green, greasy Nile. And was offered the most frightful food. If you want to broaden your mind while tightening your belt, go to Egypt.

I'd been warned in Thailand. There that extraordinary traveller, Barbara Cartland, had hotly urged me: 'Dahling! In Egypt don't even brush your *teeth* in the water!'

I took plenty of my favourite whisky which originally tasted a trifle odd mixed with toothpaste. I then bought bottles and bottles of mineral water on our lofty river boat, resolutely refusing even a sliver of ice, touched no fruit I couldn't peel, no vegetables nor even the whiff of a salad. Lettuces in these lands are usually grown on land enriched with something very nasty. Eggs are all right. Egyptian bread is excellent. Whisky is a fine disinfectant. I lost weight and felt fit.

Of our forty-strong agreeable Thomas Cook party, thirty-six were felled by the Pharaohs' curse. But our cheerful tour leader, looking with me round the dwindling breakfast tables on our river boat, *Nile Beauty*, replied: 'But this is good! First time I've ever had a full turn-out for the Valley of the Kings!'

The pale, scourged walking wounded, sustained by their spouses, staggered ashore at Luxor. We had flown there on Day Three, rising at 3.45 am in the windy Cairo night to fly south by mad Egyptair. Cairo airport was a farce, blocked in by ancient jalopies, its flight boards giving batty information, even at the boarding gates. And Egyptair is dry!

No seat allocation means that the strong and the fleet win across the tarmac. I allied myself with a sporting and amusing Deputy Governor of a London jail whom I'd spotted in the aircraft laughing with his wife at *Private Eye*. 'They'll be OK,' I knew. He was also a Welsh prop forward. We cut through a posse of sharp-elbowed French tourists at Aswan for the flight to those best-of-all marvels at Abu Simbel, on the Sudan border.

Here, stark, gigantic, on the desert cliff above the three hundred-mile-long lake created by the Aswan dam, stand two Bondish space domes. They cover the temples of Rameses II and his wife, Queen Nefartari, moved in a rare, multi-national effort from what is now the bed of the lake.

I turned the bluff and saw the four titanic statues towering over me and gasped as if winded. Like thousands before me, before Christ, I felt a slave beneath stern gods.

Approach to sites – as to people – is half the battle. We did the Pyramids of Giza all wrong on Day Two, bussing from Cairo into a crammed car park crackling with quarrelling camel owners. The vast, ugly bulk of Cheops' Pyramid shrank behind this foreground.

The best view is from the splendid dining room of the hotel (but awful dull kebabs) where Churchill and Montgomery stayed to scheme and celebrate their desert victories. There's another view of Cheops which looms over the disappointing noseless Sphinx, if you look up-tilted through the smelly bothy where we hired camels.

'See you can ride then!' chirped a small and dapper man from Cheshire, one of the minority on our tour to risk boarding these morose, snarling beasts. Sandown and Lingfield felt a long way away as I drove my mount to overtake a crawling gaggle of American tourists. The Cheshire man had been in the Yeomanry in the Middle East during World War II. As such he'd fought in Syria, in Britain's last cavalry action. I pressed him for details as our ships of the desert rocked slowly forward down the hot tarmac road.

The area is abuzz with tourists, honking coaches, grunting camels and incessant pedlars of ghastly souvenirs. We panted to quit the bus, but our guide kept us captive, lecturing on 'no slavery ever in Egypt'. We squinted up at the towering blocks unable to believe that labour had voluntarily lugged them up there. We argued. He lost his temper and, still cooped up, we began to laugh.

If you like the beauties of classical Greece, Egypt's monuments are crude, primitive and lumpish. Yet the old relics are so full of dark, sinister forces that, even back in green England, I can't forget their brooding anger.

To trace its source, I decided foolishly to enter the passage which leads into the heart of Cheops. It is a claustrophobic crack requiring awkward stooping. Thus you squeeze past Krauts wet with sweat (very free sweaters, the Germans, it's all that gassy beer). There were packs of rather whiffy Arab schoolkids, too. And when you get to the end at last, there's only the dreariest small chamber. Not a foretaste of the hereafter, I fearfully wondered, and faced the foul return. As with Avebury's great mound built by our early people where the old Bath Road now dashes west from Marlborough, I romantically believe that somewhere deep inside Cheops lies mystery aglint with treasures.

I like the freedom of the Nile, drifting one day downstream past reeds and oxen in a felucca. Abdul, its owner, a brown beanstick, grins through gaping teeth as he collects from beneath the tiller postcards from tourists from Arkansas, Australia and Amsterdam. His son shinned up and down the mast like a monkey, hoisting the white wing of a sail. At the water's edge, boys wade in circling round a huge fishing net. Girls clean black cooking pots in the tinted, tainted water. But then at Eton we had to swim in a filthy backwater filled occasionally by the bodies of dogs and once (which made them build a swimming pool for 1300 boys) with the bloated corpse of a man.

The *Nile Beauty* cocooned us cleanly and cheerfully against Egypt's dirt. In my cabin shower, I clenched my teeth against the probably poisonous water. The Egyptian crew, as willing as keen gundogs, smiled a lot.

At Luxor we moor below a steep embankment. Barefoot, robed children scamper. Biblical men with sandals slipping, flap along on tripping donkeys. Inside the creepy inner sanctuary our guide, an intelligent, well-read but sickly student with liver pains (a combination making him cross with us), eloquently quotes the high priest's morning call in that sepulchre to Horus, God of the falcon head: 'I come in peace. Wake up peacefully'.

There are fewer beggars than in Morocco but more touts: 'Dollars? Carriage ride? Genuine Pharaoh scarab?' But I defeat their swarms by pronouncing: 'Salaam' and raising a right hand like a priest. Their religious politeness requires a lengthy response. By its end, I've fled.

I push past them towards the strange, dark old Winter Palace, now a sort of hotel. Doors to empty bars open silently as we creak down corridors musty with damp. It feels like a memorial to the British Raj.

Behind, in a February garden flowery as England in June, a tiny old *dhobi-wallah* totters past us under a huge heap of laundry. 'Welcome' he mutters. Nearly all Egyptians try very hard to please. The Cairo Marriott (the one good hotel I found) which was once a palace has a lobby like the set for the Arabian Nights, dazzling with rich, smart people waiting for their chauffered limo's to glide up. Through it, at any hour of the quite chilly nights, pass pretty single ladies going about their business.

My room, overlooking the gardens, is excellent. 'Well done,' I thank the waiter bringing me mineral water for my whisky.

'Well done?' he repeats anxiously, 'But "well done" is for bifsteak, surely, Sir, for English persons.'

This charms me in Cairo's flat, grey, generally charmless city, where crazy traffic tries to kill you. Only the streets of the old bazaars have colours and the scents of spices and are a pleasure to stroll through. The museum is a must because of the Tutankhamun treasures (but they were better displayed in London) and even at the Hilton next door, the food is still abysmal.

Wonderful things to see, yes. Like the tomb of General Mere Ribar, where the bright paintings on the walls make ancient Egypt dance alive. Here's the general's vet tenderly treating his pet hyena. There's the abominable tax collector totting up the general's earnings then, as we now worry about ours.

I can't forget colossal Karnak either, heavily menacing. But frustrating, too, as hordes of hissing Japs and squawking French photographed themselves like silly puppets beneath the giant feet on Egypt's ancient stage.

TRAVEL FACTS

Egyptair, 269 Regent St., London W1 (01–734 2395)
Thomas Cook, PO Box 36, Thorpe Wood, Peterborough (0733 63200)
Kuoni, Kuoni House, Dorking, Surrey (0306 885044)
Sovereign, 17–27 High St., Hounslow, Middx (01–987 4545)
Egyptian State Tourist Office, 168 Piccadilly, London W1 (01–493 5282)

— JAMAICA —

Ireland in the sun. Tropical thunder. Warm rain dashing on brilliant flowers. Palm trees drip. Jamaican sea is as warm, sometimes as sticky, as tea and all I crave in high heat is ice-cold water to swim in.

Like that other island where John Bull once ruled, Jamaica has the same dilapidated charm, an identical malevolence and whisper of menace. But travel should not be boringly safe. There are friendly laughing people in Jamaica who entertain me richly, just like my many Irish friends. But there are the black looks and the hatred, too, and the rain falling upon little donkeys on empty, potholed roads. In summer everything's cheaper in Jamaica. But it rains.

The wild and pretty road bumping west along the coast out of Montego Bay is interrupted by dozing goats and grazing donkeys, looked after in a fashion by bright-clothed locals sleeping on their hunkers or on their feet. Colours dazzle even on the ancient battered cars, and the emerald and diamond sea is Asprey's all over. The sea is beautifully empty. But it laps poor shacks.

There is, too, an Irish mañana mood. There is no Irish word which conjures up the immediacy of 'mañana'. 'Come soon', Jamaicans sooth with white smiles when you ask for breakfast, whisky or electric light (power cuts are frequent) and certainly a telephone call. It doesn't come soon. Soon it doesn't matter. Guinness up there. Ganja down here. Marijuana is still a blissful industry. Two light 'planes, recklessly overburdened with the stuff, couldn't take off from their airstrip on the road east to Ochos Rios. They crashed and remain as warnings, nose-dived into the turf like drunks.

Three years earlier, soon after the last Troubles, I'd stayed with American friends near Round Hill, one of the grandest resorts west of Montego Bay: a lovely beach, old well-established houses in bright gardens, dining and dancing by the shore, reading a play of mine after dinner, a wife disturbed and crying walking in the banana groves.

At night our security guards, un-uniformed and so as frightening as guerillas, would slip silently across the moonlit lawns, ducking into the shadows of hibiscus and poinsettia. And semi-wild goats, strongly resembling Lenin, kept stumping into the elegant front hall.

'Are things better?' Jamaican friends shrug, 'The rich get richer ...' What's new? Freedom from the imperial yoke seldom improves the workers' lot. The millionaires at the top of the pile just grab their way to more. As tourists, the Americans have rushed in to fill the gap left by the British whose share of tourism plunged from twenty to five per cent. The Jamaicans say they'd like us back. They giggle at us, finding our serious demeanour comic, whereas the Yanks at 'Sandals', our first port of call, heartily play games. So they're like children and the locals understand this seriousness about small things.

'Sandals', a place for couples – '*definitely* no singles' affirms the manager, is at the end of the Montego Bay runway. Aircraft noise is deafening but the guests are urged by the attractive dusky hostesses to 'think positively'. So, like trained dogs, we wave at and do not curse the bellies of the jets. 'We make virtue of necessity,' said the manager comfortably.

The staff are marvellous in their cheerful wish to please. What's more, every drink is free. This, like letting children in chocolate factories at first stuff themselves silly, leads to moderation, then abstinence. Would that it were so in other matters. Delicious piña coladas stand half empty, forgotten in scores round every cheerful bar.

Tumbling out of our BA flight (top class and with an unusually happy crew), we get calypso'ed at Sandal's door. Reggae beats everywhere. Garlanded maidens shaded from ebony to honey show us to our rooms. Mine is delectable but looks about sixteen. 'She is twenty-three and spoken for,' the manager warns me. But later I can tell him, 'Actually, she's twenty-one. And leaving you.'

He knows, for Jamaica, 146 miles by 51 with a 6000 ft mountain in the middle, is as parochial as my English village. I meet again out there the daughter of a double-barrelled Dorset family, now married (somewhat to their concern) to the Jamaican owner of Sandals, of a 'plane, a motor cruiser, a Mercèdes, and three homes. He's one of the new wave of local entrepreneurs who've made it. Her voice, heavily lilted with her husband's mates, returns to Sloane with me. She is covetously eyed by my companions as she steps – dressed for her private plane back to Kingston – across the sands to see me off.

We leave for Negril on the island's western snout. It is supposed to be a hot bed of licentiousness and we are staying at 'Hedonism II – *the* place for singles'.

Heads are shaken by the more sophisticated Jamaicans: 'They're all only farmers down there!' says one. 'And what do they farm, those peasants?' retorts another. 'Only ganja!'

'Service will be poor down there, let me tell you.'

The dreadfully named 'Hedonism II' (like that of a vulgar *nouveau riche* motor cruiser) turns out to be a blundering brown barracks. What a disgraceful waste, for it's set among wild woods above a scimitar of dazzling beach. The American college kids who comprise its guests find naked bathing, 'really risqué, man'. But they have not had to endure the wrinkled old hairy horrors in Europe along Tahiti Plage and other purgatories.

Here, as at Sandals, hearty team games are the rule. 'Nood Beach High versus Prude Beach High Olympics!' they bellow, wobbling and dangling across the silvan sand.

'Only man is vile,' I mutter, swimming out to sea to avoid the heat of the shallow green water and the pubic horrors (some nastily shaved) revealed along the waterline.

A dreadlocked Rastafarian glides up on his catamaran going 'Peep-peep-peep' like a child's toy car, and chanting 'Never fear, Rasta' is near!' Giving me a pull, he tenderly steers me off the stone jetty. I find him the most gentlemanly man around and then discover that, behind his dream state, he's a brisk entrepreneur. He owns two 'cats' and a store and is expanding his business interests. He has got the best of both ends of the modern world, I think, watching him drift away – probably to a board meeting – round the next neck of the woods and still singing . . . 'Rasta' is near, never fear'.

Along the little road past the development, are rows of pretty little shacks covered in flowers which the locals let out for peanuts – a few dollars – to America's semi-hippies. I like that road much better than Hedonism II.

Among trees along the beach an American, as old and twisted as they, washed himself naked in the open. His much younger girlfriend, also naked, and pinkly embarrassed, looked away from the nasty sight. Do ugly people never look in mirrors? A very plain, very naked American girl popped out of the next straw shelter to greet us. 'Hi, honey! Hi', she murmured. I gave her the cursory glance I use when judging certain reject horses at my local country show. I did not require her to trot out to show her paces. In these circumstances my Eton headmaster could have repeated his courteous rejection of a Piccadilly prostitute – 'I have neither the time, I fear, Madam, nor the inclination'. But I missed my cue.

Below us in the steamy heat, Americans drowsily lugged their sunbeds into the warm sea and slouched in them gasping, half-submerged. Behind us: arriving bizarrely over-dressed, save for their leader, four Russians muttered beneath the trees in a tight-lipped group.

Their boss had white hair, gold teeth, 1950's shorts and a straw hat. He spoke. The others, younger, just nodded, 'Da, Da, Da ...' Were they spies or gayskis? But I was frustrated. Always one of them remained to guard their clothes and papers. It was not a nice place.

East of Montego Bay, the Royal Caribbean is a different thing. The hotel has a graceful charm and good food. From it, I visited one of Jamaica's notorious 'Great Houses'. Rose Hall is haunted by the White Witch who, one hundred and sixty years earlier, had murdered her three husbands – poisoned, strangled, and stabbed. Then in an excess of Freudian complexities, she not only slept with some of her stud slaves but watched them being flogged to death beneath her balcony. Our guide said, 'Not for one million dollars, man, would I sleep in Rose Hall.'

My favourite hotel was Shaw Park at Cutlass Bay, near Ochos Rios, where we did the tourist thing and shinned up slippery Dunn's River Falls. We happily overtook two squawking American groups on the way. We are led by a grumpy Rasta guide (we won't hold hands as he insists).

Shaw Park triumphantly combines the essence of a foreign holiday and of Jamaica in particular. Sophisticated one end and wild jungle the other. At this end, jolly bars, a disco and a madly patriotic owner resembling David Niven who raves about everything British. At the other end is the forest on the water's edge by a river. Black fisher folk squat, gossiping and snoozing beneath an upturned boat. One runs blithely along the silver beach and is accosted by two girls, one dark and butch, one fair and sexy, who say they are Polish, but speak German.

They vanish joyfully into the bushes with the black man.

TRAVEL FACTS

Air Jamaica, 36–7 Piccadilly, London W1 (01–734 1782)
British Airways, PO Box 10, Heathrow Airport, Hounslow, Middx (01–759 2525)
Kuoni, Kuoni House, Dorking, Surrey (0306 885044)
Caribbean Connection, 93 Newman St., London W1 (01–631 3650)
Tradewinds, 66–68 Brewer St., London W1 (01–734 1260)
Jamaican Tourist Office, 1 Lowther Gdns., Prince Consort Rd., London SW7 (01–493 3647)

— MIAMI AND THE
BAHAMAS CRUISE —

The beautiful, high society lady from Miami kindly came to the *Sunward II* to meet her Long Island girlfriend and me. We'd been on a Bahamas cruise to faded pink Nassau, snorkelling on a desert island, then Freeport and back.

'You must have been with a lot of swells,' she exclaimed, 'cos the first man I saw coming off was very distinguished and Gucci all over!'

The Miami lady should know, for she comes from the nobs' woody and flowery suburb of Coconut Grove. Her family built and richly furnished Vizcaya, that astounding pseudo-Spanish palace, with gardens like Versailles, lapped by the sea. It's open to the public and is well worth a visit – and not only to escape from Miami centre. It proves that not all Miami is grey fanged, high-rise, tripper blocks on the beach nor black slums nor Hispanic knifings. Eighty years ago when it began, Miami was created for the swells. Part lingers sweetly on.

It was our cruise ship's Greek '*maitre d*' who was 'Gucci all over'. Drinking with us on our first night out of Miami on *Sunward II*'s deck under the velvet indigo night, looking down on the stars reflected in the frothing wake, he told us haughtily: 'Of course, Norwegian-Caribbean does well – there are two hundred million lower middle-class Americans longing to come on our cruises!'

Miss Long Island who, with a senior and far richer admirer, has sailed the Atlantic in a state room in the QE2, took this tetchily. I'd warned her our cabin might prove to be a closet, out of which we'd both be only too keen to come, and quickly, too. But there was quite enough room without playing knights' moves at chess. Kim, our inscrutable Korean steward, kept it spick and us punctual.

'Dinner, dinner, sir and madam! Eight o'clock. You second sitting.'

'No, Mr Kim, we're going ashore.'

There is a lot of ashore on this four day cruise from Miami to the Bahamas and back again. As there should be on all. What's a boat but a hotel that moves? You want to see how the land lies everywhere it stops.

The Greek *maitre d'* added: 'This boat is bottom of our line of five. The *Norway*, once the great *France*, is biggest passenger boat afloat and something else.'

Some Western prancing (jeans and foolish Texan hats) leapt around on the open deck. A too loud disco dissuaded most couples from erotic dancing. The rest were refeened.

Americans in their hundreds feel at home on boats like these and behave quietly and politely, much better than the Brits abroad. They make noises only in Europe because they feel uneasy amongst us strangers.

Miss Long Island had told me that *her* cruise brochure had suggested that the *Sunward II* would be loose with swinging singles. 'You'd be better on your own,' she suggested. But the only (female) singles sighted were the croupiers, all Brits because few Americans are trained and the rest won't work the long hours.

But there was a twenty-strong blush of honeymoon couples, into whose private welcome party in the ship's nicest bar we blundered. 'Champagne we've had and cream gateaux, and it all makes us feel real special,' twittered a clean, teenage bride.

The Greek had fiddled the computered *placement* to get us seated with the only two other lively couples we encountered all cruise. These were well-off Californians filling in four days before their long and boozy Super Bowl weekend at Tampa on Florida's west coast. The Super Bowl is terribly boring to a Brit. What's more, 'you can't possibly *go* to Tampa,' barked a great Kentuckian friend to me. 'Everyone *comes* from Tampa!'

On our other side sat a Hispanic couple who never spoke. She, desirably voluptuous, looked daily sulkier, and he paler. We drew libidinous conclusions.

Florida is dark with non-English speaking immigrants. 'Butter, please,' asked Miss Long Island one morning from a middle-aged Cuban couple. 'No comprende,' they muttered. I remembered some Spanish and discovered they had left Havana seventeen years before to live in Miami. But they still don't need English to ask for bread and butter in Florida.

Next down the table was a family of four from the freezing Mid-West, whence the cruises draw most of their sun-seekers. The violet-rinsed ma made my day with her comment: 'You look just like George C. Scott.'

I hesitate, because I can't instantly recall the man's face.

'General Patton,' she chirps. 'So distinguished.'

But all life's leg-ups lead to slippery banana skins. Our huge rolypoly black waiter butts in with a chortle: 'Ah sure can't grab yah ac-*cent*. Ah know yah not English, anyways!' (He works six months solid on the four-day and three-day Bahamas winter cruises for every six weeks holiday.)

The food he plonks down sounds temptingly Norwegian but, till the last night, is plain small-town American – the market, after all, for which they cater.

We leap ashore delightedly at Nassau: Georgian squares, George V red pillar boxes, and a splendid black lady bossing the tourist office. Always use tourist offices in any new land. The people in them usually have so little to do they're keen to help. The roguish negress used to perform, she tells me delightedly, at Al Burnett's naughty night club, The Stork, in Swallow Street, where I passed many a merry evening as a trainer celebrating winners and drowning losers. I think she was the one who did strange things one night with a green silk scarf and then tormented a lusty major-general with it ...

She recommends Cable Beach for swimming, the Straw Market for haggling, and dinner in Graycliff. The one white lady in the office whispers: 'Better not walk there at night. Safer in a taxi.'

Old, battered American taxis drive us around New Providence Island at fantastic expense. You need wads of dollars on these cruises. Drinks on board can't be signed for either. Silly psychology, for everybody orders more freely if they don't have to fish out notes, particularly in a fifteen-knot breeze. Even two local piña coladas or two rum and tonics cost almost a fiver, so rich is the dollar, so feeble our pound.

Nassau's hilltop is bewitchingly dilapidated. Close to the Governor's grand residence, where the unhappy Duke of Windsor and the former Mrs Simpson worked out their penance, are empty town houses, closed hotels and clubs, and gardens becoming jungles. What a waste of elegance. The new hotels, violent and stark, rear up over the lovely beaches miles out of town.

The epicurean Graycliff is a splendidly furnished two-hundred-and-fifty-year-old colonial home, now turned into a hotel and restaurant at prices to make even a New Yorker wince. Stone-crab claws for starters are £9 a head! *Fruits de Mer* £35 each! The cheapest potable wine (Californian Sauvignon is always good value) turns out here to be £25 a bottle. And the wine list runs up to Latours at £1,150 a bottle! Who can come here now?

In the 'Spooning Gallery', the exiled Windsors played cards. More recently, I read in the Visitors' Book, there have been Liverpool's Beatles, several gold-laden sheiks, and a couple from Solihull who wrote 'Funtastik'.

A more sensible and pretty little place to eat is The Cellar, set in an attractive garden on an uphill side street.

Cursing Graycliff's £90 bill, I am cajoled to the casino complex on neighbouring Paradise Island. What a misnomer! It is a sad inferno of gamblers praying dully for a touch of self-relief under gigantic roof-mirrors. Americans are generally deprived of casinos – lucky devils – Vegas, Reno and Atlantic City are exceptions to US laws. So this ghastly place on Paradise Island is crammed with them hanging gloomily around clanking fruit machines, chattering roulette wheels and packs slapped down by snake-eyed, waxen-cheeked croupiers. It's like Hell's airport waiting for the last plane out.

'I've gambled enough with the bigger things in my life,' I grumble, 'to be turned on by a silly little spinning ball.'

Then a Mafia posse, in their uniform of black silk suits, wide shoulders and white ties, make me lower my voice. Minced round by henchmen, they oil their way across into an inner private parlour, where they will bet away your and my life savings in half an hour.

Next day, all is a sapphire heaven on the line's private empty island. We go snorkelling. Thick fish flocks, in budgie blues, yellows and greens, brush and nibble our legs and arms, and greedily feed like finches from the bread in our snorkel leader's pockets. No crowds. Silence bar the surf's hiss. For lunch, fresh hot dogs at rough green tables beneath the palm trees. Black ladies with home-made crafts have rowed across from another island to sell them cheaply from little thatched huts.

Freeport, on Grand Bahama, is like a warmer Milton Keynes. New, neat roads, scrupulously clean, await life. Docks are blank concrete and smelly oil refineries. A tasteless, modern Moorish complex set in the middle of nowhere is called 'International Bazaar'. But, rooked £6 a head by a hefty taxi driver (four couples squeezed into his car), Miss Long Island and I will not now retreat. The rest have decanted at the Bazaar. But we push on till emerald sea and creamy sands flicker on our right between pines and palms.

'Stop!' We've reached the far and unspoilt end of Lucayan Beach.

Don't be dismayed by the customary high-rise façade of the Atlantik Beach Hotel. Trade is poor, so the car hire girl immediately offers me discounts equivalent to a couple of taxi rides. More particularly, because the hotel is one selected by Swiss travel agents rather than British and American ones, the food is two classes better.

Glorious beach, with only ten others on it. Cheerful attendant. Big, blue, sparkling pool. Jokey and efficient barman and waiters. Top-class piña coladas and the best grouper fish cooked Creole style that we've had on the whole trip. A young, witty calypso singer with his tall, blind, black drummer quietly and cleverly serenade us beneath an ancient olive.

Dreary façades often hide life's better things, we thought, embarking for the last night's cruise to Miami. But, especially in the two-faced Caribbean, you have to push through to find them.

TRAVEL FACTS

Pan Am, 14 Old Park Lane, London W1 (01–409 0688)

British Airways, PO Box 10, Heathrow Airport, Hounslow, Middx (01–759 2525)

Virgin, 7th floor, Sussex House, High St., Crawley, West Sussex (01–938 3611)

Norwegian Caribbean Line, 3 Vear St., London, W1 (01–493 6041)

Royal Caribbean Line, Bishops Palace House, 2a Riverside Walk, Kingston-upon-Thames, Surrey (01–541 5044)

Carnival, Equity Cruises, 77–79 Gt. Eastern St., London EC2 (01–729 1929)

Bahamas Tourist Office, 23 Old Bond St., London W1 (01–629 5238)

— MAURITIUS —

My travelling companion, fiercely independent and averse to public jostle, seemed ominously unsuited to a Club Med. 'Furthermore,' I asked their British boss in wintry Brompton Road, 'aren't Club Med guests all swinging teenagers?'

'Completely wrong!' retorted M. Boeuf, who, with Gallic tartness has picked '1066' for his London telephone number. 'Go to Mauritius. You will see.'

I'd falsely warned my companion we'd live in straw huts, wear only beads and use slit trenches. I was wrong and she did not believe me. But our arrival at the Club's Pointe aux Canonniers, on the most beautiful tropical island I've ever seen, was a little inauspicious.

The lady took against the Chef. Not the good English cook there but the 'Chef of the Organisers' as Club Villages call them. Clad only in loin cloth and flower garland, with a backing group of beauties similarly undressed and varying in hue from petite ebony to bouncy auburn, the Chef led welcome chants and rattled off his orders in staccato French. This I might have found hilarious if it hadn't been noon and 90°F and we'd left Heathrow at 3.30 pm the day before. (Air Mauritius – super, crew charming).

Indeed, on our last night we fell about laughing in the lovely garden lit by flaming torches, as we watched, their songs merging in the mass gurgling of ten thousand frogs, a similar welcome meted out to a jet-struck squad of Ilford junior management.

But Boeuf was naturally right. Though there's a fine seductive set of bronzed, leggy model girls, nubile gymnasts and husky males, middle-aged French bourgeois couples predominate. They keenly compete in tennis tournaments, at volleyball, and queue to water-ski and for trips in the glass-bottomed boat to gaze at the wondrous sea-shells and coral. These my companion buys by the score, haggling with a swarthy boatman on the strand. They will prove irksome to lug home but look really pretty in her Hampshire bathroom.

We meet a horsey Irish couple (the only other English speakers there) who read my books. They are active from pearly dawn into the warm night. 'This is our sixth Club Med. We love them. This is the best.' And the pretty, much-travelled wife used to work for British Airways and so knows her islands in the sun.

Very senior couples take excursions around this exotic island. At our dinner table the first night – the French rush in at eight exactly, though the village has no clocks – we join our group: two abstemious spinsters from Lille, a Calais pork butcher, an elegant government official from nearby Réunion Island, and a teenage couple, he girlish, she masculine, silently fumbling each other's white thighs.

In our canvas-shaded Mini-Moke we wind down lanes under the fabulous flame trees past huge sweet-scented laburnums. Bougainvillaea bursts out of crofts and round tiny shops marked *'Boulangerie'* or *'Grande Ouverture!'*

We walk across the Club Med's springy lawns outside our air-conditioned, neat apartment. The gardens flash with red, darting cardinal birds, squawking mynahs and cooing doves. Past the frangipani, under the palms we stroll along the next door public beach of Mon Choisy. Behind the canna lilies and the hibiscus buzzes another day of Club Med action.

Here it's a Hindu holiday. Dark families picnic under the pine fringe. They call out to us in French. *'Ça va?'* is the current catchphrase. Pretty children with bare feet boot balls about the silver sand. They splash in the warm, clear emerald sea. Far out, like a bouncing white pearly necklace, the surf rumbles on the protective coral reef.

The people are of every shade, black, coffee, tawny, yellow, and white. But all announce they love *'la reine'* whose head appears on the rupee bank notes. 'We are all Mauritians,' they happily declare.

Along the road under shady trees, groups of mixed faces laugh together, waiting for buses, waving at tourists. They seem the happiest people I've come across for years.

Green seas of sugar cane roll across the island's interior, split up by mounds and rows of piled-up lava rock. The core of Mauritius, first Dutch, then French for a century, then ours till Independence, is an imperial central mountain range. Its peaks fantastically squirl against the sky like a child's drawing of fairy hills.

The creeds are mixed, too. Here's a white Muslim mosque next to a grey Catholic church by the white beach at Grand Baie. Round the corner is a Hindu temple. Red prayer-flags wave in tiny garden shrines. Stone walls hide the seaside villas of the rich.

Signposts mix languages, too. We drive past Trou aux Biches, where there's a lovely restaurant with a sea view infinitely more beautiful than the South of France, and on to Goodlands. We visit Pamplemousses, once the French Governor's home and now – 'Second best botanical gardens in the world,' says our expensive black guide, leading us past lily ponds and palms which flower but once every hundred years and then, like a swan's song, die.

Gardening ladies in kingfisher saris doze under trees. The place is an arbour of spices: incense trees, nutmeg, cinnamon, verbena, eucalyptus of course, and a tree called '*quatre spices*'. In front of the Governor's residence stand the remains – looking like a metal four-poster – of the frame on which the late and greatly loved Prime Minister, a Hindu, had been ceremoniously cremated three weeks earlier.

Nearby, below an old sugar cane mill and distillery once sweated over by African slaves, is a lolling heap of hundred-year-old, gigantic tortoises, resembling in their wrinkled guile and drooping eyes, a bevy of our own retired prime ministers.

Grand Baie is my favourite village: coves, yachts, palms and restaurants. We dine Chinese at La Pagoda and at midnight listen to 'Sega' and sung in a French patois by four locals as the laid-back moon leaves her wake across the water.

Shopping in Port Louis, the jumbled little capital, is fun and frightening. My companion has her handbag snatched in the jostling market but seizes the thief like an Amazon while the locals leap about longing to beat him down with sticks. 'Ver' sorry,' he mutters with Mauritian courtesy. '*Je m'excuse*' and wriggles off.

We buy necklaces of coral, jade and shells in The Argonaut next to the main bank and then look for a business appointment at a numbered address. But the main street has no numbers. Even the local police don't find this odd. Our new friend, third generation Mauritian but hailing originally from Alsace, finally makes contact with us at the marvellous hotel called the Saint Géran Sun. He brings his beautiful blonde French-bred girlfriend. 'We often don't have any addresses here. Everyone knows each other by name. And our people do love thumping thieves!'

Denis and Sophie join us for a delicious dinner, '*Cuisine Française*', at this hotel on the east coast which ranks for me and my sophisticated companion in the top three seaside hotels of the world. Excellent wines, particularly a *blanc de noir* (a type of rosé) brought in from South Africa. The beef comes almost as far: two thousand miles from the high ranches in Kenya.

The crabs are sadly disappointing, but the sea is alive with good fish. An oyster seller on the beach recommends what seems only a café at Perrybère. But we eat shrimps in brandy and fish from the Indian Ocean cooked Creole fashion with sweet and sour sauce. The food's less than £1 each and the wine only a little more. What you pay for the journey you'll save on incredibly cheap, delicious Mauritian meals.

On our last night, dreading our dawn departure, we swing to the music at the Saint Géran, with our shadows flatteringly extended across the quiet sea.

TRAVEL FACTS

Air Mauritius, 49 Conduit St., London W1 (01–434 4375)
Club Mediterranée, 106–108 Brompton Rd., London SW3
(01–581 4766)
Kuoni, Kuoni House, Dorking, Surrey (0306 885044)
Sovereign Worldwide, 17–27 High St., Hounslow, Middx
(01–987 4545)
Mauritius Government Tourist Office, 49 Conduit St., London W1
(01–437 7508/9)

Greece The Gallery at Tyrens. This part impresses with its antiquity; the rest I found overrated and litter-ridden.

Greece Fishermen, cats and chickens taking lunch in the taverna by the land-locked harbour of Tolon.

Greece The awesome amphitheatre of Epidaurus, a magic place quite apart from its amazing acoustics.

...ece Looking north over Mystras ...ards Sparti. In the distant mountains ...previous night I nearly slithered ...the hair-pin dirt track.

Hungary Budapest: the statue of St. Stephen, Hungary's first king is enclosed on the hilltop of Pest by the "Fishermen's Bastion". Fabulous views from the bastion and the Hilton just round the corner to the left.

Hungary Szentendre village (St. Andrew) on the Danube a short drive out of Budapest is full of art galleries, craft shops and excellent privately-owned restaurants.

Rome While the students sat, sang, smoked or snoozed on the Spanish Steps, the Travelling Companion was racing like a blonde borzoi through the rich shops nearby.

Florence Looking down on the Piazza della Signoria gives a pretty good feel of Florence - even down to the tourist coaches. Never try to drive in the city; you can walk everywhere.

Madeira Looking down on the port of Funchal where you find the best restaurants. Behind us stands world-famous Reid's Hotel where elderly cosseted Brits sit in the lovely gardens in February reading yesterday's "_Times_" to see how many of their friends have snuffed it back in freezing Britain.

Switzerland Elder daughter Kate negotiates a bridge above Lenzerheide. We have walked down from the summit of the Rothorn and I have nearly fallen into the stream.

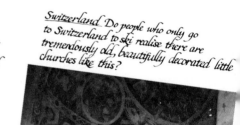

Switzerland Do people who only go to Switzerland to ski realise there are tremendously old, beautifully decorated little churches like this?

— KENYA SAFARI —

Our forty-four year old Dakota bounced dustily down in the bush and was lumbering over us again on its way to the next Kenyan game reserve before we were into the Land Rover. We jolted through the amazingly verdant savannah of the Masai-Mara to Keekorok Lodge.

I'd told the travelling companion: 'Washing in a bucket, sleeping under the stars', but Kuoni pampered us round our exploration of four very different reserves.

Two porters stagger across the lawn under the lady's baggages. Why do women's flimsy clothes weigh so heavily, and why can't they ever travel light? Why must they mind what they wear out at the back of beyond?

Tea and sandwiches are butlered to our bungalow. And five elephants, plus baby, pace past fifty heavy feet away, squelchily munching the grass round the water hole which is their magnet. Quitting bungalows, sundowners, and early suppers (excellent fruit and salads flown up from Nairobi), the photographic hunters rush forth in a chatter of shutters.

But these people, Americans, Krauts, French and a few Brits are hideous. As we learn to study game, we involuntarily study our fellows, and are appalled. Burnt scarlet thighs, warthog-faced, buffalo-bellied, rhino-bottomed, and gibbering like monkeys, the human race seems even worse against the lovely animals – cheetahs, gazelles, lionesses and giraffes – which really live there. What must the poor beasts think of horrible homo sapiens who, by invisible wits, overtook them?

I long to ride a horse across the rolling green plains, laced with rivulets, hatched with thickets. In one such, we seek a leopard sleeping after his kill up in a high thorn tree.

'If you ride,' murmurs Leonard, our black Bantu driver-guide, 'first the leopard or lion kill horse, then eat you.'

The other four in our safari van are Republican Irish. Like the game outside, we stalk each other's conversation warily. Do we believe them all a nation of IRA hyenas? Do they suppose we support the rhino Paisley's herd?

Suddenly, we are all thrilled kids when we start spotting. We point and gasp and grunt – 'Cheetah there! Half right! Three lionesses on that hump!'

The vast African sky is a pale dome spotted with tennis ball clouds, sketched by buzzards gliding on the hot air and by revolting vultures, too, waddling in to gulp the lion's kill.

We see more hordes of game and birds in the Masai-Mara than anywhere else. But its abundance sucks in an excess of vehicles and honking Yanks.

One elegantly disdainful cheetah lounges on his mound, staring at a half-moon of eight clicking, jabbing safari vans, four feet from him. He rises like a ballet dancer among this huddle of human apes. He sprays his thorn tree to mark it and lopes away. Suddenly, he swings, glares and hisses, fangs bared at an old Land Rover lumbering up. 'Probably his family were all killed by Tanzanian poachers in old Land Rover like that,' murmurs Leonard sadly.

The inside of Masai-Mara is such a green and pleasant land you feel so comfortable you could pat the lionesses. Outside, all is changed. Dusty, grim, hostile. Across the over-grazed wilderness, the thin Masai cattle limp. Their owners stare angrily.

On an arduous day's drive north to Samburu, a very different sort of reserve, we pass more facets of Kenya's kaleidoscope. We pause among the rich hill farms – green glades, golden crops, gum trees – where the English milords once lived like princes. A few still do.

Two Irish ladies dressed for Blackpool in dazzling shorts and bulging tops, teeter high-heeled along the dirt road to ease lobster limbs. Simultaneously, two young Masai warriors in full war gear pad into sight with their sinister lope, spears at the ready, jogging towards us. Past they go without a glance. Leonard, with lowered eyelid, whispers, 'Strange sights on country roads!'

Samburu has a proper air of African menace. Desert. Dust. Hostile, spiky mountains. And urgency to pass the road blocks – where sinister Somalis proffer swords – before the gates close at dusk. In we nip. Eighty yards from our old thatched hut, repulsive crocodiles doze and slither across the orange mudflats like ghastly fogies in St James's clubs.

The river flows only in the spring and autumn rains. But along its banks stand great trees. In one bough, softly lit, hangs a fresh haunch: bait for the expected leopards. We dally over an excellent dinner. The African night chitters, clicks, and howls. Suddenly, our Irish fellow travellers whisk us off. A leopard has sprung lithely on to the bough and is boxing at the bait with lethal pad.

But sixty other guests, oblivious of real-life savagery at their elbows, are staring ahead at an old film projected whirringly on to the screen by the river.

Next day, we hear that a second leopard, stronger but coming later, found the food gone and, quarrelling over frontiers, killed a beautiful cheetah.

Dik-dik, the tiny deer, have their territories, too. They mate for life and when one dies the other celibately mourns.

We re-cross the Equator – sun hot, air deliciously cool, six thousand feet up here – and straddle the line for silly photographs while reluctantly buying trash from pedlars.

On to renowned Tree Tops. No wonder our shrewd Queen was so disappointed at the new construction when she re-visited the place. And it's far too full of pushy, loud Americans, oil-rich from huge tax-free salaries from the Gulf.

Only when night has fallen and their honking ceases does Mrs Rhino, with her half-bold, myopic son, come to the salt lick twenty feet below us by the pool and clash heads with a bloody-minded waterbuck.

Outspan, where Baden-Powell lived till his death, is charming, and Nyeri still feels a British garrison town. In its tiny churchyard in uneven graves lie teenaged soldiers killed thirty years ago during The Emergency. An elderly Lancers colonel, a much decorated flight lieutenant, and Baden-Powell's own grave, marked with the Scout sign of a dot inside a ring, which means 'I have gone home'.

So to our favourite reserve, Lake Naivasha and its dream-like Lake Hotel. Great lawns, huge trees and flower beds. Servants bringing tea. Ghosts of stiff-collared officers and settlers with their long-gowned ladies sweeping past before the vanished governors. The lake is confetti-full of flamingos, pelicans and cormorants. An angry mother hippo guards her baby and we steer well clear.

On Crescent Island, we walk alone, the loudest human sound our footfalls in the hot, dry grass. We are completely surrounded by herds of Thomson gazelle, zebra, waterbuck and giraffe. Pairs of haughty fish eagles stare down on us like judges at criminals in the dock.

For, just behind the screen of peace and beauty, savagery throbs. On one bank of this great, shallow lake, Joy Adamson was butchered by her cook. On the other, we take tea with a famed foreign authoress-photographer who lived with the Masai, sustained by their diet of blood and milk. Her red-eyed mongoose hangs round her neck and eats her scone. In a garden shed stands her husband's aircraft, with a bullet hole in it from a trip just made to Uganda to rescue a friend in need.

Jolting back under the bowl of night, the truck's lights pick up a series of tall pyramids: anthills. Each is unknown to its nearest neighbour. Yet, each is a civilisation of sorts. Those thousands stars which glitter above us in the African night are bigger suns than ours. Under Africa's pervasive spell, we feel we're only ants in an immense universe.

TRAVEL FACTS

Kenya Airways, 16 Conduit St., London W1 (01–409 0277)
Kuoni, Kuoni House, Dorking, Surrey (0306 885044)
Abercrombie & Kent, Sloane Sq. House, Holbein Pl., London SW1 (01–730 9600)
Thomson Holidays, Greater London House, Hampstead Rd., London NW1 (01–439 2211)
Kenya Tourist Office, 13 New Burlington St., London W1 (01–930 3837)

— CANYONLANDS, USA —

Lord! What a fearful place!

Our helicopter, twitchy as thistledown, leapt from the flat, pine-stippled plateau.

'And there she lies!' bellowed the pilot into my headset.

The Grand Canyon, one mile deep, yawned below like Hell's jaws snapping at a fallen spirit. Sinister at sunrise. Bloodthirsty as the Arizonian sun plunged behind a far horizon which looked like the Planet of the Apes.

Into this maw, striped pink, green, grey and chrome yellow, you could tip every temple, every cathedral built by puny man since he began to worship gods. They'd be a mere pile of pebbles in that horrendous chasm which extends longer than the road from Leeds to London.

At night I meet two deer grazing the hotel's lawn on the canyon's lip. At dawn, a long, grey animal with a bushy tail like a fox pauses, pad raised, to regard me, just another mammal speck beside this prehistoric gulf.

Dawn floods the multi-coloured bands of stone, each one signifying a million years or so. But who can grasp the meaning of aeons? Fossilised sharks' teeth tell of ancient oceans here before the world's convulsions and before the dinosaurs and pterodactyl roamed. Our history is simply the blink of someone's eye.

The hotel El Tovar is a splendid black-timbered Edwardian Scottish baronial shooting lodge. Maddeningly long delays for dinner with faint voices booming out names into a crowded bar, but it was excellent when we got it. 'Nice to have a gentleman from Europe,' the frilly little *maitre d'* bows, 'who knows about food and wine.'

But I was thinking with admiration about the one-armed major from the Civil War who last century led his surviving cockleshell heroes through the mad rapids of the river below. Repeatedly wrecked, always in awe, he was the first white explorer of the canyon. Don't miss the spectacular short film shown in the local village.

I'd flown to Phoenix with Kuoni to join a coach-load of elderly Americans on a week's tour of Canyonlands – 'Ninety per cent of our people are over fifty,' chirped our bright British-born guide. Tours up to two weeks include Los Angeles, Las Vegas and San Francisco.

Three other Brits less experienced in the States than I were soon amazed. 'Those Americans are so nice, so warm, so friendly!' The locals had come from fifteen different states. But Brits are rare in the Canyonlands, and though that's our loss, we get nicely spoilt by the Americans.

Phoenix has erupted since I was there five years ago riding a Quarter horse in the Catalina Mountains. Americans are awful about heartless cities and about city sprawl. Their boring grids of streets – don't they know nature abhors straight lines? – devour the desert and its crazy cacti. Automobile smog hovers already over the city. Northerners who sought Arizona's perfect air now move out to build two million dollar nests on the red flanks of Camelback Mountain just above our excellent resort, La Posada, in Scottsdale.

Americans may ruin their cities. But my goodness they save their countryside! Three glorious National Parks on the borders of Arizona and Utah: Page, Bryce and Zion. Here is the base of the potent Mormon cult. The scenery is naturally stupendous: wild, immense, and technicolored. Human intrusion, like a good teacher with a child, is minimal yet helpful. In tiny museums are courteous young guides. All of us, like not smoking in church, stand respectfully, speak quietly, in the great lap now enfolding us.

Whizzing across America's largest Indian reservation from Page, I see the remnants, taciturn and forlorn, of the Navajo nation. Lonely shacks, mobile homes, upturned old cars like dead turtles in the poor land. Behind a sheep flock, a young brave, with glossy raven hair bobbing, lopes sadly along. The desolate dispiritness is the same as that of South Africa's cursed Bantu homelands.

A well-to-do Negro couple on our coach murmur to me about America's guilt. 'Would our guide be so sympathetic about the Indians, do you think, if he wasn't born English?'

We stay at Page in the Lodge on the water's edge of Glen Canyon. Stone valleys have been dammed to change it into the glittering aquamarine and enormous Lake Powell. View from hotel superb: food ghastly, service worse. Where once were stones, flotillas of houseboats bob about like ducks on deep water. One houseboat, more of a mansion-liner, is large enough for a top deck swimming pool and its own helicopter pad. The rich fly up here in their private planes from Phoenix or Los Angeles.

I hitch a lift in a Cessna across this crazy new lakeland. We fly low over the *Mesas* which are small plateaux with their tops sliced off in other eras to make them look like fortresses. On the top of one gallops a herd of wild Indian horses. Deep down there is the sullen Indian reservation. It's like a landscape by Dali, with grotesque mountains cheapened by having been given by the guides silly little names like 'Mittens'.

We are led, as into a zoo, into an old lady's solitary *hogan*, her mud-hut igloo, to watch her comb and spin wool. She mutters in the Navajo tongue to our Americanised Indian girl guide. But she takes our dollars. Her eyes look like those of her compatriots at the wind-licked trading-post. They are as black and sad as a whipped lurcher's. I push out furiously into the marvellous hot October sun and the cool fresh air. Will the last specimens of white folk, I wonder, be thus exhibited to an alien race?

The other Parks are like the Greek's classical notion of Arcadia. Oak Creek Canyon and the little village of Sedona are charming. Bryce is fantastical. I leave the noisy coach-load to dream over its crazy pink ranges under the scent of the pines. Snow lies scattered in tiny patches. The sun stings. A girl in love coming to the brink cries: 'Oh, my God! It's crazy!' and grips her lover in a wild embrace.

But for me, Zion, in its sweet sunlit gulf, with its river gurgling, trees yellowing and lush grass, is a magic transportation into a sort of Shangri-la.

TRAVEL FACTS

Pan Am, 14 Old Park Lane, London W1 (01–409 0688)
British Caledonian, Caledonian House, Crawley, W. Sussex (01–688 4222)
Kuoni, Kuoni House, Dorking, Surrey (0306 885044)
Trekamerica, 62 Kenway Rd., London SW5 (01–373 5085)
United States Travel & Tourism Administration, 22 Sackville St., London W1 (01–439 7433)

— LANZAROTE —

'You'll either love it or loathe it,' laughed jolly plump Pat of OSL Villas at Lanzarote's pretty little airport.

Lots of green paint (a prescribed Lanzarotan colour) and masses of red flowers, a combination we see all over this island. First impressions of distant islands are generally airports. At Lanzarote you know immediately that people of taste are in charge. And friendly immigration and customs, too, what's more. Perhaps the officials know that only the nicer Brits come to Lanzarote.

But would we loathe or love it?

We laughed, too. For everyone says the same thing about this bizarre, black-earthed, volcanic isle snouting up into the wild Atlantic, as far south as Cuba.

The aircraft's steps at unlovable Luton had frozen solid to the door as if, like us, longing to be dragged away into the sunshine from Britain's biting January. The Caribbean and Florida are expensive. Lanzarote is cheap and offers you six hours of sun a day and temperatures averaging 75°F.

Hills like the Scottish border are sprinkled with what the travelling companion calls 'Bethlehem houses'. There are no high-rise horrors anywhere in villages or along the miles of empty coast. Concrete brutes are banned by the proud Lanzarotans.

The island is no more like its sister Canary, Tenerife, than North Cornwall is like Blackpool. So if you like the latter, leave Lanzarote alone.

Here, a strange race, possibly akin to the Vikings, once landed on what the ancient Greeks, more beautifully, called the Hesperides, supposing they were the peaks of the lost continent of Atlantis.

Some restless magic lingers. It's not a dosy place. Not all the locals are the dark, hawkish Spaniards fancied by the travelling companion. All is house-proud clean.

At Femès, a botanical dazzle around a fisherman's church topping a mountain pass, we could have eaten our tortilla off the road, let alone the bar floor, presided over by a first beady, then flirtatious, señora. Femès is comelier even than those Andulucian *pueblos blancos* I like. Climbing up through black fields, past white cottages with green woodwork and floods of red flowers, we whipped on dark glasses against the brilliance. We tried the wine made in the village (awful) and switched to a good Rioja from mainland Spain.

Miles below the pass, there stretches a plain like a dusty Western Ireland. Beyond twinkles the sea and the hidden white beaches of Papagayo. Maps show no roads across but we followed tracks like safari drivers and found a series of tiny coves reached by hopping across the rocks.

Even Papagayo's main beach has few amenities. The surf is terrific but no-one rents out boards. So we body-surfed in emerald waves more powerful than those of Southern Africa. Somersaulting through them, we were flung up the beach. There loomed sun-scarlet, naked Krauts, whose bloated bellies blessedly hid their nether horrors. But there were not many of these monsters. Nor was nudity *de rigueur*. Then pacing towards us came an Oxford don, pince-nez glinting, six feet or more of pale thin body, muttering to himself. It was only when he had passed, I realised that he, too, was starkers. But his self-containment in his thoughts made him unaware of corporal matters. Had he absent-mindedly forgotten to dress?

On the south-west coast the beaches are glistening coal-black beneath white spume, as if your eyes had suddenly switched off the colour. We press on to Playa Blanca.

On the horizon, as the setting sun plummets like a cricket ball, lies the next island of Fuertoventura, to which we were always going to take the next ferry and always missing the time or postponing the expedition. The mountains glow flamingo pink, then ruby and finally merge into the sapphire sky.

Near the tiny port we find our favourite restaurant called the Playa Blanca. Marvellous meals of deep Atlantic fish which make the warm Mediterranean rubbish taste like bony cotton wool. Beers first to slake thirsts after swimming. Grilled prawns in garlic butter. Plump firm soles. Salad and those strange Lanzarotan salty, wrinkled potatoes. Two bottles of Marqués de Caçares, one of the best wines from Spain, and all for a tenner for two of us.

We're living cheaply, too, in a pretty white apartment in the Oasis San Antonio just behind the Playa de los Pocillos. Self-catering, a ghastly phrase, is a growing thing as holidaymakers begin to resent the regimented cattle droves of huge hotels. The Oasis embraces two little pools and is so thick with flowering shrubs that we could only hear, and barely glimpse, our neighbours. 'More *Crossroads* than *Coronation Street*', murmured the travelling companion. All were Brits, middle-aged or young with families, and smilingly polite. 'Arthur heard that

Arsenal played,' yelled one sun-tanned matron to another on a balcony, 'thaw must have come back home'.

The southwards coastal strip looks tacky but hides some adequate shops and a surprisingly elegant drinking club which we found – as often turns out – by luck out of a disaster. We'd eaten a dreadful meal in a restaurant in Puerto del Carmen called El Burro.

'No like?' demanded the lordly patron sneering at our discarded plates piled with picked-at fish.

'No.'

'Not good?' he feigned astonishment. 'It was terrible,' I said. It was our only bad meal on Lanzarote. But the couple at the next table, who had suffered the foul food silently, so admired our courage that they took us off to the drinking club in Los Pocillos. Good restaurants opposite on the seafront include La Ola and the expensive and rather chi-chi La Gaviota.

Arrecife, the little capital, is all right but not much more. In a slummy street by the port is an excellent fish restaurant, Los Troncos, where fishermen and mongers haggle prices with merchants.

Northwards stands the solitary luxury hotel on the island, Las Salinas, managed by Sheraton, and though too large when viewed from afar, has been decorated in fairly natural hues, is far from an eyesore, and was refreshingly full of quiet guests – for once: large holiday resort hotels so seldom are.

Don't feel driven to visit the grim black-brown volcanic National Park of arid larva. It's like a desert ploughed by giants into a refuse tip. You crawl round nose-to-tail in an escorted convoy of goggling, flapping trippers.

Enraged by one old lady stalling her car again in front of me, I attempted to overtake her on the lava and quickly got stuck among the flying cinders.

The lunar landscape suggests how our world might end if loonies ever pressed the button. Thankfully, we scuttled off to swim privately at Papagayo and to lunch again on the terrace in the sun of the restaurant Playa Blanca.

TRAVEL FACTS

Iberia, 130 Regent St., London W1 (01–437 5622)
OSL/Wings, Travel House, Broxbourne, Herts (0992 87233)
Lanzarote Villas, Springfield Rd., Horsham, W. Sussex (0403 51304)
Thomson Holidays, Greater London House, Hampstead Rd., London NW1 (01–439 2211)
Spanish National Tourist Office, 57–58 St James's St., London SW1 (01–499 0901)

— EPCOT, Disneyworld —

Dashing out of Spaceship Earth, I call: 'Where's the boat for Italy:' The shimmering, pimpled orb stands ten storeys high, looks like a giant golfball and contains a corkscrew journey like Dr Who's through times past and future.

Silver-clad denizens of Earth Station, EPCOT's information centre, point the way between Communicore East and West, 'See the flag!'

Taut in the chill breeze (even in Florida, January isn't always balmy) the Stars and Stripes blows spotlit in the dusk over World Showcase Plaza. 'There's the Boat Dock.' I hurry on, late for my dinner date in Italy.

Beyond the lake lie not only Italy but Germany, Japan, China and France. I could walk round Mexico, Canada or the United Kingdom and the site where they will build Morocco.

Ivor in Wonderland has been totally disorientated all the lively day. EPCOT in Disneyworld is split in twain like real life: one half, things as we'd like to have them; the other, future hopes and fears. The south half round the lake is World Showcase, a sniff of other cultures in samples from foreign nations. The north is Future World, a glimpse in eight gigantic structures of how our grandchildren may contrive to live on this planet, if batty generals don't blow it apart.

Everything is in capitals and scrupulously clean. EPCOT, on its two-hundred-and-sixty-acre site, means Experimental Prototype Community of Tomorrow. Today, weirdly dressed youths, some disguised as French Legionnaires, pick up every shred of candyfloss and every butt end as soon as it hits the ground.

The long, low boat glides up like a futuristic Thames launch. I'm its only passenger. Ironically, Future World closes at 8 pm. But, in the different countries of World Showcase, the eat-spots go munching on. My pilot is a merry-eyed Moroccan student, limpingly learning English. So we prattle in French.

'Why not dine in France then?' He points half right across the lapping water towards the reproduction French Quarter. There's a mini Eiffel Tower and the glow from those ornate lamps behind the Champs Elysées.

But I'd lunched in France in what felt as cold as any boulevard café. Before, I'd seen a fabulous film touching, like a deft Impressionist, on the glories of France.

'Makes you real want to go there,' murmured a New Yorker to her husband. It sure did. For all our arguments with our European neighbours, aren't we lucky to have them on our doorstep?

Then I shopped for chocolates in a reproduction Les Halles. Lunch wasn't cheap either, but America isn't. I was peeved with Madame at the receipt of custom.

'I'd just like an omelette and some wine,' I said.

Madame, at the desk, her French nose blue with cold, retorted: 'For snacks, try pub anglais!'

Disney's Hollywood set designers have done a grand job. In United Kingdom are bits of Tudor, Queen Anne, Victorian street lamps, a red pillar box, and shops selling Pringle, tartans, sporting prints and shortbread. A patient queue waited to squeeze into the pub.

Inside the crush, frothy American college girls were chatting up the jolly young English barmen selling Bass. There were Americans, in their silly caps, rooting for either 'Reds' or 'Raiders', with shouts at their rivals across the pseudo-Edwardian brasswork. The Super Bowl – more hyped to four times as many millions than our Cup Final – was happening in dreadful Tampa that weekend.

There were also some bemused English, humbly waiting for cottage pie in the pub's dining room and feeling as we too often do in threatening 'Abroad' the need for mates who speak as we do. There weren't many. Most Brits in Florida in winter lurk in the hideous Blackpool wedges of Miami. But that is only forty minutes south by plane. They're missing something literally marvellous in EPCOT.

I dock opposite Italy and find my host with his tempestuous Sicilian wife. She manages Alfredo's thrumming, singing restaurant: fettuccine – delicate as it should be – and some sensibly coarse red Barolo to sluice it down.

I'd dreaded all this would be like Disneyland in California. But even its setting is another world. Disneyland is gripped by grim and smoggy Californian urban sprawl. EPCOT, near Disneyworld, has been built from virgin pine forests and empty swamps in the middle of central Florida.

'It was Walt's last dream,' murmurs a clean, earnest man in the Press office. Old Walt always knew his onions. He bought not only space here but convenience for Florida's seaside resorts. Orlando, the nearest airport, joins my top five favourites of the world.

I'd planned half a day for EPCOT. I was mad. I spent three and long to go back, bringing my children.

First, I went to Mexico. It is perpetually set at evening in a country market place with Americans buzzing about buying. Or are they, too, like so much else, magically automated Disney waxworks? I peer closely in the dimness into the face of one. Will it move? Speak?

'Want sumpin', bud?' it snaps. Threatened, Americans wax fearfully angry.

I swiftly turn to admire the backcloth of what, like all else here, is theatre: a Mayan pyramid, a rumbling volcano and lightning flashing in an indigo sky. In front, a brown band enters, singing Spanish love songs. But they are real and so are the visitors eating early Mexican lunches in the candlelit Cantina San Angel.

'Oh, see The Land, man,' urged my Bahamian taxi driver, taking me from Orlando to Trust House Forte's upmarket hotel, the Viscount, on Lake Buena Vista. 'Journey through The Land, man, and it'll tell you how everything was grown, is grown, and will be growing when we're dead and gone.'

Was that a real lake under my hotel window or yet another Disney creation? In this weird World, I have to nick myself shaving to be sure that it isn't a robot writer scowling back.

TRAVEL FACTS

Pan Am, 14 Old Park Lane, London W1 (01–409 0688)
British Airways, PO Box 10, Heathrow Airport, Hounslow, Middx
(01–759 2525)
Virgin Holidays, Saxon House, Stephenson Way, Crawley,
W. Sussex (0293 775511)
Kuoni, Kuoni House, Dorking, Surrey (0306 885044)
Enterprise, 17–27 High St., Hounslow, Middx (01–409 0688)
United States Travel & Tourism Administration, 22 Sackville St.,
London W1 (01–439 7433)

— THAILAND —

'There's another famous English writer staying in my hotel,' the manager of the splendid Royal Cliff most agreeably informed me. Naturally, I leapt at this bait like a silly trout. We were eating a delicious Thai lunch at Pattaya on the coast and sat in the corner restaurant overlooking the swimming pools and splendorous gardens. I love Thai food for it combines the best of Chinese and Indian. This isn't surprising for from those roots grew the Thai nation.

I guessed at several good British authors.

'No. Barbara Cartland.'

I was astonished. Pattaya, still so pretty by day, was turned from a fishing village into an 'R and R' base for wretched GI's flown for weekends out of the pointless hell of Vietnam. At night, however, the sea front and the roads off it are a winking strip of hookers, paederasts and transvestites.

I felt this was not quite Miss Cartland's scene and said so. I was careful, naturally, to omit the word 'another' when quoting the dapper dandy of a manager. Miss Cartland does not like to be compared, let along paralleled, and my seventeen books so far – all quite unlike hers – represent about her output per month.

'Dahling!' she cried, instructing her nice son to pour me more champagne in their suite, 'Don't you know that the only place in the whole *world* to eat good French food in warm weather in January is the Oriental in Bangkok!'

I hadn't thought of it that way. A few years earlier I'd been able to afford a couple of nights in the Oriental, widely held to be the world's finest hotel. The week before driving down to Pattaya I had dined with English friends in the Oriental's restaurant across the broad river, slipping over the warm scented water in a hotel boat. We had eaten Thai food on the terrace at midnight in January and the couple, both on a second marriage, had said, beaming like Cheshire cats, that they felt as happy with one another as if they had each won a huge football pool. 'Being happily married is mostly luck,' they said and kissed.

This time I stayed in Bangkok at the Oriental's challenger, the silk-ceilinged Regent, opposite the Royal racecourse. What an unusual delight after the long haul from London to have a Thai maiden welcoming me in my room with tea, then kneeling to change my shoes for slippers. And embarrassment, too, for those of us unused to such attendance.

The Regent was being taken over by a famous hotel group but this didn't ruffle the calm of its enormous foyer. I cannot use the American 'lobby' for a pillared entrance hall as large as a football pitch and decorated like a palace. Behind the foyer is its French restaurant (good) and round the corner the Spice Market restaurant serving superb Thai food. Here the sensible rule of eating in France applies: take the menu of the day. Delicious little dishes pop up in fragrant groups and, better still, you're offered sample tastings first.

Bangkok, dead flat, five million strong, is golden with temples, jostling with motorised tricycle-taxis and a-flutter with silk. I buy my bolt of the lovely stuff (this time for my elder daughter's first dance) from Shinawat out in the suburbs. The store is by appointment to the King and less expensive than the better known Thai silk firm founded by an American flyer.

Old blue buses bursting at the seams are buzzed by manic mopeds along the broad boulevards and, on the great grey river with its Far Eastern smell, the lumbering barges are buzzed like wasps by the 'long-tailed speedboats'.

I was looked after by the busy laughing Mr Gordon George, Indian-bred and Thai-reared, who had just started his own eponymous travel agency. 'Scotsman in British army probably came to my grandmother,' he chortles when I ask about his unlikely name. Then he adds, 'If Thai person sees cobra and Indian at same time, he first kills Indian!' Squeals of laughter.

His driver, Bandit (it means scholar) is, like nearly all Thais, calm, courteous and kind. He takes me round the temples in his red BMW. The famed Golden Buddha is found surprisingly tucked away in a tiny temple off a back street in Chinatown. Solid gold, he was coated in cement to be smuggled down from the invaded north. We doff shoes. Bandit places his palms together and bobs his head to the Buddha. I follow suit and learn to use this charming Thai greeting and the words for 'Thank you' which sound like 'Karpoon krap'. The Buddha is smiling serenely as if men's foibles faintly amuse him.

Parents used to bring up baby Brits always to say 'Please' and 'Thank you'. The same phrases in a foreign language bring smiles to strangers and ease the traveller's path. The fact that you have bothered, however coarse your accent, means they will try too.

In the days when Britain was a major nation, it was the officer, sahib, and bwana classes who dreadfully shouted English at the natives. Those classes are extinct but their shameful habits have been inherited by our factory workers abroad. At least the latter possess one sound excuse for public failure: our state education thinks, like an old Blimp, that learnin' a foreign lingo is a waste o' time.

'Ninety-eight per cent Buddhists in Thailand,' says Bandit. 'Some Muslims still allowed four wives. Royal family only recently gave up concubines.'

In the 'European Palace', where the previous king was assassinated in 1946, stands a row of trim little nineteenth century cottages built for the royal concubines. 'Only foreign guests staying there now. Your Queen stayed there!' This thought tickled Bandit.

Rising at dawn in a pearl mist across the water we phut-phutted up river and then wound off along the *klongs*. Down these exotic waterways, the city as instantly turns to jungle as turning the pages of a book. Temples pass, glittering in gold and in green and blue cut glass. Floating markets coagulate under tall palm trees at crossroads of the klongs. From rows of wooden shacks on stilts people emerge to wash: their vegetables, dogs, chickens and themselves. The Thais' scrupulous cleanliness makes me feel scruffy.

On the main river's far bank Bandit takes breakfast from a stall but sends me up the vertiginous Temple of the Dawn – gigantic pagodas almost as ugly as the Albert Memorial. Below me I see saffron-robed monks pacing in their monastery garden.

The Royal Palace in the city is a grand assembly of temples, golden-domed and golden-breasted. An enormous fresco, painted two centuries ago and continually flaking, winds round wall after wall like the Bayeux tapestry. It shows in a fairy-tale Indian setting the saga of the Good King (shown in white) and his support group of friendly monkeys fending off the attacks of the Bad King (green) with all his wily tricksters. Groups of sweet Thai children goggle along. Bandit talks of 'Teacher Anna' but says 'Your film *Anna and King of Siam* not allowed in Thailand, so no-one knows if true'. He notes my doubt and adds quickly, 'But Thais getting more democratic every year'.

Mr Gordon George himself escorts me round the notorious district of Pat Pong. He is known everywhere and may be disappointed that I am not instantly suited and ready to leave him for at least an hour. Bikini-clad girls with numbers (up to eighty in one bar) pinned to them like competitors in horse trials climb up in shifts of half a dozen to dance on the glass tops. Some, weary or bored, simply move their hips and feet to the music looking down languidly at us. Other young triers work with gusto giving us the eye. 'Not expensive,' murmurs Mr

George, inviting two across to our table for a drink, 'and if you want longer, you may have next door hotel room.'

But the girl snuggling against me coos, 'You go Pattaya? You take me Pattaya. I make you very happy.'

The squads on the bar top change every fifteen minutes. 'Best see ladies move, not sit,' says Gordon George, 'you tell much more by how ladies move.' And I thought suddenly, and in a totally different context, how right he was. Women betray their characters in their walk.

Then on to a far classier place. Girls of outstanding quality and beauty (so unlike the raddled creatures of many *exhibitions fantastiques*) are doing astounding things with objects more at home in larder or kitchen. 'But they are beautiful,' I murmur. Some blow whistles and other instruments but not with their mouths. This whistling suddenly waxes urgent. In a flash the girl displaying herself on stage vanishes and is replaced immediately by three girls at least partially covered and pretending to dance with the sort of modesty you'd find in a common or garden strip. The door bursts open. Police swarm in and glower. Gordon George has vanished, too, but only into the back bar where I, ducking under tables, find him drinking quite legally. 'Ah,' he says watching me pop up, 'I see you know about police raids.'

The arms of the law soon withdraw. Within five minutes the lovely legs of naughtiness resume erotica. At my side at the large bar is an odd couple: a grey-bearded Englishman who's lived in Bangkok for years, and his aristocratic young French girlfriend. Together they study the performers on the bright lit stage with the critical attention of country folk at agricultural shows. I had never seen another woman so plainly interested in such sexual displays without becoming as plainly turned on. But the French aristo coolly pointed out some particular points of prowess.

There seem to be no plain Thai girls. There are only the smooth laughing young or bent old crones. Were the latter the former when the American troops were flown in to the beaches of Pattaya?

The warm sea below the luxurious Royal Cliff hotel is choppy one day. Thais expertly windsurf over the water towards the tropical islands. Tourists paraglide. Over the jade water gaudy fishing boats pull away. I plan to sail out there but the days have fled.

Flying on to Singapore, I sit next to a Singhalese protestant clergyman going to an ecumenical conference. 'I'm no prude,' he says, talking of Thailand, 'but isn't it demeaning picking those girls like chickens from those glass coops? And the Japanese do most terrible things to them. In that fire last week in a Bangkok brothel they'd chained the girls up and left them, you know.'

I did not. 'I like the Thais. I like their smiles, their past, their religions, their food,' I said. And left it there.

TRAVEL FACTS

Thai International, 41 Albemarle St., London W1 (01–491 7953)

British Airways, PO Box 10, Heathrow Airport, Hounslow, Middx (01759 2525)

Jetset, Jetset House, 74 New Oxford St., London WC1 (01–631 0501)

Kuoni, Kuoni House, Dorking, Surrey (0306 885044)

Champagne Connection, 93 Newman St., London W1 (01–631 3650)

Tourism Authority of Thailand, 9 Stafford St., London W1 (01–499 7679)

— NEW YORK —

The tall lawyer stooped like a stalk over my two daughters on his green Kentucky lawn, warning them about their first visit to New York.

'Up there,' he said, clenching his lips and jutting his jaw so that his words rattled out like colourless cardboard pellets, 'New Yorkers speak like this.'

The girls stared up at him wide-eyed like goslings.

'People in New York,' he went on, 'are often cross, always in a hurry, and so, I am afraid, very often rude.'

'Why?' asked the logical twelve year old. The eleven year old's face quickened with anticipation as if before competing on her pony in some exciting gymkhana.

'There are far too many people in New York City,' explained the lawyer in the tranquil drawl of the hospitable South. 'And there isn't room nor time enough for them all to make a living.'

We feared the worst and sometimes found it. The people at La Guardia as we pattered about looking for our luggage were tight-lipped, snappy and unintelligible. Yes, they were rude. The first grunting taxi driver in his grotesquely battered yellow cab set the general pattern: crouching, sweating, growling men with little English; names displayed with terrifying identikit pictures on their jolting, burning dashboards – Russians, Cubans, Israelis, Puerto Ricans, Greeks, and one blue-black hyped-up gentleman from Haiti singing in full blast French a native calypso. One very nice Scotsman drove us home from the theatre and there was a jolly black man whose name was White.

'If I don't answer,' read the sign in the oven-hot taxi, leaping over the collapsing roads, 'it's not because I'm deaf. I just don't like talking.'

He stuck a paw backwards around his bullet-proof window for the money for the toll bridge. Manhattan, like a giant's fortress loomed to our left beyond the East River. 'It looks,' the children said, 'just like on telly. But hotter and bigger and crosser.' Few New York taxi drivers know where they're going. How blessed are we in London when we can afford a taxi. And even with our absurdly numbered, wandering, and changing one-way streets, we can give the most remote address and relax. Never so in New York. The girls were quicker than I in picking up the patois.

They grasped that it's hopeless in Manhattan to ask even for the well-known, excellent Halloran House Hotel on Lexington Avenue. ''Lex' 'tween 49th and 48th Streets,' the girls learned to snap out.

The taxis in a yellow surf spurt from one stop light to the next but we always find the hospitable Halloran House.

The girls also quickly understood Manhattan's logical, but boring, grid system for roads. 'All the avenues go north and south, Daddy, and the streets go east and west from Fifth Avenue.'

At the Halloran House all is friendly. My daughters, nicely unspoilt and totally unused to hotels, begin to lug their suitcases across the steaming sidewalk. No one but a damn fool or a divorced dad confined to split school holidays ever tries holidays in New York between June and October.

The taxi driver silently grabs his fare. When I first flew into Fleet Street from my snug executive's desk in the City that famous foreign correspondent, now good novelist, Noel Barber, told me, 'I get all my best quotes from taxi drivers and always use the local telephone directory to get some reasonable sounding names and addresses to attribute them to!' He would not have got far in New York City.

But inside the cool lobby of the hotel, the mood is instantly warmer. A tall waistcoated bellhop with a white carnation swoops up all our suitcases under an arm.

'First time in N'Yawk?' he asks us. The elevator is swooshing up to the twenty-second floor and Jane's ears pop. She nods. 'Better tie up your shoe lace then,' suggests the bellhop amiably, 'N'Yawk's a bad place to have an accident!'

The girls have never slept higher than three floors up. Will they be dizzy? They dash from one bedroom to another squealing, '*Six* telephones! *Three* bedrooms. *Gosh!*' The Halloran House, fifty years old and quite recently redone, has done us proud.

The girls ring each other up and me in silly foreign voices while we're showering. They chat to Room Service, occasionally complaining, 'Daddy, I can't understand what he says. I think he must be German or something.' Having been only to Kentucky before where everyone speaks the pleasantest sort of English and have agreeably easy British names, my daughters are baffled by this polyglot city. They cannot possibly say of it as they said of my beloved Kentucky, 'But this isn't Abroad, Daddy, it's full of all your friends!' I have just two good friends and my literary agent who live in Manhattan and a few more out on Long Island. But that's all.

Three continental breakfasts plus orange juices and various cokes and whiskys over the weekend cost me £120. 'Where's the Empire State, Daddy? What are those two huge ones at the bottom?' – (The World Trade Centre towers) 'And what's that huge one near here with the top sort of shaved off?'

I am absolutely silent. I fend off further difficult questions. From up here New York looks wondrous, even beautiful.

'Hungry?' I ask. 'Starving! That lunch on the aeroplane from Louisville was almost as bad as Air France.'

Airlines should, as banks do now, and as Jesuits have always done, woo our children as their future clients. Once Air France (who normally feed you well – especially on their internal Paris–Nice route) had offered my children, due to upset schedules, Heathrow's packaged plastic muck. The girls have not forgotten it and may never do so.

Sweating like footballers, we weave through the crowds on the still grilling sidewalks. We peep into Bloomingdale's. The girls are impressed. 'It's a bit like Harrods. Is it expensive? Let's leave shopping till our last day.' They observed that prices in America had doubled since their first visit to Kentucky two years before. What a bargain the States were when a pound bought $2.40 and I could afford to take my Manhattan friend out to '21'. At that rate of exchange (ludicrously high) dinner for three at one of New York's top spots cost me £80 in English terms. The current rate made it £137. Never forget to discount what seem only small fluctuations in the rate.

We dive into the cool of Hamburger Heaven and sit at the marble counter. Everyone else is ordering their meals in three seconds and eating them in a minute. We ponder over burgers, milk shakes, pies, omelettes, and ice creams. The black lady is very patient. Then she shouts our orders down a telephone. She has that pinkish-saffron overlay of colour on face and hair that I only see in New York. '*Shure* you want milk shake *and* pie *and* ice cream *and* a double beefburger, honey?' she asks one daughter.

Later without request, nor commenting on our defeat, she pops the vast uneaten slabs of our meal into a bag for us. 'Take that home, honey, and thank you for bringing your two lovely daughters in here.' The Burger Heaven blowout cost $20.

For the theatre – Twiggy and Tommy Tune in *My One and Only* – we are picked up by an English girlfriend, an artist who lives in New York, but who has only that afternoon returned jet-lagged from two months holiday in Scotland. She is arguing with a taxi driver outside the

Halloran House. 'Oh, my God,' she gasps, kissing us all, 'it really is a culture shock coming back to New York.'

Next day it's frenzied sightseeing starting with a whizz up to the roof of the World Trade Centre. 'Better than the Empire State,' says the merry girl from the *I Love New York* office. 'You'll see fifty miles around (like London to Oxford), on a clear day.' It is clear. And it is thrilling.

A babel of tongues from other awe-struck visitors on the top. 'We're the only people here who aren't foreign,' says Jane. I see exactly what she means. However feeble in practice the special relationship does spring from shared beginnings. But Kate corrects her, 'Here we're foreign, too, though'. I know a Welsh peer who, like Nancy Mitford's 'Uncle Matthew', never leaves England for holidays. He grunts 'I had enough of bloody Abroad in the war.'

The Staten Island ferry (25¢ the return ride) reminds us we're on a huge continent for it's full of American sightseers who know even less about New York than we do. 'Where're you from?' they ask one another. 'Is that Noo Jersey? That Governor's Island? You from England?' They are from New Mexico, Montana, and New Orleans – further from New York than London lies from Moscow.

On the ferry's bows the girls watch a strange, sad lady in a scarlet dress singing mournful Spanish songs to herself. Then the boat barges into the wooden piers of Staten Island.

After lunch we go to New York's latest bit of pretty re-development: South Street Seaport which has all the vivacity of an Italian town.

Then the highlight: helicoptering around Manhatten. The sky is buzzing with other choppers. An Italian family of three shares ours. The fat Mama crosses herself as we dip, drop, bank and swoop around the Statue of Liberty and then flutter away high over Broadway. Vertigo grips me. But 'There's our hotel!' squeak the girls, dangerously gripping the door handle as the helicopter heals over at forty-five degrees to give those who can face it a better view.

That night to *A Chorus Line* on its record breaking run. Like the curate's egg, I thought, and feeling guilty that some parts were too naughty for the girls. Then dinner at Sardi's spotting stars among the cartoons and in the flesh. The bill for four is $120. The service is superb. Beneath the ice-cold air conditioning Jane shivers. I put my jacket round her small shoulders and then a table napkin on top. Our red-coated waiter smiles and observes courteously, 'Ah, the latest fashion from Bonwit Teller!'

On a day of green peace on Long Island, we stroll around

Westbury, a mansion built by the Phipps family only thirty years earlier but in William and Mary style, and now very much a stately home, lapped by gardens designed by an American Capability Brown. How Croesus-rich that family must have been to have lived here in such style well into the 1950s and with what good taste. English, of course. Furniture by Chippendale and Hepplewhite. Pictures by Constable, Gainsborough, and Reynolds. I feel immensely proud that Britain has produced such beauty and immensely sad that, fallen on bad times, we've had to sell them. We are to America as ancient Greece was to Rome.

From the seaside on the north shore we see Connecticut and there's the start of the Atlantic where thousands of miles, a different world away, but only a month earlier the girls were surfing in North Cornwall.

Our last dinner is at that wonderfully crazy establishment Maxwell's Plum, haunt of celebrities. 'Aren't the women smartly dressed,' says Kate, 'far smarter than the men! And look,' she whispers, 'that's Crissy Evert Lloyd at the very next table.' Hand in hand with her husband John, the star of the tennis courts smiles at my daughters.

Next day, after shopping, the children finally vanished up the fallopian tube at JFK leading them into their TWA jumbo's belly. It is 7 pm and 98°F at Kennedy. Over there in England where they go to school, it will be midnight and under 50°.

My downcast spirits are uplifted by a concert that night in the Lincoln Center. The splendid American national anthem played with vigour – for it is the start of the orchestra season – stirs me mightily. On this extraordinary nation with all its virtues and faults we must depend. But they understand our mutual debt very much better down there in the green peace of Kentucky. There I sit by the wide Ohio, sixteen hundred miles from the sea, yet broader than is the Thames at London. I'm reading Chekhov's short stories again; he might have enjoyed the irony of this independent Englishman's devotion to America.

TRAVEL FACTS

British Airways, PO Box 10, Hounslow, Middx (01–759 2525)
TWA, Oxford St., London W1 (01–636 4090)
Virgin, 7th floor, Sussex House, High St., Crawley, W. Sussex
(01–938 3611)
B&B: Home Base Holidays, 7 Park Ave., London N13 (01–886
8752)
B&B: Urban Ventures, 139 Round Hey, Liverpool (051–220 5848)
United States Travel & Tourism Administration, 22 Sackville St.,
London W1 (01–439 7433)

— HONG KONG —

This dinner party in Hong Kong is like those I enjoy along the upper reaches of Chelsea. But that's the South China sea out there and the brooding Republic of China, waiting to take back its child which the British fostered and turned into a capitalist.

Chinese servants flit about, silently serving delicious European food flown in from Australia and California. The company is English, Chinese, German, Eurasian. The men are in shirtsleeves. Their women, twice as elegant as in London, richly dress up.

A spry young English merchant banker assures me across his dinner table: 'A man of *reasonable* intelligence who works at it should be able to make a million pounds out here in six or seven years.' No one, bar me, shows any surprise. He passes the champagne.

'How *many* millionaires?' He repeats my question. 'Why, my bank manager has three hundred clients each worth £30 million or more!'

Below us once stood the old Repulse Bay Hotel with its ticking fans and crimson lights, now long pulled down like everything else in Hong Kong where to be ten years old is to be out of date. The nights boom with the sound of rebuilding. On the beach below stands the garish temple of the Chinese sea gods where I once walked hand in hand and a touch of love with someone who lived here.

What contrasts! Just behind the grand hotels, the great high-rise banks and trading houses, I step immediately into Chinatown. Whiffs of jasmine and joss sticks, Cantonese cooking on the street braziers crackling at street corners. Barely a word, barely a Hollywood cinema poster, in English. Shops flame with Chinese symbols, voices babble, hawk, argue – everything's haggled over.

One jostling block from the gliding Rolls-Royces of Hong Kong's sterling millionaires, traders squat on the stones of Cat Street flogging antiques, some of which presumably fell off the backs of rickshaws.

Glamorous hotels front squalid doss-houses, everywhere fluttering with drying laundry. Beautiful cosmopolitan people drift into the Captain's Bar in the Mandarin in Central; a quarter mile away, the redlight district of Wanchai honks and tonks, known to every poxy sailor round the globe.

Yet in the pleasant countryside flowers bloom all year and in Big Wave Bay on the island's south eastern corner we swam at the end of

January. The girl wasn't surprised. 'Don't you know the sea here's warmer in winter than Bondi Beach in summer?' The South China Sea in Hong Kong's brief winter from mid-January to early March is warmer, too, than the North Sea at the height of our summer.

I like the archipelago which at dawn reminds me of the Aegean. We set off to explore Cheung Chau Island, an hour's trip by ferry west past the latest immigrants' settlements, then south-west towards Lantau Island. On the island's harbour-side the market's in full babble. Brown chicken are cooped in huge bowl-like baskets. An old crone sells fish and sea snakes. Chow dogs saunter. Pet birds hop in cages. Bright green vegetables glisten on stalls. Someone says, 'The Chinese enjoy shopping so much they go twice daily for the fun of it'. Two men polish a new sampan with a power-sander making the air sweet with wood scent. Incense wafts from a temple by a playground where school children leap at basketball.

Bamboo shoots burn in the dark temple. On a bench before the altar an old man kneels, bows thrice, then casts two lucky pieces of wood: two smooth sides up mean good luck: two rough sides bad; one each is so-so.

Behind, a family builds a huge high-pooped new junk on a slip-way. Down the shopping alleys tea, sizzling prawns and pork in rolls of batter are sold from stalls. There's one rich house, with lion-dogs at its door of open ornate poles, flanked by poems from that part of mainland China whence the family originated. I pry into the large hall. It's kept, rich Chinese fashion, as the ancestor shrine.

I drive through the tunnel under the harbour to Kowloon-side and lunch at Shatin, the world's newest, grandest racecourse. Here, they simply sliced the tops off great hills and filled up an entire sea bay to lay out the track and construct the grandstands.

The Royal Hong Kong Jockey Club, together with the Hong Kong and Shanghai Bank and the Governor, still constitute the colony's triple power. 'But the greatest of all three,' a Chinese tycoon whispers to me, 'is the Jockey Club.' All the top tycoons are members.

I'm the only Englishman at this table for sixteen on top of the gigantic grandstand, where so recently the sea was lapping. Chinese members outnumber Europeans four to one. These vastly rich men possess an oriental swanlike superiority; they glide with grace. I feel a crude peasant at a royal reception, aware that China was a civilised society a thousand years before our early British ancestors started to grunt about in woad.

Here's a young Chinese tycoon educated at Millfield. 'They didn't know quite how to treat me,' he laughs. 'Whether to snap their fingers at me like a Chinese waiter or ask my father for £50,000 more to educate more poor English boys!'

'Until a century ago', he reminds me, 'our emperors wouldn't let barbarian Europeans set foot in China!'

He has two architects over to lunch in Hong Kong. They come from the Republic where he is building hotels. Suave and distinguished, they were imprisoned during the Cultural Revolution and made to work on farms for eight years. 'But we Chinese are very patient,' they smile at me. These intellectuals with ivory faces, wearing tunics of dove-grey silk, look at me with absolute confidence and a tinge of pity.

Two beautiful, brilliant Chinese girls come to the table. One heads a stockbroking business, the other is a leading barrister. One was schooled in England, the other married an American. But European women seldom marry Chinese men.

Rolls-Royces in a purring herd ooze away from Shatin racecourse. There are more Rolls here per square mile than anywhere else in the world. One solid gold one cost £1.25 million. Its number plate alone – lucky because it carries four 'eights' – cost £100,000. 'Fours' are bad numbers; they mean death.

A dashing English bachelor volunteers to whirl me round the city's low life. He shows me the sampan brothels oiling about on the scum-green water of the Typhoon Harbour. And then the dingy 'Fish-roll Stalls' once busily staffed, he tells me, with nimble-fingered, exquisite Thai girls.

'But the police have cracked down on all that,' he sighs. 'And I love Asian girls. So smooth, and they never smell. Those Thai girls used to make £20,000 in a few years here for their marriage dowries. Then they went back to Bangkok, got married and got bored!'

One Chinese girl in a fish-roll stall was an American's nanny in the daytime. Another worked in Hong-Kong's equivalent of Harrods.

He points out, too, but steers us well clear of the dreaded 'Ballrooms' where Chinese whores are viciously guarded by their bare-waisted heavily-tattooed minders. Instead, we drift into an elegant 'Topless'. From one mirrored room to another octagonal bars like a honeycomb are presided over by naked females surrounded by goggling drones.

I find the dark lady in the first bar so repellent that I'm relieved when my guide murmurs to me: 'She was a man till she had the sex change last year.'

Suddenly, from the adjoining bar, arises the slurred shouting of our National Anthem. We weave in to investigate. A very drunk Englishman, endeavouring to stand erect, and partly recognising me, greets me with the shout, 'What'll win the Grand National, blast you?' He then crashes on top of a titanic negress who might, so great is her protuberant belly, be totally naked.

But behind the counter of this octagonal bar, and laughing happily, stands a young blonde of great beauty structured to dominate a centrefold. The cold air conditioning does cheeky wonders for her breasts about which Solomon would have sung. Bending closer, I murmur compliments, and touch.

'Darling, how sweet of you.' She speaks, amazingly, with the voice of a Sloane Ranger. Germans, Australians, Scandinavians and Britons crane over her as she raffles her knickers for ten dollars a time. She glows like a flame within this close circle of desire.

'Why,' I naturally ask her later, 'do you do it?'

'I just love all you men lusting all round me, darling.'

Later still, finding that her luxury flat is near our excellent Excelsior Hotel, I'm bold enough to offer her a lift home when her job's done.

'Really sweet of you, love. But I've my own Ferrari.'

TRAVEL FACTS

Cathay Pacific, 7 Appletree Yard, Duke of York St., London SW1 (01–930 7878)

British Caledonian, Caledonian House, Crawley, W. Sussex (01–668 4222)

British Airways, PO Box 10, Heathrow Airport, Hounslow, Middx (01–759 2525)

Sovereign Worldwide, 17–27 High St., Hounslow, Middx (01–987 4545)

Jetset, Jetset House, 74 New Oxford St., London WC1 (01–631 0501)

P & O Air Holidays, 77 New Oxford St., London WC1 (01–831 1234)

Hong Kong Tourist Office, 125 Pall Mall, London SW1 (01–930 4775)

— INDEX —

Abercrombie & Kent 164
Abu Simbel (Egypt) 144–5
Adamson, Joy 163
Aegean Turkish Holidays 132, 135
Africa *see* Egypt, Kenya, Mauritius, Morocco
Ag. Georgios (Gr.) 117
Agadir (Mor.) 119
Aigues Mortes (Fr.) 88
Ainhoa (Sp.) 109
Air Europe 38, 64, 69, 118
Air France 17, 26, 34, 39, 41, 52, 89, 182
Air France Holidays 41, 52, 89
Air Jamaica 151
Air Malta 127
Air Mauritius 160
Air Portugal 81, 93, 106
Alayor (Men.) 75
Albufeira (Port.) 106
Alburquerque, Duke of 36
Algaiarens (Men.) 77
Algarve 103–6
    Albufeira 106
    beaches 104–6
    Cape St Vincent 104
    Carvoeiro 106
    golf 103, 105
    Lagoa 106
    Lagos 104
    Loulé 106
    Milfontes Vila Nova 103, 104
        castle 104
    Monte Gordo 106
    Portimao 105
    Quarteira 106
    Quinta do Lago 105
    Sagres Baleeira hotel 104

São Bras 106
Santiago 103
    castle 103
surfing 106
tennis 105
Vale do Lobo 105
Vilamoura 105
    Dom Pedro hotel 105
Vila Real 106
wind surfing 104
Alitalia 6, 21
Amboise (Fr.) 14
America, United States of *see* Canyonlands; Epcot; Mississippi, river; New York
American Express 9, 13, 21
Amsterdam 10–13
    'brown bars'/cafés/restaurants
        Gijsbrecht van Amstel 12
        Hotel American 11
        Oyster Bar 11
        Speciall 12
    canals
        Heren 12
        Princess 10
    museums
        Rijksmuseum 11
        Van Gogh 11
    Pulitzer hotel 10
    'red light' districts 10–11
Andalucia 111–14
    Arcos 112
        castle 112
    beaches 111
    bull fighting 113
    Castellar 113
    El Bosqué 111–12
        Hostal inn 111–12
    Grazalema 112

Hostal inn 113
Guadalquivir, river 111
Jerez 111
Jimena 113, 114
   castle 113
Puerto de Santa María 111
Ronda 113
   Reina Victoria hotel 113
San Roque 114
Sanlúcar 111
Ubrique 113
vineyards 111
Andalucian Express Train 114
Angers (Fr.) 14
Anglia Holidays 98
Annigoni 6
Antibes (Fr.) 49
Antoinette, Marie 24, 39–40
Arcos (Sp.) 112
Arecife (Lanz.) 170
Argolian Gulf (Gr.) 57
Argos (Gr.) 58
Arilas (Gr.) 117
Arizona *see* Canyonlands
Arles (Fr.) 86–7
Arrow Holidays 106
Arta (Maj.) 68
artists *see* Annigoni; Caravaggio;
   Chagall; Michelangelo;
   Millet; Rembrandt;
   Tintoretto; Van Gogh;
   Vermeer
Ascain (Fr.) 107
Asia *see* Hong Kong; Thailand;
   Turkey
Asklepios (Gr.) 59
Aspirot, Madame 107
Aswan (Egypt) 144–5
Athens (Gr.) 57
Auden, W. H. 8
Aulan, Marquis d' 33
Austria *see* Vienna
Austrian Airlines 9
Austrian Tourist Office 9

Avis car hire 3, 35, 39, 59, 91, 92
Ay (Fr.) 31

B&B: Home Base Holidays 185
B&B: Urban Ventures 185
Bad Godesberg (Ger.) 97
Baden-Powell, Robert 163
Bahamas 152–6
   beaches 154–5
   Freeport 155
      Atlantic Beach Hotel 155
   Nassau 154
      Cellar restaurant 155
      Graycliff hotel 154
   New Providence Island 154
   Paradise Island 155
   snorkelling 155
Bahamas Tourist Office 156
Bangkok (Thai.) 175–8
Barber, Noel 181
Barbizon 39–41
   hotels
      Clef d'Or 41
      Le Bas-Breau 40
   Fontainebleau château 39
   Fontainebleau forest 39
   Ile de Beauté restaurant 41
   Musée Ganeé 41
   Vaux-le-Vicomte château 40
   Versailles 40
Basle (Switz.) 94
Basque country 107–10
   Ainhoa
      Ithurria restaurant 109
   Ascain 107
      Hotel de la Rhône 107
   Bayonne 108
   beaches 109
   Biarritz 107–10
      Marbella hotel 107
   Came 107
   Capbreton 109
   Larressore 108
   pelota 107, 108

sailing 109
St Jean-de-Luz 109
St Pée
   château 108
   Hotel de la Nivelle 108
San Sebastián 109
surfing 109
Bayonne (Fr.) 108
beaches *see* Algarve; Andalucia;
   Bahamas; Basque country;
   Brittany; Corfu; Cyprus;
   Estoril; Gozo; Hong Kong;
   Jamaica; Lanzarote;
   Madeira; Majorca;
   Maurtius; Menorca;
   Morocco; Paxos;
   Peloponnese; Provence;
   Thailand; Turkey
Beauregard château (Fr.) 16, 17
Belgium *see* Bruges, Brussels
Belgium Tourist Office 30, 45
Belgium Travel Service 30, 45
Bernini, Giovanni 19
Biarritz (Fr.) 107–10
Big Wave Bay (HK) 186–7
Bitez (Turk.) 134
Bizot, Christian 31
Blois (Fr.) 15, 16
   château 14
boating *see* cruises; pedallo boats;
   sailing
Bodrum (Turk.) 132–5
Boeuf, M. 157
Bonaventure 127
Borg, Victor 125
Bough, Frank 50
Boyer, M. 32, 33
Bracieux (Fr.) 16
British Airways 13, 21, 26, 30, 35,
   41, 45, 60, 135, 143, 149,
   151, 156, 174, 179, 185, 189
British Caledonian 26, 41, 167,
   189
British Midland 13

Brittany 128–31
   beaches 129–30
   Cancale 129
   Château des Ormes 128–31
   Dol-de-Bretagne 128, 129, 130
   Le Tronchet 130
     Hostellerie l'Abbatiale 130
   Le Vivier 129
   pedallo boats 130
   Plage du Petit Port 129
   Rothéneuf 128
   Sables-d'Or-les-Pins 130
   sailing 129
   St Hacut
     Le Terrier restaurant 130
   St-Jacut-de-la-Mer 130
   St Malo 128
   St Servan 128
   tennis 130
Brittany Ferries 110, 128, 131
Brittany Ferries Camping 131
Bruges 42–5
   Basilica 43–4
   Béguinage 42, 44
   Burg, the 43
   canals 42
   Les Halles 43
   Nôtre Dame hotel 42–3
   restaurants
     De Snippe 44
     De Witte Poort 44
     Kastel Minnewater 44
     T Kluizeken 44
   St Jacob's church 44
Brussels 27–30
   Astoria hotel 27
   'City 2' 28
   Grand Place 28, 42
   Hôtel de Ville 28
   Mannekin-Pis 28
   museums
     Maison du Roi 28
     Place Royale 27
   Quai aux Briques 29

restaurants/bars
  Armes des Bruxelles 28
  Belle Moulin 29
  L'Ecailler du Palais Royal 29
  La Chaloupe d'Or 28
  La Morte Subite 29
  Maxim's 42
  Rugby Man 29
  Vincents 28
Sablons
  Grand 28, 29
  Petit 28
shops 28
Budapest (Hung.) 82–4
bull fighting see Andalucia;
    Camargue
Bull, Peter 71

Cadogan 123
Cairo (Egypt) 144–7
Cala Gat (Maj.) 68
Cala Pregonda (Men.) 76
Cala Ratjada (Maj.) 65–9
Calypso's Cove (Gozo) 125
Camargue 86–9
  Aigues Mortes 88
    restaurants
      Camargue 88
      Les Remparts 88
  Arles 86–7
    Jules César hotel 87
  bull fighting 86, 88–9
  Etang de Vaccarès 86
  Le Cailar 88
    Le Sanglier hotel 88
  Le Grau-du-Roi 88
  Les-Saintes-Maries-de-la-Mer
    86–9
    Brûleur de Loupes restaurant
    88
  Mistral wind 87, 88, 89
  Nîmes 86–7
    Cheval Blanc hotel 86
    Le Courbet restaurant 87

Roman arena 86
  vineyards 87
Camara de Lobos (Mad.) 92
Came (F.) 107
camping see Brittany
canals see Amsterdam; Bruges
Canary Islands see Lanzarote
Cancale (Fr.) 129
Canyonlands 165–7
  Glen Canyon 166
  Grand Canyon 165
  Indian reservation 166–7
  La Posada 166
  Lake Powell 166
  Mormons 166
  National Parks
    Bryce 166, 167
    Page 166
    Zion 166, 167
  Navajo Indians 166–7
  Oak Creek Canyon 167
  Page
    Lodge hotel 166
  Phoenix 165, 166
  Scottsdale 166
  Sedona 167
Canvas 131
Cap Ferrat (Fr.) 49
Cap Martin (Fr.) 49
Capbreton (Fr.) 109
Cape Arila (Gr.) 117
Cape St. Vincent (Port.) 104
car hire see Avis; Hertz
Caravaggio 20
Caravela 81, 93
Caribbean Connection 151
Carnival, Equity Cruises 156
Cartland, Barbara 144, 175
Carvoeiro (Port.) 106
Cascais (Port.) 80
Castellar (Sp.) 113
castles see Algarve; Estoril;
    Hungary; Peloponnese;
    Turkey and see châteaux

Cathay Pacific 189
Cavalaire (Fr.) 50
Cavalière (Fr.) 50–1
Chagall, Marc 33
Chalons-sur-Vesle (Fr.) 33
Chambord château (Fr.) 14, 16
Champagne 31–4
  Ay 31
  Bollinger, House of 31
  Châlons-sur-Vesle 33
    Assiette-de Champenoise
     restaurant 33
  Champillon 33
    Royal Champagne restaurant
     33
  Épernay 31
  Fontenay-Tresigny 32
    Le Manoir hotel 32
  L'Epine 33
    Armes de Champagne hotel
     33
  Marne, river 31
  Piper-Heidsieck 33
  Reims 31–3
    restaurants
      Le Chardonnay 33
      Les Crayères 33
      Le Florence 33
  Sept-Saulx 33
    Cheval Blanc hotel 33
  vineyards 31–3
Champagne Connection 179
Champillon (Fr.) 33
châteaux see Barbizon; Basque
    country; Brittany; Loire,
    river; Provence and see castles
Château des Ormes (Fr.) 128–31
Château de Pray (Fr.) 14
Chenonceaux château (Fr.) 15, 17
Cheung Chau Island (HK) 187
Chinon château (Fr.) 14
Chur (Switz.) 53
Ciudadela (Men.) 76
Cleopatra's Island (Turk.) 132

Clery (Fr.) 15
Club Mediterranée 157–60
Club Tropicana (Maj.) 61–4
Cologne (Ger.) 97
Comino (Malta) 124
Corfu 115–18
  Ag. Georgios 117
  Arilas 117
  beaches 117–18
  Cape Arila 117
  Corfu Town 115
  Damia 117
  Ipsos 117
  Kassiopi 116, 117
  Paleokastritsa 117
  Sidari 117
  wind surfing 118
Costa de los Pinos (Maj.) 68
cruises:
  river see Mississippi, river; Nile,
    river; Rhine, river
  sea see Bahamas
Cumberledge, Mrs Nora 66–7
Cutlass Bay (Jam.) 151
C. V. Villas 70, 72, 73, 118
Cyprus 99–102
  beaches 100
  Curium 99
  Episkopi 100
  Fontana Amorosa 101
  Hotel Berengaria 101
  Lania 101
  Latchi 101
  Limassol 99
    Churchill hotel 99
  Maroni 101
  Paphos 101
  Pissouri
    Bunch of Grapes restaurant
     100
  Polis 101
  Troodhitissa monastery 101
Cyprus Airways 102
Cyprus Tourist Office 102

Dalaman (Turk.) 132
Damia (Gr.) 117
Dan Air 53
Danube Travel 85
Davos (Switz.) 53
Deià (Maj.) 61
Disney, Walt 80
  and see Epcot
Disneyworld *see* Epcot
Dol-de-Bretagne (Fr.) 128, 129, 130
Domecq, José Ignacio 111
Dors, Diana 80
Dunn's River Falls (Jam.) 151
Durrell, Gerald 116
Düsseldorf (Ger.) 95, 97

Eger (Hung.) 85
Egypt 144–7
  Abu Simbel 144–5
  Aswan 144–5
  Cairo 144–7
    hotels
      Hilton 147
      Marriott 146–7
    Giza 145
    Karnak 147
    Luxor 144, 146
      Winter Palace hotel 146
    Nile, river 144–7
    pyramids 145–6
Egyptair 147
Egyptian State Tourist Office 147
Eisenhower, General 32
El Busque (Sp.) 111–12
Elizabeth, Empress 8
Engelfred family 50–1
Enterprise 174
Epcot 172–4
  Lake Buena Vasta
    Viscount hotel 174
Epernay (Fr.) 31
Eperon, 'Arfer' 50
Epidauros (Gr.) 57, 59, 60

Estoril 78–81
  beaches 78–81
  castles 79–80
  golf 79
  Hotel Palacio 78–9
  Cascais 80
    Hotel Albatroz 80
    João Padeiro restaurant 80
  Guincho 80
    Muchaxo hotel 80
  sailing 80
  Sintra 79
Etang de Vaccares (Fr.) 86
Eugen, Prince 9
Eurocamp 128–31

Falcon 135
Fayence (Fr.) 51
Femes (Lanz.) 168
Finney, Albert 71
Florence 3–6
  apartments
    Residence Palazzo Ricasoli 3
  bars/cafés/restaurants
    Bar Gilli 5
    Harry's Bar 5
    Hotel Baglioni 6
    La Posta 5
    Paoli 6
    Pastkowski 5
    Trattoria Cammillo 6
  frescoes 4, 6
  hotels
    Hotel Baglioni 6
    Hotel Lungarno 5
  palaces
    Medici-Riccardi 4
    Uffizi 5
    Vecchio 5
  Piazza della Republica 4
  Ponte alla Carraia 5
  Ponte Vecchio 5
  San Lorenzo church 4, 6
  shops 4

Florida *see* Epcot; Miami
Fontainebleau (Fr.) 41
  château 39
  forest 39
Fontenay-Tresigny (Fr.) 32
Forbes, Sir Hamish 134
Formentor (Maj.) 61
Fouquet, M. 40
France *see* Barbizon; Basque
      country; Brittany;
      Camargue; Champagne;
      Loire, river; Paris; Provence
Francois I 16
Frank, Anne 12
Freedom Holidays 60
Freeport (Ba.) 155
French Government Tourist
      Office 17, 26, 34, 41, 52,
      89, 110, 131
French Leave 17, 34, 89, 110
French Railways *see* SNCF
French Travel Service 52, 110
Freud, Sigmund 8
Fuertoventura (Lanz.) 169, 170
Funchal (Mad.) 91, 93

Gaios (Gr.) 70, 72
George, Gordon 176, 177, 178
German Tourist Office 98
Germany *see* Rhine, river
Giza (Egypt) 145
Glen Canyon (USA) 166
golf *see* Algarve; Estoril; Marbella
Goodlands (Mau.) 158
Goulamine (Mor.) 122
Gozo 124–7
  beaches 124–5
  Calypso's Cove 125
  Cornocopia hotel 124, 125
  Eclipse restaurant 125, 126
  Marsalforn Bay
    Il-Kartell restaurant 126, 127
  Mgarr 125
    Gleneagles Bar 127

Ramla 125
    sailing 127
  Ta' Cenc 126
  Victoria 125, 126
  Xaghra 124, 126
  Xlendi 127
Gozo Holidays 127
Grace, Princess 49
Grand Baie (Mau.) 158, 159
Grand Canyon (USA) 165
Grasse (Fr.) 51
Grazalema (Sp.) 112–13
Greece *see* Corfu; Paxos;
      Peloponnese
Greek Islands Club 73
Grinzing (Aus.) 7
Guadalquivir, river (Sp.) 111
Guise, Duc de 16

Hayes & Jarvis 114
Henry III 16
Hertz car hire 3, 70
Hohenlohe, Prince 36
Holiday Club International 64
Holland *see* Amsterdam; Rhine,
      river
Hong Kong 186–9
  beaches 186–7
  Big Wave Bay 186–7
  Cheung Chau Island 187
  hotels
    Excelsior 189
    Mandarin 186
  Lantau Island 187
  'red light' districts 186, 188–9
  Shatin racecourse 187–8
  Typhoon Harbour 188
  Wanchai 186
Hong Kong Tourist Office 189
Horizon 38
horses *see* Lippizaner horses;
      Spanish Riding School *and*
      see racecourses
Hungary 82–5

Budapest 82–4
  Basilica 84
  'Coronation' church 84
  hotels
    Forum 83
    Hilton 84
  Opera House 82–3
  Redoubt restaurant 83
  Eger 85
    Park Hotel 85
  Lippizaner horses 85
  Szentendre 84
  Szilvásvárad 85
  Visegrád castles 85
Hungarian Tourist Office 85

Iberia 38, 69, 77, 114, 171
Inn-Tent 128–31
Ipsos (Gr.) 117
islands see Bahamas; Corfu;
    Cyprus; Gozo; Hong Kong;
    Lanzarote; Jamaica;
    Madeira; Majorca;
    Menorca; Paxos
Italian State Tourist Office 6
Italy see Florence; Rome

Jacques, Charles 39
Jamaica 148–51
  beaches 148, 150
  Cutlass Bay
    Shaw Park hotel 151
  Dunn's River Falls 151
  Montego Bay 148
    hotels
      Royal Caribbean 151
      Sandals 149
  Negril 149–50
    Hedonism II hotel 149–50
  Ochos Rios 148, 151
  Rose Hall 151
  Round Hill 148
Jamaican Tourist Office 151
Jerez (Sp.) 111

Jetset 179, 189
Jimena (Sp.) 113, 114
Just Motoring 34

Kalikavak (Turk.) 135
Karnak (Egypt) 147
Kassiopi (Gr.) 116, 117
Kenya 161–4
  Keekorok Lodge 161
  Lake Naivasha reserve
    Lake Hotel 163
  Masai-Mara reserve 161–2
  Nyeri 163
  Outspan 163
  Samburu reserve 162
  Tree Tops 163
Kenya Airways 164
Kenya Tourist Office 164
Khashoggi, A. 37
Klimt, Gustav 8
KLM 13
Koblenz (Ger.) 98
Köln-Dusseldorfer Line 94, 98
Königswinter (Ger.) 97
Kosmas (Gr.) 59
Kuoni 56, 143, 147, 151, 160,
    164, 167, 174, 179

La Cadière d'Azur (Fr.) 49–50
La Garoupe (Fr.) 49
La Posada (USA) 166
Lagoa (Port.) 106
Lagos (Port.) 104
Lake Buena Vista (USA) 174
Lake Naivasha reserve (Ken.) 163
Lake Powell (USA) 166
Lakonia, vale of (Gr.) 60
Lantau Island (HK) 187
Lanzarote 168–71
  Arrecife 170
    Las Salinas hotel 170
    Los Troncos restaurant 170
  beaches 169

Fèmes 168
Fuertoventura 169
    Playa Blanca restaurant 169,
        170
    Oasis San Antonio 169
    Papagayo 169, 170
    Playa de los Pocillos 169, 170
        restaurants
            La Gaviota 170
            La Ola 170
    Puerto del Carmen
        El Burro restaurant 170
    surfing 169
Lanzarote Villas 171
Larressore (Fr.) 108
Launder, Frank 50
Le Cailar (Fr.) 88
Le Castellet château (Fr.) 50
L'Epine (Fr.) 33
Le Grau-du-Roi (Fr.) 88
Leonidion (Gr.) 59
Le Rayol (Fr.) 51
Le Tronchet (Fr.) 130
Le Vivier (Fr.) 129
Lenzerheide (Switz.) 53–4
Les Lecques (Fr.) 50
Les Saintes Maries-de-la Mer
        (Fr.) 86–9
Lichfield, Patrick 80
Lippizaner horses see Hungary
Lisbon (Port.) 78
Loches château (Fr.) 14
Loggos (Gr.) see Longos
Loire, river 14–17
    Amboise 14
        Château de Pray hotel 14
    Angers 14
    Beauregard château 16, 17
    Blois 15–16
        château 14
    Bracieux
        Le Relais restaurant 16
    Chambord château 14, 16
        St Michel hotel 16

Chenonceaux 15, 17
    château 15
Chinon château 14
Cléry 15
Loches château 14
Montrichard
    tollhouse restaurant 17
Olivet 15
Orleans 14, 15
    La Cremaillière restaurant 15
St Dye-sur-Loire 16
    Manoir Bel Air hotel 16
vineyards 15
Long Island (USA) 183–4
Longos (Gr.) 72
Louis XI 15
    XIV 40
    XVI 24
Loulé (Port.) 106
Lufthansa 98
Luxor (Egypt) 144, 146

Maclean, Alistair 86
Madeira 90–3
    beaches 92
    Camara de Lobos 92
    Funchal 91, 93
        restaurants
            Golfino 93
            Le Jardin 93
            Romano 93
        hotels
            Reid's 90–1, 93
            Savoy 90–2
    Porto Moniz 91
        Cachalote restaurant 91
    Porto Santo 92
    Seixal 91
    vineyards 91
Magazia (Gr.) 72
Magic of Italy 3, 6, 19, 21
Mahler, Gustav 8
Mahon (Men.) 75
Majorca 61–9

Artà 68
beaches 61–8
Cala Gat 68
Cala Ratjada 65–9
  hotels
    Aguait 68
    Sea Club 66–7
    Tony's Bar restaurant 68
Club Tropicana 61–4
Costa de los Pinos 68
  hotels
    Europa 68
    Port Verde 68
Deià 61
Formentor 61
Palma 65
pedallo boats 64
sailing 64, 68
snorkelling 64, 68
wind surfing 64
Malev Airlines 82, 85
Malta 124
  Comino 124
  Valetta
    hotels
      Coronthia Palace 124
      Phoenicia 124
  and see Gozo
Maltese Tourist Office 127
Marbella 35–8
  golf 35
  hotels
    Fuerte 36
    La Cabana 37
    Los Monteros 35–6
  Puerto Banus 37
    Don Leone restaurant 37
  tennis 37
  Torremolinos 35
March family 68
Marne, river (Fr.) 31
Marseilles (Fr.) 49
Masai-Mara reserve (Ken.) 161–2
Masalforn Bay (Gozo) 126, 127

Mauritius 157–60
  beaches 158
  Club Mediterranée 157–60
  Goodlands 158
  Grand Baie 158, 159
    La Pagoda restaurant 159
  Mon Choisy 158
  Pamplemousses 158–9
  Perrybère 159
  Point aux Canonniers 157
  Port Louis 159
    Saint Gérain Sun hotel 159,
      160
  sailing 159
  tennis 157
  Trou aux Biches 158
  water skiing 157
Mauritius Government Tourist
    Office 160
Medici, Catherine de 17
    Cosimo 4
Menorca 74–7
  Alayor 75
    Bennetts restaurant 75–6
  Algaiarens 77
  beaches 76–7
  Cala Pregonda 76
  Ciudadela 76
  Mahon 75
  Menorca Country Club 77
  Reclau 77
  sailing 76, 77
  supernatural 75–7
  villa 74–5
Meon 106, 115, 127
Meon's Book of Beaches 76
Mgarr (Gozo) 125, 127
Miami (USA) 152
Michelangelo 19, 43
Michelozzo 4
Milfontes Villa Nova (Port.) 103,
    104
Millet, Jean 39
Mississippi, river 139–43

Natchez 139–41
New Orleans 139
Vicksburg 142
Mistral wind see Camargue
Monaco 49
Mon Choisy (Mau.) 158
Monemvasia (Gr.) 59
Mons (Fr.) 51
Monsarrat, Nicholas 125
Montauroux (Fr.) 51
Monte Carlo 49
Montego Bay (Jam.) 148–9, 151
Monte Gordo (Port.) 106
Montrichard (Fr.) 17
Mormons see Canyonlands
Morocco 119–23
   Agadir 119
      Hotel Europa 119–21
   beaches 119–20
   Goulimine 122
   Tafroute 122
   Tiznit 122
Moroccan Tourist Office 123
Mototrain 22, 108
Muldain (Switz.) 55
Mundi Color 38, 69, 114
Murk, Mr 53, 55
Mykinae (Gr.) 57, 58
Mystras castle (Gr.) 59, 60

Nafplion (Gr.) 58
Napoleon 41
Nassau (Ba.) 154–5
Natchez (USA) 139–41
National Greek Tourist Office 60,
   73, 118
National Holidays 98
National Parks (USA) see
   Canyonlands
Navajo Indians see Canyonlands
Negril (Jam.) 149–50
Netherlands National Tourist
   Office 13
New Orleans (USA) 139

New Providence Island (Ba.) 154
New York 180–5
   Empire State Building 183
   Halloran House Hotel 181
   Lincoln Center 184
   Long Island 183–4
   restaurants
      Maxwell's Plum 184
      Sardi's 183
   shops 182
   South Street Seaport 183
   Staten Island 183
   World Trade Center 183
Nierstein (Ger.) 98
Nijmegen (Hol.) 95
Nile, river see Egypt
Nîmes (Fr.) 86–7
Norwegian Caribbean Line 156
Nyeri (Ken.) 163

Oak Creek Canyon (USA) 167
Oasis San Antonio (Lanz.) 169
Ochos Rios (Jam.) 148, 151
Olivet (Fr.) 15
Olympic Airways 60, 73, 118
opera houses see Vienna; Hungary;
   Budapest
Orlando (USA) 173
Orleans (Fr.) 14, 15
OSL Villas/Wings 77, 123, 171
Outspan (Ken.) 163

P & O Air Holidays 189
Page (USA) 166
Paleokastritsa (Gr.) 117
Palma (Maj.) 65
Pamplemousses (Mau.) 158–9
Pan Am 143, 156, 167, 174
Paradise Island (Ba.) 155
Papagayo (Lanz.) 169, 170
Paris 22–6
   Arc de Triomphe 22, 24
   bandits, child 25
   Bois de Boulogne 24

cafés/restaurants/buffets
    Gare d'Austerlitz 23
    La Cascade 24
    Tronchet 25
Faubourg St Honoré 24
Gare d'Austerlitz 22–3
Jeu de Paume 23
Longchamp racecourse 24
Louvre 22, 23
Madeleine 24, 25
Orangerie 24
Palais Royale 24
Place de la Concorde 23, 24
shops 24
Tuileries Gardens 23, 25
Versailles 22
Paris Travel Service 26
Pataya (Thai.) 175
Paxos 70–3
    beaches 72
    Gaios 70, 72
    Longos (Loggos) 72
    Magazia 72
    sailing 70, 72
pedallo boats see Brittany; Majorca
Pegasus 6, 9, 21
Peloponnese 57–60
    Argolian Gulf 57
    Argos 58
    Asklepios 59
    Athens 57
    beaches 57–9
    Epidauros 57, 59, 60
    Kosmas 59
    Lakonia, vale of 60
    Leonidion 59
    Monemvasia 59
    Mykinae 57, 58
    Mystras castle 59, 60
    Nafplion 58
        castle 58
    Sparti 59
    Tiryns 57, 58
    Tolon 57–8

Iris hotel 58
Spilia restaurant 58
Tyros 59
wind surfing 58
pelota see Basque country
Perrybère (Mau.) 159
Phoenix (USA) 165, 166
Plage du Petit Port (Fr.) 129
Playa de los Pocillos (Lanz.) 169,
    170
Pointe aux Canonniers (Mau.) 157
Poitiers, Diane de 17
Polignac, Prince de 33
Pontin's 61–4
Port Louis (Mau.) 159, 160
Portimao (Port.) 105
Porto Moniz (Mad.) 91
Porto Santo (Mad.) 92
Portugal see Algarve; Estoril;
    Madeira
Portuguese National Tourist
    Office 81, 93, 106
Provence 49–52
    Antibes 49
    beaches 49–50
    Cap Ferrat 49
    Cap Martin 49
    Cavalaire 50
    Cavalière 50–1
        Hotel Surplage 50–1
    Fayence 51
    Grasse 51
    La Cadière d'Azur 49–50
        Hostellerie Bérard 50
    La Garoupe 49
    Le Castellet château 50
    Les Lecques 50
    Le Rayol 51
    Marseilles 49
    Mons 51
    Montauroux 51
        La Marjolaine hotel 51
    sailing 49, 50, 51
    St Cézaire 51

St Tropez 51
  vineyards 50
  water skiing 51
Puerto Banus (Sp.) 37
Puerto de Sante Maria (Sp.) 111
Puerto del Carmen (Lanz.) 170
pyramids *see* Egypt

Quarteira (Port.) 106
Quincho (Port.) 80
Quinta do Lago (Port.) 105

racecourses *see* Hong Kong; Paris;
    Thailand: Bangkok
Ramla (Gozo) 125
Reclau (Men.) 77
'red light' districts *see* Amsterdam;
    Bangkok; Hong Kong
Reims (Fr.) 31–3
Relais et Chateaux Association 55
Rembrandt 11
Rhine, river 94–8
  Bad Godesberg 97
  Basle 94
  Cologne 97
  Düsseldorf 95, 97
  Koblenz 98
  Königswinter 97
  Nierstein 98
  Nijmegen 95
  Rotterdam 94
  Xanten 95
Rome 18–21
  Borghese Gardens 20
  cafés/restaurants
    Cafe de Paris 20
    dal Bolognese 20
    Passetto 19
    Rosetta 20
  Caracalla, Baths of 20
  Castel Sant'Angelo 18
  Fontana de Trevi 20
  Hippodromo 20
  Hotel Columbus 18

Navona Square 19
Pantheon 20
Papal audience 18
Piazza del Popolo 20
St Peter's 18–19
Santa Maria church 20
shops 20
Ronda (Sp.) 113
Rose Hall (Jam.) 151
Rotheneuf (Fr.) 128
Rotterdam (Hol.) 94
Round Hill (Jam.) 148
Royal Air Maroc 123
Royal Caribbean Line 156

Sable d'Or les Pins (Fr.) 130
Sabena 30, 45
safari *see* Kenya
Sagres (Port.) 104
sailing *see* Basque country;
    Brittany; Estoril; Gozo;
    Majorca; Mauritius;
    Menorca; Paxos; Provence;
    Switzerland; Turkey
Samburu reserve (Ken.) 162
Scottsdale (USA) 166
Sedir (Turk.) 132
Seixal (Mad.) 91
Sept-Saulx (Fr.) 33
Shatin racecourse (HK) 187–8
St Cézaire (Fr.) 51
St Dye-sur-Loire (Fr.) 16
St Hacut (Fr.) 130
St Jacut de la Mer (Fr.) 130
St Jean de Luz (Fr.) 109
St Malo (Fr.) 128
St Moritz (Switz.) 53
St Pee (Fr.) 108
St Servan (Fr.) 128
St Tropez (Fr.) 51
San Bras (Port.) 106
San Roque (Sp.) 114
San Sebastian (Sp.) 109
Sanlucar (Sp.) 111

Santiago (Port.) 103
Saxe, Marechal de 16
Scott, Mrs Lurton 142
Sealink Travel 34
Sidari (Gr.) 117
Sidonia (USA) 166
Sintra (Port) 79
SNCF (French Railways) 110
snorkelling see Bahamas; Majorca
Sovereign 6, 9, 81, 85, 147, 160,
    189
Spain see Andalucia; Basque
    country; Lanzarote;
    Majorca; Marbella;
    Menorca
Spanish National Tourist Office
    38, 64, 69, 77, 114, 171
Spanish Riding School see Vienna
Sparti (Gr.) 59
Speedbird 143
Sportz (Switz.) 55
Staten Island (USA) 183
Stevenson, Robert Louis 39
Sunmed 60, 118, 135
Suntours of Witney 81, 93
supernatural see Menorca
surfing see Algarve; Basque
    country; Lanzarote wind
    surfing see Algarve; Corfu;
    Majorca; Peloponnese;
    Switzerland; Thailand
Swiss National Tourist Office 56
Swiss Travel Service 56
Swissair 56
Switzerland 53–6
    Chur 53
        Hotel Stern 53
    Davos 53
    Lenzerheide 53–4
        Sunstar hotel 53–4
    Muldain 55
        Gasthof Junkerhaus
            restaurant 55
    sailing 53

St Moritz 53
    Sportz 55
        Guarda Val restaurant 55
    wind surfing 53
    Zurich 53
Szentendre (Hung.) 84
Szilvasvared (Hung.) 85

Ta' Cenc (Gozo) 126
Tafroute (Mor.) 122
Taylor, Roger 105
tennis see Algarve; Brittany;
        Marbella; Mauritius
Thai International 179
Thailand 175–9
    Bangkok 175–8
    beaches 176
    Budda, Golden 176
    'European' Palace 177
    hotels
        Oriental 175
        Regent 175–6
        Royal Cliff 175, 178
    Pat Pong 177
    Pattaya 175
    racecourse: Royal 175
    'red light' districts 177–8
    restaurants
        Royal Palace 177
        Spice Market 176
        Temple of the Dawn 177
    wind surfing 178
Thomas Cook 102, 144, 147
Thomson Holidays 26, 38, 56, 66,
    77, 93, 102, 118, 119, 123,
    164, 171
Time Off 13, 26, 27, 30, 45
Timms, Timothy 57
Timsway Travel 57, 60, 102
Tintoretto 5
Tiryns (Gr.) 57, 58
Tiznet (Mor.) 122
Tolon (Gr.) 57–8
Torremolinos (Sp.) 35

Tourism Authority of Thailand 179
Townsend Thorensen 17, 45
Tradewinds 151
Trans-Europe Express 18
travel agents
  America, United States of 143, 167, 174, 185
  Austria 9
  Bahamas 156
  Belgium 30, 45
  Cyprus 102
  Egypt 147
  France 17, 26, 34, 41, 52, 89, 110, 131
  Germany 98
  Gozo 127
  Greece 60, 73, 118
  Holland 13
  Hong Kong 189
  Hungary 85
  Italy 6, 21
  Jamaica 151
  Kenya 164
  Lanzarote 171
  Madeira 93
  Majorca 64, 69
  Mauritius 160
  Menorca 77
  Morocco 123
  Portugal 81, 106, 114
  Rhine, river see Germany
  Spain 38, 114
  Switzerland 56
  Thailand 179
  Turkey 135
Travel Club of Upminster 106
Travelscene 13, 85
Tree Tops (Ken.) 163
Trekamerica 143, 167
Trou aux Biches (Mau.) 158
Turkbuku (Turk.) 135
Turkey 132–5
  beaches 133–4

Bitez 134
Bodrum 132–5
  castle 133–4
Cleopatra's Island 132
Dalaman 132
Kalikavak 135
sailing 133, 134, 135
Sedir 132
Tarkbuku 135
Turkish Airlines 135
Turkish Tourist Office 135
Typhoon Harbour (HK) 188
Tyrou (Gr.) 59

Ubrique (Sp.) 113
United States see Canyonlands; Epcot; Mississippi, river; New York
United States Travel & Tourism Administration 143, 167, 174, 185
Utah (USA) 166

Vale do Lobo (Port.) 105
Valetta (Malta) 124
Van Gogh, Vincent 11
Vaux-le-Vicomte château (Fr.) 40
Vermeer, Jan 11
Versailles (Fr.) 22, 40
VFB 17, 52, 89
Vicksburg (USA) 142
Victor Holidays 30
Victoria (Gozo) 125, 126
Vienna 7–9
  Amadeus hotel 8
  amusement park 9
  cafés/restaurants
    Beim Novak 9
    Grunewald 8
    Hawelka 8
    Kahlenberg 9
    Lehman's 8
    Olivenhain 9
    Rathausplatz 8

Sachers 8
Smutny's 8
Grinzing 7
Mayerling hunting lodge 9
National Library 9
Opera House 8, 9
palaces
    Belvedere 9
    Hofburg 9
    Schönbrunn 9
St Stephan's cathedral 8
shops 8
Spanish Riding School 9
vineyards 7
wine pubs 7
Vilamoura (Port.) 105
Villa Real (Port.) 106
Villaseekers 77
vineyards see Andalucia;
    Camargue; Champagne;

Loire, river, Madeira; Provence;
    Vienna
Virgin 156, 174, 185
Visegrad castles (Hung.) 85

water skiing see Mauritius;
    Provence
West Indies see Bahamas; Jamaica
wind surfing see Algarve; Corfu;
    Majorca; Peloponnese;
    Switzerland; Thailand
Windsor, Duke and Duchess of
    79, 154
Winter Inn 17, 42, 45

Xaghra (Gozo) 124, 126
Xanten (Ger.) 95
Xlendi (Gozo) 127

Zurich (Switz.) 53